ABSOLUTE
BEGINNER'S
GUIDE

TO

Tablet PCs

Craig F. Mathews

 800 East 96th Street,
Indianapolis, Indiana 46240

D1341695

Absolute Beginner's Guide to Tablet PCs
Copyright © 2004 by ToolKits, Inc.

International Standard Book Number: 0-789-73049-9

Library of Congress Catalog Card Number: 2003110531

Printed in the United States of America

First Printing: December 2003

06   05   04   03   4   3   2   1

Trademarks

All terms mentioned in this book that are known to be trademarks or service marks have been appropriately capitalized. Que Publishing cannot attest to the accuracy of this information. Use of a term in this book should not be regarded as affecting the validity of any trademark or service mark.

Warning and Disclaimer

Every effort has been made to make this book as complete and as accurate as possible, but no warranty or fitness is implied. The information provided is on an "as is" basis. The author and the publisher shall have neither liability nor responsibility to any person or entity with respect to any loss or damages arising from the information contained in this book or from the use of the CD or programs accompanying it.

Bulk Sales

Que Publishing offers excellent discounts on this book when ordered in quantity for bulk purchases or special sales. For more information, please contact

U.S. Corporate and Government Sales
1-800-382-3419
corpsales@pearsontechgroup.com

For sales outside of the U.S., please contact

International Sales
1-317-428-3341
international@pearsontechgroup.com

Associate Publisher
Greg Wiegand

Acquisitions Editor
Michelle Newcomb

Development Editor
Kevin Howard

Managing Editor
Charlotte Clapp

Senior Project Editor
Matthew Purcell

Copy Editor
Kate Welsh

Indexer
Mandi Frank

Proofreader
Jennifer Timpe

Technical Editor
Sean Campbell

Team Coordinator
Sharry Lee Gregory

Interior Designer
Anne Jones

Cover Designer
Dan Armstrong

Page Layout
Michelle Mitchell

Contents at a Glance

Table of Contents

About the Author

Craig F. Mathews has been an IT professional for more than a decade, a passion that has recently expanded to include entrepreneurship. He is CEO of Toolkits, Inc., which helps organizations align IT capabilities with their business strategy and goals. He is also the founder of TabletGuru.com, a site dedicated to the advancement of the Tablet PC as well as to teaching people how to use them.

A member of Mensa and a Beta Gamma Sigma graduate of UNC's Kenan-Flagler Executive MBA program, Mathews blends business and technical perspectives to create smart, usable tools, and to train and consult. He frequently speaks and consults on topics as varied as IT strategy, homeland security, and leadership principles.

When not writing, Mathews enjoys time with his wife and two sons, Austin and Jameson. He is a pilot, a potter, and a risk junkie. He lives in Raleigh, NC and loves to explore, learn, and experience the joy and freedom God has provided for each of us.

About the Tech Editor

Sean Campbell began his career as a college instructor in the early 1990s at Purdue University. He has continued to work with a wide range of Microsoft technology ever since leaving Purdue. Sean then began to pursue consulting and training engagements with Chicago companies. In 1998, Sean joined ARIS corporation and taught Visual Basic and SQL Server courses as well as working on consulting engagements centered on these technologies.

Sean has been one of the principal sources of ASP .NET, Windows Forms, .NET CF, and SQL Server expertise at 3 Leaf Solutions, as well as being a leading expert on code development in C#, VB .NET, and T-SQL. Sean has also been author of many different seminars for Microsoft on technologies such as SQL Server, ASP.NET, .NET Remoting, .NET Security, MMIT, and the .NET CF. In addition, Sean has been responsible for signature content such as the recent 101 VB.NET samples made available to Visual Basic developers on MSDN. He holds several Microsoft certifications (MCDBA, MCSD), and he has led many consulting projects at 3 Leaf Solutions, including SQL Server installations and configurations, as well as upgrading a large GIS application from DAO and Access to ADO and SQL Server, as well as numerous .NET projects.

Currently Sean specializes in investigating new technologies for 3 Leaf in a variety of areas related to his expertise. Sean gets most of his kicks out of working with new Microsoft product releases while they are early in their development prior to release to the general public.

When not working Sean loves spending time with his family, taking in the Pacific Northwest, reading (History primarily), and taking in any baseball game he can.

Dedication

To Julie, my wife of 15 years, who has provided love, support, and encouragement, as well as two awesome sons. I love you with all my heart.

Acknowledgments

Thank you to all of the people who helped create this book. Thank you to Sam Johnson for letting me try out my first Tablet PC. Thanks to Rick Kughen for dealing straight and working extra-hard to bring Que and me together on this project; to Michelle Newcomb for making it all work and handling the details; and to Kevin Howard for his development efforts. Thank you to Matt Purcell, my project editor, Sean Campbell for technical editing, and Kate Welsh for copy editing. Thanks also to the other editors, graphics professionals, and others who helped make my first book a reality. Thank you all for helping me realize a life-long goal.

We Want to Hear from You!

As the reader of this book, *you* are our most important critic and commentator. We value your opinion and want to know what we're doing right, what we could do better, what areas you'd like to see us publish in, and any other words of wisdom you're willing to pass our way.

As an associate publisher for Que Publishing, I welcome your comments. You can email or write me directly to let me know what you did or didn't like about this book—as well as what we can do to make our books better.

Please note that I cannot help you with technical problems related to the topic of this book. We do have a User Services group, however, where I will forward specific technical questions related to the book.

When you write, please be sure to include this book's title and author as well as your name, email address, and phone number. I will carefully review your comments and share them with the author and editors who worked on the book.

Email: feedback@quepublishing.com

Mail: Greg Wiegand
Associate Publisher
Que Publishing
800 East 96th Street
Indianapolis, IN 46240 USA

For more information about this book or another Que Publishing title, visit our Web site at www.quepublishing.com. Type the ISBN (excluding hyphens) or the title of a book in the Search field to find the page you're looking for.

INTRODUCTION

If you just got a Tablet PC or are interested in learning more about what a Tablet PC can do, you've picked up the right book. I won't treat you like you're an idiot or a dummy—just someone who is new to the Tablet PC.

With that said, I will write from the perspective that you're not new to computers, just to Tablet PCs. If you need more help with Windows XP, please pick up the excellent book on the subject by Shelley O'Hara, *Absolute Beginner's Guide to Microsoft® Windows® XP*. It can help you understand the basic operation of Windows XP, which is beyond the scope of this book.

What I will guide you through in this book are the aspects of Windows XP and hardware that are specific to the Tablet PC. In addition, I will walk you through how others use the Tablet PC, and how you can extend the capabilities of your Tablet PC through additional software and hardware.

Some Key Terms

I use the terms *click* and *tap* interchangeably, because they perform the same action in most cases. When you can do only one or the other, I use the appropriate term. Tapping with a pen selects items just like clicking a mouse button, just as double-tapping performs the same operation as double-clicking.

Some Things to Keep in Mind

Because each computer can be customized to the user's needs, I will have to make some assumptions about how you use your Tablet PC. As you see figures and the steps I take you through to perform actions, please keep in mind the following:

- There are often several ways to perform an action. If the action you use is different from what I show, don't think you're doing something wrong if it works for you. I've tried to provide the quickest method to accomplish each task, but another way may make more sense for you.

- Your Windows setup may look different from the one shown in the figures in this book. For example, you may be using a different background image for your desktop, or you may choose a different style for your Start Menu.

- Your particular Tablet PC is probably different from the one I used when writing this book. Because of this, you will probably have different options and idiosyncrasies that are not covered in this book. I have tried to make most of the examples generic enough to be useful to all Tablet PC users, but there may be some differences that you need to account for.

The Basic Structure of This Book

This book is divided into seven parts, with each part being further divided into several chapters. There are also a couple appendices that list additional resources and that provide a quick reference to commonly used actions.

Part I, "What Makes the Tablet PC Special?," is your introduction to the Tablet PC. This section covers the benefits of the Tablet PC over other computer platforms, including a general introduction (Chapter 1), comparisons of the Tablet PC to other platforms (Chapter 2), and usage scenarios that help you understand how others use the Tablet PC (Chapter 3).

Part II, "Configuring and Using Your Tablet PC," walks you through the basic features of the Tablet PC hardware and software, helping you configure the Tablet PC for your specific needs. This section covers both the hardware configuration (Chapter 4) and operating system configuration (Chapter 5) of your Tablet PC.

Part III, "Using Included Applications," covers Windows Journal (Chapters 6 and 7), Tablet PC Input Panel (Chapter 8), and Speech Recognition (Chapter 9), which are the primary tools that are unique to the Tablet PC. Grasping these tools will make you a power Tablet PC user.

Part IV, "Data Communication and Protection," is a primer to wireless networking (Chapter 10) and data management and protection (Chapter 11). This section helps you protect your system from data loss and prying eyes, as well as helps you connect to wireless networks at home and during your travels.

Part V, "Using Other Included and Free Applications," shows you how to use applications such as Sticky Notes (Chapter 12), various PowerToys that can be downloaded from Microsoft (Chapter 13), and for the lighter side, Inkball and other games such as Pool for the Tablet PC (Chapter 14).

Part VI, "Using Microsoft Office 2003 with the Tablet PC," discusses only the aspects of Office applications that are different with the Tablet PC. Office 2003 offers excellent integration with the Tablet PC through integrated inking capabilities. Some aspects of Office XP will also be covered. The Office suite itself will be covered in Chapter 15, while Chapter 16 will deal with OneNote specifically, which is one of the killer apps for the Tablet PC.

Part VII, "Extending Your Tablet PC," discusses add-on hardware (Chapter 17) and software (Chapter 18) that can help you get the most out of the Tablet PC. These add-ons are not free, but depending on your needs, may offer significant benefits over your base configuration.

Have a great time learning to use your Tablet PC!

Conventions Used in This Book

This book explains the essential concepts and tasks in an easily digestible format. At the beginning of each chapter is a bulleted list of *In This Chapter* highlights that provides you with a framework for what you are about to learn. At the end of each chapter, under the heading *The Absolute Minimum*, you can review the main points covered in the chapter.

In addition, several icons appear throughout the book to direct your attention to a *note* that provides more detailed information, a *tip* that can help you perform a step more efficiently, or a *caution* to help you steer clear of a potential problem. Following is a brief description of each icon:

Notes provide additional information about the subject matter covered in a particular section. You can safely skip these notes and still learn the basics.

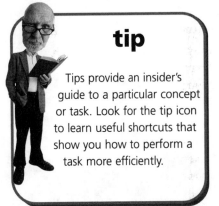

tip

Tips provide an insider's guide to a particular concept or task. Look for the tip icon to learn useful shortcuts that show you how to perform a task more efficiently.

caution

Cautions point out common user errors and problem areas to help you avoid the mistakes that hundreds of other users have already made. To avoid trouble and stay on the right track, read the cautions.

Let Me Know What You Think

I love to get feedback, positive and negative. If you discover some topics that I missed, or see things in the book that really struck a chord with you, please let me know. Feel free to email me at abg-tpc@TabletGuru.com. You can also find additional information and answers to questions about the Tablet PC at www.TabletGuru.com. Thanks for reading this book!

PART 1

WHAT MAKES THE TABLET PC SPECIAL?

1

INTRODUCING THE TABLET PC

There's no getting around it: The way you work with the Tablet PC is different from the way you work with all other computers. It's not just a touch-screen tablet, it's not just a laptop, and it's not just a Windows-based computer. It's different.

The fact that the Tablet PC is different scares lots of people, but it doesn't have to. In this chapter, I'll walk you through some of the basic aspects of the Tablet PC, including what you give up when you choose it for your main computing platform, what you get for switching, the common pitfalls people face when switching, and the new thinking processes you need to adopt to get the most out of your Tablet PC.

Your Digitizer Pen

Let's face it. If you've used a Windows-based PC for the past ten or so years, you've grown attached to your mouse. You may have even named it and bought it a brother for when you travel. Don't worry. You can still use it with your Tablet PC.

The cool thing about the Tablet PC, however, is that you don't *have* to use the mouse if you don't want to. In fact, in many situations, it's faster and easier (and takes up less space) to use the digitizer pen that comes with the Tablet PC. Figure 1.1 shows the parts of the digitizer pen. I will refer to the various parts of the pen throughout the book.

FIGURE 1.1

These are the parts of the pen that I will refer to throughout the book.

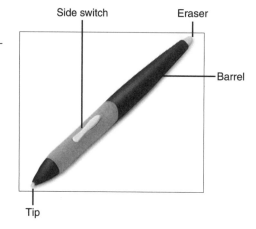

Your pen has a point on it that you use to tap items on the screen instead of clicking on items with the mouse. Most pens have at least one additional button, and many have a button on the end of the barrel, where an eraser would be on a pencil.

When you first start to use the pen, and especially if you're used to touch screen PDAs or tablets, you will invariably treat the display as if it's going to break if you touch it very hard.

Don't worry. Press with reasonably firm pressure.

Press until you start to see the screen become discolored under your pen. Then back off a bit. Now you know how hard you can press. The Tablet PC is made to take it.

tip

Don't be afraid to rest your hand on the Tablet PC's screen as you use the digitizer pen; you can use it just like an ink pen. (That's why Microsoft didn't design Tablet PCs with touch screens.)

Tap, tap, tap. Tap until you feel comfortable with how the pen operates. To get the hang of things, I suggest opening Windows Journal and just trying everything out. Don't be afraid of breaking anything. Your Tablet PC can probably handle more than what you can give it. Write, scrawl, draw, sketch, do whatever you would normally do on paper.

Question: If you try to write in an application, but you've lost your pen, what are you going to get?

Answer: Chicken scratch. Because most people can't effectively guide a mouse to create legible hand-written text. And since the Tablet PC requires you to use a digitizer-based pen instead of a touch screen for user input, if you lose the digitizer pen, you're pretty much out of luck.

> **caution**
>
> If you lose your digitizer pen, there's no other way to regain the pen interface other than buying another digitizer pen. Your PDA stylus and finger won't work. You may want to keep a spare just in case.

INK PENS AND DIGITIZER PENS

When you begin using a Tablet PC, you will begin to use a digitizer pen. A digitizer pen is a special device that communicates the pen movement to the Tablet PC. Most work passively, but some require batteries.

A digitizer pen will not have ink because it would mar the Tablet PC screen. Instead, the digitizer pen has a plastic tip that senses the pressure you exert on it, and transfers the location of the pen and the pressure information to the digitizer sandwiched behind the screen surface. This translates into the cursor moving, and also into thicker or thinner marks in pressure-sensitive applications, such as Windows Journal.

A PDA stylus will not work with your Tablet PC because it is not a digitizer pen. A stylus is just a stick that isn't as fat as your finger, allowing you to touch more specific regions of a PDA or touch-screen device.

Use your ink pen for paper, and your digitizer pen for your Tablet PC. From now on in this book, I will use the term "pen" to mean the digitizer pen.

If you lose your pen, you will not be able to move the cursor without a mouse or a replacement pen.

Don't lose your pen, or make sure you have an extra handy in case you do. In most Tablet PCs, there is a place to store the pen so that it doesn't get lost.

When you feel comfortable with the pen and the pressure you can use, try other applications, or read on.

Digitizers Versus Touch-Screen Displays

After you've really understood that the tablet can take a heavy-handed pen, rest your palm on the screen. Go on. Plop it down there. Notice that the cursor does not move if you don't have the pen in your hand. Next, try tapping buttons with your finger, and notice that nothing happens. That's because the Tablet PC's screen is not a touch screen. Won't ever be, according to Microsoft's specifications for the Tablet PC. Microsoft's theory is that people need to rest their hands on the screen in order to make it more usable.

Now that you understand what does and what doesn't work, try using the stylus from your PDA to write on the screen. Notice anything? It doesn't work, either. That's because your PDA's stylus isn't a digitizer pen, like the one that comes with your Tablet PC. Only the pen(s) that came with your Tablet PC (and those using similar technology) will work with your Tablet PC.

How to Use Your Pen Effectively

To get the most out of your pen, get to know it. Learn whether your pen/digitizer combination is pressure-sensitive or not. Figure out which way of holding it feels most comfortable to you while still giving you access to the barrel button (if present).

For most writing, use the Tablet PC just like you would an ordinary pen and paper—rest your hand on the screen and start writing, as shown in Figure 1.2.

FIGURE 1.2

Rest your hand on the screen when you write, just like you would do if you were using a pen and a paper notepad.

The sensitivity of the Tablet PC varies by machine. Get used to how much pressure it takes to make solid strokes on the tablet, and whether the strokes appear thinner with less pressure and thicker with more pressure (that is, the Tablet PC's *pressure-sensitivity*).

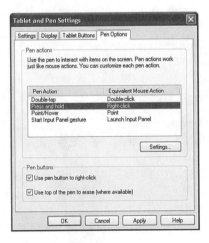

tip

Be careful how you hold your pen. Depending on how you hold it, it could be easy to click the shaft button, right-tapping where you don't want to.

Right-Tapping with Your Pen

Many people have problems with right-tapping because of the secondary button location. If your pen has a side button along the barrel like the one in Figure 1.1, your Tablet PC is probably set by default to use it for right-tapping. Right-tapping is the same thing as right-clicking with a mouse.

If you find that pressing the button on the barrel is too cumbersome, there are other ways to use the pen to right-tap. In Figure 1.3, you can see that the Tablet and Pen Settings dialog box lets you see the behaviors of your pen for right-tapping (or, as it's called in the dialog box, *right-clicking*), as well as whether the pen button is to be used for right-tapping.

FIGURE 1.3

The Tablet and Pen Settings dialog box lets you define how the pen operates.

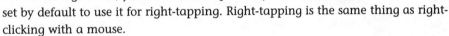

You can get to the Tablet and Pen Settings dialog box by tapping the **Start** button, tapping **Control Panel**, and then tapping **Tablet and Pen Settings**.

As you can see in Figure 1.3, "press and hold" is commonly set as another right-click option. This allows you to press the pen to the screen and hold it there for a brief moment until the Tablet PC recognizes this as a right-tap.

Use whichever method works best for you. Or use both.

The Eraser

Some Tablet PCs come with pens that have erasers. Some also have the Wacom "duo-switch," which allows you to use the back side of the side switch (a dual-action button) as the eraser. Notice in Figure 1.1 that the side switch is long; this is an example of the Wacom duo-switch pen.

If your Tablet PC does not have a pen with an eraser, you will need to select the eraser function inside your application. Not all applications support the use of the eraser button. Applications that do (Windows Journal, Corel Grafigo, and the like) can save you a bit of time when correcting your work.

The eraser, in those applications that support it, functions just like a pencil eraser in that it lets you "erase" or remove a portion of what you drew or wrote on the screen. Different applications use the eraser differently.

In Windows Journal, for example, you can select from various types of erasers, including a stroke eraser that removes an entire pen stroke instead of just a few pixels.

Tablet PC Pros and Cons

Although there are many benefits to switching to the Tablet PC from another computing platform, there are a few things that you must give up. For example, the Tablet PC has a smaller screen, no integrated removable drives, and a slower processor. But you gain handwriting and speech recognition capabilities, as well as the ability to use your computer instead of paper for almost everything.

Getting Used to Less Screen Real Estate

For me, getting used to less screen real estate was tough. I am a screen real estate hog. I used to only buy laptops with 1400×1050 displays. On top of that, I used a second 1280×1024 display. Now, I still have the external display, but my Tablet PC is only running at 1024×768.

For those of you who don't want to know the numbers, I think bigger is better when it comes to screen real estate, because a bigger screen enables you to be more efficient in your work thanks to less scrolling and application swapping. But the trade-offs for the Tablet PC functionality are worth it.

tip

Use a second screen to extend your desktop. This can help you be more productive than using the Tablet PC screen alone.

What works well for me is to use a second display. I connect an LCD flat-screen to my Toshiba Portégé 3500 whenever I am at home or work. This gives me more screen real estate to work with. Writing this book would have been much more difficult had I not had the second display, as I am constantly going back and forth between Word, Photoshop, the file system, and other applications.

But when I travel, or feel like working on the back porch, I don't have the luxury of the second display. It's not really a problem then, though, because when I'm out and about, the size of the tablet is more welcome than lots of screen space. Also, when I am working in the "mobile" mode, I usually use the pen and the tablet more directly and don't need the confusion of a mouse and second display.

Portability Versus All-in-One

Another thing I miss about my laptop is the easy access to storage devices. Sure, I can easily connect my floppy drive, DVD/CD-RW drive, and external USB 2.0 drives to the Tablet PC, but there was something about being able to burn a CD whenever I needed to transfer data to others that I miss with the Tablet PC.

That said, I don't miss having those integrated peripherals as much as I thought I would—especially when I'm traveling coach at 30,000 feet in the middle seat. There's just not enough room for it there (even on those so-called "extra leg room" flights).

In fact, I don't usually even carry my peripheral drives when I travel. I know that I can connect to the Internet, and thus email, about anywhere, which means I can transfer data even without the drives.

You can still have a CD-ROM drive and floppy drive, they just won't be built into the Tablet PC. Make sure you get one that has fast data throughput capabilities, such as Firewire, USB 2.0, or PC card interface.

But if you're a big CD burner like I was (I used to burn about 20 CDs per month), you'll find it an adjustment, just as I did. On the flip side, I now have fewer junk CDs floating around than I used to.

The portability—not to mention the extra functionality—of the Tablet PC is just too great to go back now. Because I specify the computers we purchase for the companies I work with, my perspective has changed from one of "it's gotta have everything built in" to "it's gotta have the best functionality for the person using it." I didn't used to offer a small laptop option to my users, as I figured the large screen real estate and built-in peripherals were more important than the portability. I was only half right. It totally depends on the user.

Do I Always Use It in Slate Mode?

Simple answer: No. In fact, I rarely use it in slate mode (slate mode is when the tablet is configured so that you have no keyboard or mouse connected, and you are using the pen to do all the work). Mostly, I use the Tablet PC just like a laptop: connected to screen, keyboard, mouse, and other peripherals as needed.

Does this mean it's not worth paying extra for the Tablet PC functionality? No. In fact, when I can use the same device to act like a desktop machine and also a pen and paper, I'm getting a huge bang for the buck. I have stopped using paper for almost everything. I used to take copious notes on paper for all my ideas, and then transfer them as needed to my computer. This allowed me to sketch as I thought, being a visual thinker.

I don't do that any more. Now I figure if it's important enough to think about, it's important enough to keep. Digitally. In whatever form I want.

The Tablet PC allows me to take notes in meetings—usually in slate mode. To type profusely—usually in laptop mode. To travel easily—slate mode again. Play games—laptop mode.

Put simply, the Tablet PC allows me the freedom to work the way I want when I want, without toting around a ream of notes, an extra notebook, a planner, magazines, and books. I can keep it all on my Tablet PC if it's in digital form.

In fact, I have found that I love to listen to books about as much as I like to read them. These days, instead of lugging a hardback novel on the plane, I buy a book on tape, convert it to MP3, and then listen to it on my Tablet PC or MP3 player. With a 60 GB hard drive in my Toshiba Portégé 3500, I have plenty of room to store my music, books, and work-related applications and files. I also save journals in digital form so that I can access them wherever I am. Plus, I have the capability to purchase a subscription in digital form from many journals, which allows me to read the journal in Acrobat Reader, Zinio, Microsoft eBook Reader, or other

note

You will learn when to use slate mode and when to use another mode if you have a convertible (that is, a Tablet PC that looks like a laptop, but can be converted to slate mode by swiveling the screen 180 degrees). Slate is great for reading and taking notes, while notebook mode is best for typing.

applications. This creates a significant digital library that is with me wherever I go—something you can do, too. Refer to Chapter 18 for more information on readers and content sources.

Back to the issue of using slate mode: Yes, I read in slate mode. The Tablet PC is made for it. It takes some getting used to, but the Tablet PC is a great reading platform. Just make sure you have an extra battery or two if you like to read for long periods of time.

Use the Tablet PC any way you like—it's yours. Play with it in different modes. If you bought a slate, you can decide whether you want to carry the keyboard. I couldn't work effectively without a keyboard when I write, although I am starting to really like the speech-recognition capabilities of the Tablet PC—which is why I got the Toshiba Portégé 3500. It is the fastest Tablet PC currently on the market, with a clamshell/convertible design and all the expandability I need. As you no doubt realize, different people have different needs; make sure your tablet is in sync with your needs.

Tablet PC Tutorials

The tutorial screen shown in Figure 1.4 usually comes up when you boot up your Tablet PC unless you check the Do not show me this again check box to disable it. From this screen, you can access various quick tutorials that walk you through a few of the features that come with the Tablet PC. I recommend that you watch these video tutorials before reading further; doing so will give you the big picture of what can be done with the Tablet PC, and will help you get more out of the following chapters.

FIGURE 1.4
The Tablet PC tutorials help you learn how to use the Tablet PC effectively. I recommend you go through them in addition to reading this book.

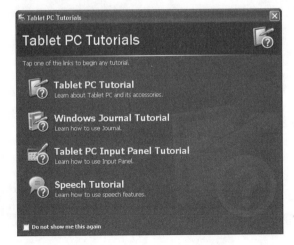

If you do not see the Tutorials page when you start your Tablet PC, tap the **Start** button, tap **Help and Support**, and then tap **Tablet PC Tutorials**. If you can't find the tutorials there, you can reach them through the file system by opening the file C:\Windows\help\latute.hta.

The Tablet PC tutorials use videos, which help deliver the content in a richer way than just this book. Together, the tutorials and this book will help you get the most out of your Tablet PC.

> **tip**
>
> Play the Tablet PC tutorials. They're a great way to get up to speed with the basics quickly. When you're finished with them, come back to this book for more depth in each of the areas.

Tablet PC Tutorial

This tutorial gives an overview of the different input methods and capabilities of the Tablet PC, which is helpful as you move forward in this book. I will repeat most of what is covered in the tutorial in this book, as repetition is one of the keys to learning.

Windows Journal Tutorial

Windows Journal is one of the cornerstone applications of the Tablet PC, which is why it is important to understand how to use it effectively. This is going to be one of your primary note-taking applications. Although I recommend Microsoft OneNote over Windows Journal in many circumstances, Windows Journal is still a powerful tool if you just need note-taking, sketching, and annotation capabilities. When you're finished with the Windows Journal tutorial, you can find more information about the application in Chapters 6, "Using Windows Journal," and 7, "Advanced Windows Journal," where I'll cover almost every aspect of the program.

Input Panel Tutorial

The Input Panel is another key application for the Tablet PC. With it, you can enter hand-written text into any application, including DOS boxes/command prompts. Use this tutorial to get up to speed on the Input Panel; for more in-depth coverage of this great tool, see Chapter 8, "Using the Tablet PC Input Panel."

Speech Tutorial

Speech is a less frequently used input method on the Tablet PC, but one of the most powerful. Windows XP Tablet PC Edition has a good recognition engine that allows you to speak naturally and still be understood. It will be helpful for you to understand at least the basics of using speech input, and the Speech tutorial is a great way to learn. After you've finished the Speech tutorial, you can get more information about speech input in Chapter 9, "Speech Recognition and Voice Control."

Getting Help

There is a fair amount of help available with your Tablet PC. The tutorials just mentioned are one form of help. Another form of help is the Help system included with Windows XP. Just tap **Start**, then tap **Help and Support**, and enter your search criteria.

The Help and Support dialog box also has additional options for support, and may even include manufacturer-specific support tools. This is a great way to learn more about your Tablet PC if you're not in a rush.

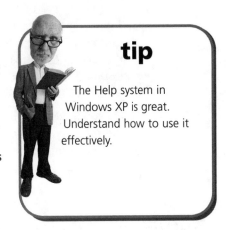

tip

The Help system in Windows XP is great. Understand how to use it effectively.

Thoughts About the Tablet PC's Future

Although the Tablet PC is relatively new, I believe it will change the way people use computers. Some people don't understand how the Tablet PC can help them. Others do. Most people I talk to about Tablet PCs say they don't see the benefit. After ten minutes with them, they usually are placing an order with their purchasing department.

Sometimes the benefits are not obvious. Once you play with one for a day or two and really think through how it could improve your processes and work style, you will probably see areas that it can help. However, not everyone reaches that conclusion, as some simply won't benefit from a Tablet PC.

For many people who are planning to buy a laptop, I recommend going the Tablet PC route instead. Prices aren't much different, and the additional functionality is incredible once you get used to it. Although Tablet PCs are not as fast as high-end notebooks, the additional functionality can benefit many—more so than sheer processor power.

Being able to sit in your easy chair, on the back porch, or in a crowded airplane or airport, and being able to get stuff done effectively without a mouse and wired network connection, makes the Tablet PC much more appealing to me than a laptop.

Sometimes I even sit on the couch in my company's lobby to work when I want to get out of my office. People looked at me funny at first; now they want a Tablet PC, too. (Especially when they see me outside on the deck working on a beautiful day when they're stuck inside.)

The Tablet PC enables a different way of work and life. Do you keep a paper planner? Good. You may want to until FranklinCovey releases version 4 of their TabletPlanner. Version 2 works great, but it still doesn't incorporate the Weekly Compass, a core part of the Franklin Planner. According to sources at FranklinCovey, the Weekly Compass will not be incorporated until version 4. Once the Weekly Compass is included, TabletPlanner will become even more of a killer app for the Tablet PC.

Do you have impromptu meetings in the hallway? Not the domain of laptops. But the Tablet PC can be effective to take notes, pull up information, and even record the conversation for reference later.

Wireless is here to stay. So is the Tablet PC—whether the critics "get it" or not.

The Absolute Minimum

Here are the key points to take away from this chapter:

- Rest your hand on the display. It's not a touch screen, so you can touch anywhere you want with your fingers and nothing will happen.
- Use an external display to extend your screen real estate when in the office.
- Try your Tablet PC in different modes and circumstances to see how you like to use it best. It accommodates multiple modes of operation.
- Use the Tablet PC tutorials to get a quick overview of how to use your Tablet PC, and then jump back into this book to learn more.

2

WHY THE TABLET PC?

This chapter will help you understand why the Tablet PC is such a powerful new computing platform. After you read this chapter, you will be better informed about how a Tablet PC can benefit you and your organization. Realize that people have different computing needs, and that some find the Tablet PC incredibly powerful, while others don't see the benefit.

What Is the Tablet PC?

The Tablet PC is a notebook computer that can operate without a keyboard. Instead, Tablet PCs receive input via the use of a special pen or via speech input. Pen input (called digital ink on the Tablet PC) enables the user to write on, and interact directly with, the computer screen, bypassing the hand-cursor disconnect often encountered with mouse input.

Although the Tablet PC can receive input via digital ink, it should not be mistaken for a simple pen computer. Most pen computers are touch-screen devices, which can actually impair productivity for those who need to rest their hand on the tablet to draw or write. The Tablet PC, on the other hand, does not employ a touch screen, which means you can use it more like a real-life notebook. The pen input of the Tablet PC makes it a perfect platform for taking notes, sketching, painting, and marking up documents and drawings.

When used as a slate (keyboard removed or hidden), it is also an excellent reading platform for digital eBooks and magazines, as well as Acrobat files and Word documents. You can keep most of your reading materials on your Tablet PC for reference any time, instead of having to lug around a carload of books.

The Tablet PC Value Proposition

The Tablet PC enables or enhances the following:

- **Note taking**—You can take notes directly on the Tablet PC in your own handwriting, which enables you to keep all your notes and files together on your computer.

- **Efficient digital collaboration**—The Tablet PC's direct annotation capability fits well with electronic conferencing. You can mark directly on a virtual whiteboard or mark up a document with the pen instead of a mouse, making your annotations more direct.

- **Speech recognition and voice control**—Use your voice to control the Tablet PC and dictate to your favorite word processor.

- **Ultimate portability**—The Tablet PC is more mobile than most laptops, yet has a larger screen surface and higher usability than PDAs.

- **eBook reading**—The Tablet PC makes it easy to read books and journals directly on the tablet.

- **Electronic forms**—You can use your Tablet PC to fill out and sign forms and documents directly on the tablet. This is useful for mobile sales forces, databases, and those who deal often with contracts.

- **Built-in wireless networking (on most models)**—Built-in Wi-Fi allows for anywhere access to corporate data and Internet applications. Many offices and public locations now offer wireless access for their patrons and business partners.

- **Mark up documents without thinking about the software**—Instead of thinking about how to use mark-up software, a Tablet PC enables you to annotate documents with your handwriting to identify items that need to be changed. This can also be used for marking up drawings done in CAD and other applications.

As you can see, the Tablet PC is an exciting new device that will change the way many people interact with their computers. The size of the Tablet PC and the pen input are the features that people notice most, and tend to be the primary reasons that most people get a Tablet PC. The size of the Tablet PC makes it less conspicuous, and thus more accepted, in meetings. The pen input changes the basic interactions with the computer.

In other pen-based machines, the operating system was not designed to make the pen input significantly different from a mouse. With Windows XP Tablet PC Edition, however, the operating system (OS) handles the pen input and allows the user to keep handwritten notes as handwriting—no conversion is required. And because the OS now deals with digital ink, a person can search for notes that are still in handwritten form. Windows XP Tablet PC Edition converts handwriting to text in the background so that it can use the handwriting for searches.

Comparisons to Other Platforms

Many look at the Tablet PC and think it's a cool toy. It is, but it's also a serious business machine. It's important to know the differences between the Tablet PC and other machines before you buy one, and it's helpful to know the differences if you use multiple devices.

Laptops

Laptops are excellent devices for what they're supposed to do: Replace the desktop for mobile users. Laptop prices have dropped to within $1,000 of their desktop counterparts. In addition, the performance of many laptops rivals that of the desktop—although laptops will always lag a bit.

The Tablet PC extends the benefits of the laptop to include direct pen input, which enables people to easily take notes, draw, edit graphics, and deal with the computer more naturally.

In general, Tablet PCs are lighter than laptops in both weight and performance. Most tablets that shipped immediately after the Tablet PC launch had processors in the 800 MHz range, while their laptop cousins were touting speeds exceeding 2 GHz.

Although 800 MHz may seem acceptable for many, the Tablet PC is called upon to perform additional tasks that most computers are not asked to perform. Speech and handwriting recognition take processor horsepower, as does the digitizer interface itself. Newer Tablet PCs are mostly at or above the 1000 MHz (1 GHz) in processor speed.

note

Tablet PCs are more capable than laptops in every way but screen real estate, processing power, and internal drives. That may sound significant, and it is, but many can benefit more from the extra capabilities of the Tablet PC than from those factors.

Desktops

Unfortunately, the Tablet PC is slower than most new PCs, and with a price tag hovering around two to three times higher than a desktop, this can be troubling. Of course, if you have a desktop PC and haven't considered replacing it with a laptop, you may not benefit much from a Tablet PC anyway. If, however, you have been waiting for a more natural input method, you frequently deal with digital photographs and graphics, or you travel often, then the Tablet PC may be a great tool for you.

Many people do not realize that write-on digitizer displays are available now for use in graphics applications. Designers, however, have been using them for some time. Wacom has several models that attach to your desktop or laptop PC and allow you to write directly on the screen, just like the Tablet PC. However, you will lack mobility with this solution. If you don't need to move around a lot and still want the pen interface, consider these, but beware. The cost of a digitizer display is close to the price of a Tablet PC, if not more.

Pocket PC and Other PDAs

For most people, even die-hard PDA users, the screen on a PDA is just too small. The Pocket PC interface is excellent compared to other offerings, but it still comes up short when dealing with more than a small checklist. In addition, most PDAs do not have a great way to input large amounts of data. Although external keyboards can be attached, the screen is still too small for much useful work. Even so, the Pocket PC does remain more mobile than the Tablet PC.

Other Pen-Based Computers

One of the key differences between Tablet PCs and other pen-based computers is that the Tablet PC is not a touch-screen device. This is both good and bad, depending on your viewpoint. The Tablet PC is designed to use a pen for input. You cannot use a finger, stick, pencil, or anything else to write on the tablet. This is great for most of us who rest our hands on the tablet. Touch screens, on the other hand, require a hands-off approach—otherwise, you will select something accidentally with the heel of your hand.

In addition, the Tablet PC has the backing of Microsoft's Windows XP Tablet PC Edition. This provides handwriting and speech recognition, as well as numerous other tools and third-party add-ons. Other pen-based computers, many of which use Windows CE or an older version of Windows, do not have that. Any application that runs on Windows XP also runs on Tablet PCs.

note

The main differences between Tablet PCs and other pen-based computers are the operating system and the digitizer versus touch-screen interface. For most people, the Tablet PC operating system is much better than any other pen-based operating system.

Certain applications require touch-screen input, and some do not. If you need touch-screen input, don't get the Tablet PC unless you want to use the pen a lot. According to sources, the Tablet PC platform will not support touch-screen functionality in the future.

Table 2.1 compares the various computer platforms: Tablet PCs, laptops, desktops, PDAs, and other pen devices.

TABLE 2.1 Computing Platform Comparison

Criteria	Tablet PC	Laptop	Desktop	PDAs	Other Pen Devices
Operating System					
Able to use a form of Windows	Yes	Yes	Yes	Yes	Yes
Linux capable	Yes	Yes	Yes	Sometimes	Yes
Other OS capable	No	Yes	Yes	Yes	Yes

TABLE 2.1   (continued)

Criteria	Tablet PC	Laptop	Desktop	PDAs	Other Pen Devices
Input Capabilities					
Keyboard	Yes	Yes	Yes	Yes	Yes
Mouse	Yes	Yes	Yes	No	Yes
Stylus (digitizer)	Yes	Yes	Yes	Sometimes	Yes
Finger/pen (touch screen)	No	Yes	Yes	Yes	Yes
Handwriting recognition	Yes	Sometimes	Sometimes	Sometimes	Sometimes
Voice recognition	Yes	Sometimes	Sometimes	Sometimes	Sometimes
Portability	Medium/ high	Medium	Low	High	Medium/ high

Tablet PC Differences

There are three basic hardware designs of Tablet PCs, and several mutations from each of those that add value in particular areas.

Differences in Hardware

As shown in Figure 2.1, Tablet PCs come in three basic designs:

- **The slate**—A slate Tablet PC is an excellent choice for those who want the lightest device and who are focused on pen input (handwriting and sketching). If you type often, you can connect a keyboard and mouse to a slate, and in some cases, a slate can be docked. When you're traveling with a slate, you will either need to carry a keyboard along with you or use the pen exclusively.

- **The convertible**—A convertible Tablet PC has the clamshell design of a typical laptop, with a screen that can be twisted and folded down to create a pseudo-slate machine. Although convertibles tend to be a bit bulkier than true slates, the benefits of the built-in keyboard often outweigh the extra weight.

■ **The hybrid**—Hybrid Tablet PCs feature a special keyboard that easily attaches and detaches. When detached from the keyboard, the hybrid becomes a light slate; otherwise, it functions like a convertible. When attached to the slate, the keyboard can be folded over so that both may be carried together. (One down side of this design is that when keyboard and slate are folded up, the screen is exposed, which could lead to screen damage.)

FIGURE 2.1

The three types of Tablet PCs: from left to right, the slate, the convertible, and the hybrid.

Each design has its own strengths and weaknesses; Table 2.2 highlights the key differences between the designs.

TABLE 2.2   A Comparison of Tablet PC Form Factors

Trait	Slate	Hybrid*	Convertible
Speed	Most are around 800–866 MHz	1GHz and above over 1GHz	Ranges from 800MHz to well over 1GHz
Display size	10"–12"	10"	10"–12"
Pen type	Varies	Active	Mostly passive
Keyboard	Separate	Integrated or detached	Integrated
Weight	Light to heavy	Light	Light to Mid

HP/Compaq has the only hybrid currently on the market.

The Absolute Minimum

Keep the following points in mind:

- The Tablet PC is a powerful new platform, and as such, you may need to play around with it to fully understand its capabilities.

- The Tablet PC is different from other computers and pen-based systems. Understand the differences to get the most out of it.

- There are three types of Tablet PCs—the slate, the convertible, and the hybrid. Each has its own benefits and uses.

3

USAGE SCENARIOS

This chapter shows some scenarios outlining how different people can use the Tablet PC to make their lives better. The goal of this chapter is to help you understand how the Tablet PC is used, and the ways in which it can benefit you. As you read each scenario, note the things that apply to you. Likewise, if you think of a Tablet PC feature that ben-efits you but that isn't mentioned here, write it down as well.

The Photographer

The photographer works mostly in the studio, where he uses a high-end digital SLR camera and his Tablet PC to take studio pictures primarily for magazines. With his Tablet PC, he can preview and edit images with the ease of a pen interface.

Toolkit

note

- **Slate style Tablet PC**—This style of Tablet PC offers great mobility.
- **Canon EOS-1Ds digital SLR camera**—This 11.1 megapixel SLR is the professional's dream. It can handle lenses from other Canon SLRs, which makes it perfect for a studio in which the photographer might need to shoot digital one day and film the next.

Most of the hardware and software mentioned in this chapter is covered in Chapters 17, "Hardware Options," and 18, "Useful Software"; for this reason, the descriptions of these products will be brief here.

- **Adobe Photoshop**—The photographer uses this program for image manipulation and perfection.
- **Corel Paint 7**—This is yet another program that enables the photographer to create interesting effects with his photos.
- **Microsoft Office 2003**—The photographer uses this suite of products to handle the business end of things.
- **LCD Projector**—This is great for projecting images for client preview.

Value Proposition

The photographer likes his Tablet PC because it is portable and has a pen interface. He can move the Tablet PC with him as he takes shots from various parts of his studio. This lets him preview the pictures he just took, and enables him to access photographic tools to improve the images on the spot.

Day in the Life

The photographer enters his studio, and starts his day by checking email and his calendar. He will be doing a product photo shoot in the morning and a studio portrait for a family in the afternoon. He sets up the studio to prepare for the product shoot, and then sets up his camera, taking a few test pictures before his client arrives. While he waits, he downloads the test pictures to his Tablet PC through a fire wire (IEEE 1394) connection.

After his test shots are downloaded to his Tablet PC, he views them, and then sends one to his printer via the Wi-Fi network in his studio. The client likes what she sees in the sample photograph, but asks to change a couple things. The resulting image of the first product is just what the client wants, thanks to the interaction of digital imaging and the photographer's Tablet PC. The photographer shoots three more products, and then edits them in Photoshop, balancing the lighting and color for perfect photos. The client is pleased and leaves, CD containing the perfected digital pictures in hand.

After lunch, the family arrives for their studio portrait. The photographer has already set up the studio for them, and this time has his Tablet PC connected to the camera and a projector so that the family can see each picture as it is taken. The PC-camera interface allows for a preview of what the camera sees on the Tablet PC, and thus, on the screen—so the family can see themselves.

After two hours of shooting, the photographer displays the pictures on the screen for the family to select the ones they want. After choosing ten pictures, the family leaves and the photographer switches to post-production mode, editing the images with his pressure-sensitive pen directly on the Tablet PC using Photoshop. After a couple more hours of editing the images, the photographer prints the photos on his large-format photo printer and is done for the day.

Summary of Benefits

Features	Benefits
Pen input	Makes photo editing easier
Digital camera	Provides ultimate photographic freedom
Adobe Photoshop	Can be used to perfect photographs
Corel Paint 7	Increases photographic creativity
LCD projector	Offers image previews for clients

The Construction Supervisor

The construction supervisor is responsible for keeping construction projects moving forward on a tight timeline and noting any problems or potential problems.

Toolkit

- **Rugged slate style Tablet PC**—This style of Tablet PC offers great mobility.
- **Digital camera**—This can be used to capture pictures of construction issues and progress.
- **Bluetooth adapter**—This is necessary for data communication with other Bluetooth-enabled devices.
- **Bluetooth mobile phone**—This can be used to connect to the Tablet PC for wireless Internet access.
- **Adobe Photoshop Elements**—This program is used for photo manipulation.
- **Mi-Forms**—This program is for data capture.
- **FranklinCovey TabletPlanner**—This program is used for time and task management.
- **Adobe Acrobat**—This program is used for digital document creation.
- **AutoDesk VoloView**—This program is used for CAD markups.

Value Proposition

The most important thing for the construction supervisor is flexibility and easy information sharing. Using the Tablet PC, she does not have to remain in a construction trailer to deal with paperwork, and can quickly share data and images of what is happening in the field.

Day in the Life

The construction supervisor checks her email when she gets to the site and finds out that plans have changed: An inspector will arrive this afternoon instead of tomorrow, causing a shift in some priorities.

At 8:00, she uses her Tablet PC to connect to a virtual meeting with a few other people in three offices. Everyone can see images coming in real-time from a Web camera set up at the construction site. Using Microsoft NetMeeting, the construction supervisor can open a CAD drawing on her computer and share the application with others in the meeting, allowing them to see the drawing and even annotate it. After 15 minutes, the meeting ends and everyone is back on track.

The construction supervisor opens TabletPlanner and adjusts the priority of items on her task list. She then fires off a few quick emails to some project team members to keep them in the loop about the day's changes. Then she walks around the construction site, taking pictures of the work completed the day before, noting anything that needs attention. During this process, she also uses Mi-Forms to note any critical information. When finished with the walk-through, she puts the pictures into Windows Journal and makes notes about each picture. She then prints the combined pictures and notes to the PDF Writer and posts the resulting PDF to the project's Web site for team members to review and comment on. She also submits the Mi-Forms data changes to the database server for tracking.

The construction supervisor then talks to several of the crews on-site to let them know what's happening and that they need to get some critical items finished before the inspector arrives. By lunch, the main issues have been taken care of, and the site passes the inspection and gets the required permit.

Summary of Benefits

Features	Benefits
Bluetooth adapter and phone	Enables easy, in-the-field data communications with other team members
AutoDesk VoloView	Can be used to mark up CAD drawings in the field, speeding the update process
Digital camera	Eliminates film costs and produces instant results
Mi-Forms	Enables forms-based information entry

The Consultant/Project Manager

The consultant works for a management consulting firm, and is on the road most days of the week. Because of the extreme traveling and the need to stay connected with the project team, The consultant is thrilled to have a Tablet PC.

Toolkit

- **Convertible style Tablet PC**—This style of Tablet PC is ideal for high text demands.
- **Noise-canceling headset**—Using this type of headset makes using the Tablet PC's speech-recognition features much easier.
- **Bluetooth adapter**—This is necessary for data communication with other Bluetooth-enabled devices.
- **Bluetooth mobile phone**—This can be connected to the Tablet PC to enable wireless Internet access.

- **Microsoft Office 2003**—The consultant/project manager uses this to prepare documents and email.
- **Microsoft OneNote**—This program is great for creating free-form notes and for brainstorming.
- **FranklinCovey TabletPlanner**—This program is used for time and task management.
- **Adobe Acrobat**—This program is used for digital document creation.
- **Microsoft eBook Reader**—This program can be used to read electronic periodicals and other documents on the Tablet PC.
- **Microsoft Visio**—This program is ideal for creating diagrams and flowcharts.
- **Microsoft Project**—This program aids in project management.

Value Proposition

The Tablet PC is more portable and useful while traveling than even a lightweight laptop computer. The ability to take notes and draw directly on the screen to capture thoughts makes it more powerful than other computers. Combined with TabletPlanner and other applications, the consultant can run every bit of his work life from the Tablet PC, including keeping up with periodicals and news.

Day in the Life

The consultant wakes up in his hotel room and turns on his Tablet PC, checking email and gathering his thoughts. He takes his Tablet PC with him to the hotel gym, having downloaded the latest edition of *The Wall Street Journal* and the local paper. While he rides the stationery bicycle, he can read his periodicals and prepare his mind for a day full of meetings and action.

After his workout and preparation for the day, he drives to the client's office and sits down at his desk. On the way into his office, the wireless network connection on the Tablet PC connects him to his home office and downloads recent information from a knowledge management Web site, storing the information for off-line retrieval. His files are also synchronized at the same time, so that if he loses or damage his Tablet PC, he will have backup files at the home office.

After checking his email and synchronizing TabletPlanner to Outlook, he heads off for his 9:00 meeting with the CEO of the client company. When he arrives, he connects his Tablet PC into the conference room projector and opens his PowerPoint presentation. About five minutes into his presentation to the CEO and her staff, the consultant wants to make a point, and uses his pen to annotate a PowerPoint slide—without stopping the presentation.

The consultant is thanked for his insight and is given approval to continue with the project to the next milestone. The CEO is complimentary about how the consultant kept up with everything on such a tight timeline project.

When the consultant returns to his office, he opens Windows Journal and makes some quick notes and sketches, outlining the key points in the next phase of the project. He then uses Visio to turn the rough ideas into professional graphics. He connects to his company's knowledge portal and starts a chat session with two of his colleagues in other parts of the world. They discuss best practices for the next phase of his project, and he comes away with a new viewpoint that saves him several weeks on the project. One of his colleagues sends him a link to a document she recently had published on the company intranet, allowing the consultant to get moving on the project even faster.

Summary of Benefits

Features	Benefits
Wireless networking	Enables access to information in many locations
Bluetooth adapter and phone	Enables in-the-field data communications with team members
Microsoft Office 2003	Allows for the creation of business documents and email
Microsoft OneNote	Allows for the use of free-form text, graphics, handwriting, and audio recording
FranklinCovey Tablet Planner	Keeps life organized
Digital document readers	Keeps all reading materials in one place

The Salesperson

The salesperson sells computer networking hardware and services, and often needs access to configuration tools when on a sales call.

Toolkit

- **Convertible style Tablet PC**—This style of Tablet PC is ideal for high text demands.
- **Bluetooth adapter**—This is necessary for data communication with other Bluetooth-enabled devices.

- **Bluetooth mobile phone**—This can be connected to the Tablet PC to enable wireless Internet access.
- **Microsoft Office 2003**—The salesperson uses this to prepare documents and email.
- **Microsoft OneNote**—This program is great for creating free-form notes and for brainstorming.
- **FranklinCovey TabletPlanner**—This program is used for time and task management.

Value Proposition

The Tablet PC enables the salesperson to access product information, a configuration tool, spreadsheets, and anything else she needs—all while on the road, giving her more face time with clients.

Day in the Life

The salesperson arrives at the office, Tablet PC in hand. She has a busy day ahead of her, but has an early meeting at the office, where she takes notes using her Tablet PC. After the meeting, she catches up on email and administrative issues, and then heads to her car with just her Tablet PC.

When she arrives at her first appointment of the day, at the headquarters of a pharmaceutical company, she meets with her client, who is ready to upgrade part of his network. She can guide him in the purchasing process through her knowledge, and by quickly finding specifications from her complete product line on her Tablet PC. She recommends a particular server and integration services, and he looks over the specifications. She connects to the client's Bluetooth printer with her Tablet PC and prints the specifications and quotation right then, saving a day's lag time while she's out of the office. Because she has access to her company's custom configuration tool through secure wireless Internet access, she is assured that the solution she is selling will work great for her client.

When she leaves the company's office, order in hand, it is an hour later, and she heads for her second appointment across town. While on her way, she gets a call from another client asking for a rush order of a network switch to replace the one that just died. She pulls over into a parking lot. The salesperson says she'll get something quick, hangs up, connects her Tablet PC to the office via her Bluetooth phone connection, and checks inventory of networking switches. She does not have any of the specific model in stock, so she checks her distributor's inventory. They have one, and she places the order, confirming same-day delivery via a courier service.

Because the distributor is only an hour away, the switch will arrive at her client's in two hours, allowing time for order processing.

She calls her client back, tells him the switch is on its way, and asks if she can have a loaner delivered immediately to get users back on the network. He says he has an older hub that he is using for now, so he can get by until the switch arrives in two hours. He thanks her for her responsiveness and promises to write a glowing testimonial about her service.

Summary of Benefits

Features	Benefits
Wireless networking	Enables wireless access to information
Bluetooth adapter and phone	Allows connectivity to other devices
FranklinCovey Tablet Planner	Keeps life organized
Digital document readers	Keeps all reading and sales materials in one place
Microsoft Office 2003	Aids in business-document creation
Microsoft OneNote	Enables the creation of free-form notes to capture the essence of a meeting

The Executive

The executive runs a medium-size product-oriented company. She travels often and spends a fair amount of time in meetings. She is comfortable with technology, but really likes the pen interface on the Tablet PC.

Toolkit

- **Convertible style Tablet PC**—This style of Tablet PC is ideal for high text demands.
- **Noise-canceling headset**—Using this type of headset makes using the Tablet PC's speech-recognition features much easier.
- **Bluetooth adapter**—This is necessary for data communication with other Bluetooth-enabled devices.
- **Bluetooth mobile phone**—This can be connected to the Tablet PC to enable wireless Internet access.
- **Microsoft Office 2003**—The executive uses this to prepare documents and email.

- ■ **Microsoft OneNote**—This program is great for creating free-form notes and for brainstorming.
- ■ **FranklinCovey TabletPlanner**—This program is used for time and task management.
- ■ **Microsoft eBook Reader**—This program can be used to read electronic periodicals and other documents on the Tablet PC.
- ■ **Windows Journal**—This program is ideal for taking notes and sketching ideas.

Value Proposition

The executive spends a fair amount of time in meetings, yet is mobile as well. Access to information at any time is important for decision making, so the wireless network access and the integration with a cellular phone for Internet access is important. The lightweight and natural input capabilities of the Tablet PC make it a winner for the executive.

Day in the Life

The executive logs on to email over breakfast in the morning via a wireless link to her Internet router. Her schedule reminds her of her son's game that night, and she tells him she intends to be there to cheer him on.

After saying goodbye to her family, the executive heads for the office, where she immediately prepares fore the first meeting of the day. When she gets to the office, her Tablet PC connects to the wireless office LAN (after she enters the required password for security). The presentation she worked on last night is uploaded to her assistant, who checks it for accuracy and fills in any gaps.

When the executive gets to her first meeting, she turns her Tablet PC into a slate format device for taking notes. Although someone else records the meeting, the executive can take notes and sketch ideas directly on the Tablet PC with a pen.

After the meeting, the executive saves her Microsoft OneNote notes, which are synchronized automatically with her network file store. This enables the executive's assistant to turn notes into text, refine the sketches, and return the information to the executive without the need for explicit data transfers and communication.

The executive then checks her TabletPlanner for the tasks for the day and begins working on her highest priority item—a presentation for a new product launch that afternoon. She looks in the file store on her machine, and finds that the presentation she worked on last night has been updated by her assistant while the executive was in the meeting. She looks the presentation over, thanks her assistant for the extra slides she didn't think about, and runs through the presentation a couple times before heading for the airport.

The executive checks off the task in TabletPlanner and then moves to her next item—some reading. The executive's assistant found some articles of interest, highlighted the pertinent parts, and dropped them in the executive's Reading folder on her Tablet PC. Because the articles are in Acrobat format, the executive can read the articles directly on her Tablet PC while riding to the airport.

Once at the airport, she checks in, and then connects to the airport's wireless network (she has an account because she frequents the airport). When she is connected, she checks her email, where she finds some last-minute statistics and information on competing products that will help her in her presentation later that day. Because the executive will be traveling only for the day, she carries only her Tablet PC case, complete with extra batteries (charged, of course). The executive can use her Tablet PC in line, on the plane, and in the taxi more effectively than any laptop. The pen-based input makes the Tablet PC more effective in confined spaces.

After her presentation and the lauds of the crowd at the announcement of her company's newest product, she flies back home and heads for her son's game.

Summary of Benefits

Features	Benefits
Wireless networking	Enables wireless access to information while on the move
Bluetooth adapter and phone	Enables on-the-go data communications
FranklinCovey TabletPlanner	Keeps life organized
Digital document readers	Keeps all reading materials in one place
Microsoft Office 2003	Aids in business-document creation
Microsoft OneNote	Enables the creation of free-form notes to capture the essence of a meeting

The Doctor

The doctor is constantly moving around her office and the hospital in which she works. Accessing patient information on her Tablet PC makes it easier to review case files regardless of her location.

Toolkit

- **Convertible style Tablet PC**—This style of Tablet PC is ideal for high text demands.
- **Bluetooth adapter**—This is necessary for data communication with other Bluetooth-enabled devices.
- **Digital camera**—This can be used to capture pictures of patient issues, such as rashes and wounds.
- **Noise-canceling headset**—Using this type of headset makes using the Tablet PC's speech-recognition features much easier.
- **Dragon Naturally Speaking**—This program is perfect for higher-quality speech recognition and for its medical dictionary.
- **Microsoft Office 2003**—The doctor uses this to prepare documents and email.
- **Mi-Forms**—This program is for data capture.

Value Proposition

The doctor likes the portability, speech input, pen annotation ability, and natural note taking that the Tablet PC provides. Indeed, using the Tablet PC can save the doctor several hours a week, which can then be spent on other cases. Speech recognition can reduce staff requirements and the time needed to transcribe voice recordings. Pen annotation is often faster and more meaningful than using a keyboard. Windows Journal and InfoPath enable the doctor to take notes naturally and unobtrusively.

Day in the Life

The doctor arrives at her office at 7:30. Her Tablet PC is on her desk, where it synchronizes with the database server and uploads patient information for the day. Throughout the day, the Tablet PC will synchronize with the custom software in the hospital's database to ensure that the doctor always has the most current information, and to ensure that the server has the latest information from the doctor's Tablet PC.

After checking her case load, she looks up some information about an obscure disease that she thinks one of her patients may have contracted. Searching through the hospital's medical reference tools online, she finds that her initial diagnosis was correct, and makes a note on the patient's chart on her Tablet PC.

At 8:00, she picks up her Tablet PC and heads for her first patient. Because the Tablet PC has all the patient information she needs, and because the Tablet PC is tied to her calendar, the appropriate information automatically appears on the Tablet PC's screen when the doctor walks to the patient's room. She refers to her Tablet PC and the Mi-Forms application displayed there instead of picking up a clipboard. She talks with her patient and takes pen-based notes directly in Mi-Forms. She takes a picture of an infected area on the patient, sending the image directly to the patient's file for reference. When she is finished with the patient, the doctor makes medication notes on the Mi-Forms application, which automatically triggers a process for medication retrieval and delivery.

Every person who comes in contact with the patient records information on the patient's chart in the Mi-Forms application. This ensures that all actions are documented, and that some mistakes can be caught before they become problems (such as medications that conflict with a patient's allergy being flagged for doctor's review before processing). Any such mistakes caught will be brought to the doctor's attention on the Tablet PC. The primary physician for a patient will always be notified of activities and changes related to that patient.

Because the Tablet PC is in constant communication with the hospital's central servers, the doctor is always notified of changes immediately. The doctor's personal schedule is in the server, which allows scheduling experts to make appropriate adjustments to schedules based on patient needs and physician case loads. The Tablet PC allows everyone to stay in communication, and reduces miscommunication and patient record problems.

Summary of Benefits

Features	Benefits
Pen input	Allows for the annotation of patient information
Speech input	Increases text input speed and frees hands
Wireless networking	Provides access to information throughout the hospital or clinic
Digital camera	Allows for immediate documentation
Digital document readers	Keeps all reading materials in one place
Microsoft Office 2003	Aids in business-document creation
FranklinCovey Tablet Planner	Keeps life organized
Mi-Forms	Enables forms-based information entry

The Attorney

The attorney is responsible for several clients and cases. To keep up with demands, she has turned to the Tablet PC. It has helped her keep notes in a single place and to easily share those notes with colleagues. The Tablet PC also helps her to stay in touch with others so she can more quickly accomplish her work.

Toolkit

- **Convertible design Tablet PC**—This type of Tablet PC is ideal in this situation because it allows for quick keyboard use when needed.
- **Noise-canceling headset**—Using this type of headset makes using the Tablet PC's speech-recognition features much easier.
- **Dragon Naturally Speaking**—This program is perfect for higher-quality speech recognition and for its legal dictionary.
- **Microsoft Office 2003**—The attorney uses this to prepare documents and email.
- **Microsoft OneNote**—This program is great for creating free-form notes and for brainstorming.
- **Adobe Acrobat**—This program is used for digital document creation, and for transferring sealed digital documents.

Value Proposition

The attorney likes the portability, speech recognition, pen-annotation ability, and natural note taking of the Tablet PC. The Tablet PC can save her several hours a week that can be spent on other cases, or with her family. Speech recognition can reduce staff and time needed to transcribe voice recordings, and pen annotation is often faster and more meaningful than using a keyboard. Windows Journal allows the attorney to take notes naturally and unobtrusively.

Day in the Life

The attorney checks her email and calendar and notices that a colleague has asked for some comments on an active case. She dictates an email back to the colleague into the Tablet PC. At 8:30, she prepares for her 9:30 court hearing by downloading all relevant case files to her Tablet PC and reviews her notes on the case. At 9:00, she heads to the courthouse carrying only her Tablet PC. She no longer needs to lug around a large briefcase filled with papers and files.

Because the courthouse has a Wi-Fi network that is accessible by attorneys, she can cross-check a few facts with a colleague back at the office via email, not disturbing the quiet of the courtroom with a phone call. Facts verified, she approaches her seat in front of the judge and gets underway with the trial. During the testimonies, the attorney can take notes in Microsoft OneNote, and can organize the notes as she proceeds. Because of her ability to quickly cross-reference digital information, she finds the answer to a question a testimony sparked, and is ready for cross-examination. When she cross-examines the witness, the information she found helps tear down the testimony and win her the case.

After her stint in court, she goes to a witness's house on another case and asks some questions, again taking notes on her Tablet PC with Microsoft OneNote. This time, though, she can record the conversation in Microsoft OneNote so that she can be sure that her notes are accurate. With Microsoft OneNote, the attorney can easily move her note nuggets, allowing her to rearrange her thoughts easily on the virtual paper. This allows her to see relationships between ideas more readily.

When she is finished with her interview, she returns to her office and submits her notes to her assistant, who cleans up the documents, checks for accuracy against the audio recording, and submits the file to the server.

Summary of Benefits

Features	Benefits
Pen input	More natural than a mouse
Speech input	Saves typing and transcription time
Wireless networking	Offers connectivity on the fly
Microsoft Office 2003	Aids in business-document creation
Microsoft OneNote	Enables the creation of free-form notes and graphics, and features handwriting and audio recording

The Real Estate Agent

The real estate agent deals in residential properties and prides himself on finding the perfect house for each person.

Toolkit

- **Convertible style Tablet PC**—This style of Tablet PC is ideal for high text demands.

- **Bluetooth adapter**—This is necessary for data communication with other Bluetooth-enabled devices.
- **Bluetooth mobile phone**—This can be connected to the Tablet PC to enable wireless Internet access.
- **Digital camera with Bluetooth**—This can be used to capture pictures of homes that might interest clients.
- **Navman GPS 4400 GPS receiver**—This program enables users to find directions and track travel progress.
- **FranklinCovey TabletPlanner**—This program is used for time and task management.
- **Microsoft Office 2003**—The real estate agent uses this to prepare documents and email.
- **Adobe Acrobat**—This program is used for digital document creation.

Value Proposition

The Tablet PC can reduce paperwork in the office and allow the agent to spend more time in the field with clients. With a completely mobile setup, he can connect to the office and the Internet while in the car, allowing more timely access to information.

Day in the Life

The real estate agent doesn't even go to the office much any more. Instead, he begins his day at home by checking recent MLS additions that meet his clients' criteria. He finds a new listing for one of his clients, and emails her the listing to let her know. He also inputs the addresses for most of the homes he wants to visit for the day and has his Tablet PC tell him the optimal driving route.

He takes his Tablet PC in the car with him, connecting it to a GPS and letting it tell him directions via voice prompting. He arrives at his first appointment, picks her up, and confirms the houses she wants to see. He pulls up the first address and reviews the map quickly to confirm the shortest route.

When they get to the first house, the agent grabs his Tablet PC and goes to the door, unlocking it for his client. He walks around the house with her, telling her details such as the builder's reputation and identifying any quality issues in the house, such as excellent or poor craftsmanship. He makes digital notes about the house on the listing that he pulled from MLS, and these notes are tied to the listing number in Mi-Forms so that he can refer to them later as well as share the comments with colleagues. After looking around, they both decide that the house is not quite what she is looking for, so they head to the next house.

While she is looking around the second house, he connects to the Internet via his Bluetooth phone, and checks MLS for anything new. He finds one that may suit his client, and imports the listing to Mi-Forms, which he can mark up. He adds the address to his navigation program and it now becomes the fourth stop of the morning.

After they leave the second house, having declared it a possibility, they go to the third, which is not for her. When they reach the fourth (the house that just got listed), she immediately likes what she sees. When they enter the house, they discover that it is perfect for her. The builder is reputable, and the construction quality is excellent. In addition, the floor plan and upkeep is great as well.

The client decides that this is what she is looking for, and the agent recommends driving around the neighborhood to look for any issues. They find none, and she decides to place an offer. Because the agent has everything he needs on his Tablet PC, he parks in a nearby parking lot, pulls up the contract template, and fills in the details while the client is excited. He then faxes the contract to the seller's agent via his Bluetooth phone connection, and the first part of the deal is done.

The agent and the client return to her house, and they part company pleased with the morning's success. Later that day, the agent gets confirmation that the seller has accepted the offer.

Summary of Benefits

Features	Benefits
Bluetooth adapter and phone	Enables in-the-field data communications with the office and MLS.
Digital camera	Allows for a quick listing creation at the client's house.
GPS receiver and software	Guides the real estate agent through voice prompting as turns approach, and provides a digital, constantly updated map of the area.
FranklinCovey TabletPlanner	Keeps life organized.
Microsoft Office 2003	Word is the basis for the agent's contracts. Excel enables him to show mortgage options and compare financing packages.
Adobe Acrobat	Keeps all reading materials in one place. The agent can easily create digital documents of MLS listings and other information. These documents can then be marked up to include notes and other information.

The Home Inspector

Home inspectors must take lots of notes in order to provide value to their clients. One of the problems has always been taking notes in the field and then transcribing them back at the office—until now.

Toolkit

- **Convertible style Tablet PC**—This style of Tablet PC is ideal for high text demands.
- **Digital voice recorder**—The home inspector can use this to dictate notes.
- **Dragon Naturally Speaking**—This program is perfect for higher-quality speech recognition.
- **Bluetooth adapter**—This is necessary for data communication with other Bluetooth-enabled devices.
- **Digital camera with Bluetooth**—This can be used to document findings.
- **FranklinCovey TabletPlanner**—This program is used for time and task management.
- **Microsoft Office 2003**—The home inspector uses this to prepare documents and email.
- **Adobe Photoshop Elements**—This program can be used for basic photo manipulation.
- **Mi-Forms**—This program is for data capture.
- **Microsoft Visio**—This program is ideal for generating floor plans on the fly.
- **Windows Journal**—This program is ideal for taking notes and sketching ideas.

Value Proposition

Due to the nature of the job, the home inspector is constantly out of the office. In the past, even small laptop computers needed to be set down somewhere before they could be used to enter information; lugging one around did not make sense. The Tablet PC changes all that. Now the home inspector has a tool that can be carried almost everywhere, and can replace the clipboard, the voice recorder, and the calculator.

Day in the Life

The home inspector has two inspections due today, and downloads maps for each onto his Tablet PC. He reads over the notes from the real estate agent who hired him for the inspections, and prepares the background material for each.

Opening Mi-Forms, he enters as much information as he has about the location, does some background research into the neighborhood and comparable properties, and enters that information into Mi-Forms as well.

He takes his Tablet PC and drives to the house, where he meets the prospective homeowners and their real estate agent, informs them of the background information he discovered in his pre-inspection, and then gets to work.

He picks up his digital voice recorder and walks around the house, dictating notes that will be automatically transcribed by his Tablet PC when he synchronizes the two. Because the voice files are stored digitally, he can run the sound file through voice recognition later, correcting anything he needs to.

While he walks through the house measuring and dictating, he takes pictures with his digital camera. When he gets back to where he left the Tablet PC running, he downloads the pictures through his Bluetooth wireless connection. While the files are downloading, he processes the voice files and ensures that the measurements are accurate.

He then walks through the house quickly, Tablet PC in hand, to sketch the basic floor plan. He inserts his drawing from Windows Journal into Visio and overlays the sketch with a more refined drawing using Visio's basic architectural tools. All told, he spends about 20 minutes doing this.

When finished inside the house, he takes his Tablet PC outside and begins taking pictures and making notes in Mi-Forms. Because his camera and Tablet PC are in close proximity, the Bluetooth connection is active, and the files from the digital camera are automatically displayed on his Tablet PC screen.

When he finishes the house inspection, he enters most of the data into his Mi-Forms inspection form, where the data can be automatically massaged and fed into a report for the client. He reviews his findings and clarifies any ambiguous notes. All the information ends up in Mi-Forms.

The pictures he took are fed into Photoshop Elements, where they are cleaned up with a few taps of the pen, and annotations are made to identify points of interest. The pen makes this process quicker. The pictures are then linked with Mi-Forms data elements so that the report can be generated quickly. Although the entire inspection was done with just a modicum of time savings, his report is all but complete when he leaves the house, potentially saving hours of time back in the office. All he has to do is cross-check his facts and clarify recommendations, then email the report to the client.

He does the same work with the second inspection, and when he returns to the office, he returns a few phone calls, opens his Mi-Forms application, and generates the inspection reports for each property. He double-checks the accuracy, digitally signs the documents, and emails them to the client.

Summary of Benefits

Features	Benefits
Speech input	Allows for text input while the user does other things
Bluetooth adapter	Allows wireless connectivity
Digital camera with Bluetooth	Enables instant visual documentation
Cordless headset	Enables users to roam free
Microsoft Office 2003	Aids in inspection-report creation
Mi-Forms	Allows for forms-based information entry
FranklinCovey TabletPlanner	Keeps life organized

The Insurance Adjuster

The insurance adjuster evaluates vehicles for damage and assesses the costs to repair vehicles, if repairable. She often works outside the office with her clients, and wants to take up as little of each client's time as possible.

Toolkit

- **Convertible style Tablet PC**—This style of Tablet PC is ideal for high text demands.

- **Noise-canceling headset**—Using this type of headset makes using the Tablet PC's speech-recognition features much easier.

- **Dragon Naturally Speaking**—This program is perfect for higher-quality speech recognition.

- **Microsoft Office 2003**—The insurance adjuster uses this to prepare documents and email.

- **Adobe Acrobat**—This program is used for digital document creation.

- **Digital camera**—This can be used to capture pictures of the policyholder's vehicle.
- **Bluetooth adapter**—This is necessary for data communication with other Bluetooth-enabled devices.
- **Bluetooth mobile phone**—This can be used to connect to the Tablet PC for wireless Internet access.
- **InfoPath**—This program can be used for data capture.

Value Proposition

Instead of taking notes while looking at the vehicle, then looking up part and labor costs, the insurance adjuster can now use the small, wireless Tablet PC to take notes, take pictures, and look up information without ever having to return to the office.

Day in the Life

The insurance adjuster arrives at the office, checks email, and responds to a few messages. Two new cases have notified her that that they will be in this morning, and she pulls up the information on their policies to determine their coverage.

When the first client arrives, the insurance adjuster takes her Tablet PC out to the client's vehicle, ready with the client's file open and the claim form partially completed. The claim form uses InfoPath 2003, which allows the insurance adjuster to enter information into a form, and then upload the information into the company database system using XML.

The insurance adjuster greets the client, and then walks around the vehicle, taking pictures with the digital camera inserted into the Tablet PC's PC card slot. The camera is sufficient to capture the details required, while not being separate from the Tablet PC. After several pictures are taken, they are dragged into the InfoPath application, where they are stored with the client's electronic claim file.

The insurance adjuster then asks some questions about the accident and enters the answers into the Tablet PC, using the machine's voice-recognition capabilities. Because the client was able to drive the car to the office, the insurance adjuster can access her network and server-based applications, which enable her to handle all claim-settlement tasks without returning to the office. After she submits the claim to her server, it goes through processing, which aggregates the information from InfoPath and other sources and creates a report in Word. Then, a check is automatically printed for the client. The insurance adjuster enters the office to retrieve the report and the check, and then sends the client on his way.

Later in the day, the insurance adjuster gets a call while at lunch. One of her clients was involved in a collision, and the car is not movable. While she finishes her lunch, the insurance adjuster connects her Tablet PC to the Internet via the Bluetooth connection with her phone. She can download all necessary information on the client's policy, and has populated as much of the InfoPath application as possible without entering anything herself.

She gets the rest of her lunch to go, and travels to the client's vehicle, and completes the report in a similar fashion to the first. However, because she is out of the office, she maintains her data connection through her Bluetooth phone and a Virtual Private Network (VPN) link back to the office, which ensures security. After submitting the InfoPath data to the server, she drives back to the office, where the check is waiting. The client can wait for the money, but the insurance adjuster wants to provide the highest level of service, so she delivers it on her way home that afternoon.

Summary of Benefits

Features	Benefits
Wireless networking	Allows access to information when roaming
Speech input	Enables hands-free text input
Bluetooth adapter	Allows connectivity to other devices
Microsoft Office 2003	Aids in document creation
InfoPath	Allows for forms-based information entry

The Service Technician

The service technician is a TV repairman who works on many brands on site. He needs ready access to product manuals and service tracking tools.

Toolkit

- **Convertible style Tablet PC**—This style of Tablet PC is ideal for high text demands.
- **Canon i70 portable printer**—This can be used to provide a service ticket to the customer.
- **Navman GPS 4400 GPS receiver**—This program enables users to find directions and track travel progress.

- **Microsoft Office 2003**—The service technician uses this to prepare service tickets and email.
- **Adobe Acrobat**—This program is used for viewing and annotating PDF files.
- **Windows Journal**—This program is ideal for taking notes and sketching ideas.

Value Proposition

The Tablet PC allows the service technician to have access to hundreds of manuals without having to tote more than four pounds. It also provides instant access to the information he's looking for.

Day in the Life

The service technician gets called out to a customer location to fix her TV. He knows the brand, and an idea of the issue, so he brings the spare parts he thinks he'll need.

When he arrives on site, he looks at the TV, assesses the problem, and then opens it to replace a component. The service technician is unfamiliar with this particular TV, so he consults his Tablet PC for the proper repair procedure. Within seconds, he has the information he needs, and gets the part from the truck. The manual is vague in one area, and he has to tinker to properly fix the TV.

Half an hour later, he has the part replaced, has tested the TV, and has documented the repair process on his Tablet PC. He even has updated the online manual with some handwritten notes so that others can benefit from his experience. The repair document gets saved in the customer's repair history electronic folder and can be accessed by other technicians to determine proper procedure. The manual will be synchronized with the server at the office so everyone will have updated manuals.

The service technician prints the customer's repair ticket and receipt on the battery-operated printer by connecting the Tablet PC to the printer via infrared.

Summary of Benefits

Features	Benefits
Pen input	Enables handwritten forms input
Portable printer	Prints documentation for customers
GPS receiver and software	Guides the technician through voice as turns approach
Microsoft Office 2003	Aids in creating service reports and receipts
Adobe Acrobat	Enables users to view digital product manuals

The Student

The student is in college, and uses the Tablet PC for her everyday computing, including class notes. Her school requires every student to have a laptop, but the student chose the Tablet PC because it does so much more.

Toolkit

- **Convertible style Tablet PC**—This style of Tablet PC is ideal for high text demands.
- **Computer-ready backpack**—The student uses this to carry the Tablet PC and books.
- **Digital camera**—This can be used to capture pictures of college life.
- **Logitech QuickCam for Notebooks**—This still/video camera is ideal for video chats.
- **Logitech Internet Chat Headset**—The student uses these for online voice chatting, video conferencing, and speech recognition.
- **Sony ECM-ZS90 switchable stereo zoom microphone**—The student uses this microphone to capture audio in lectures and meetings.
- **FranklinCovey TabletPlanner**—This program is used for time and task management.
- **Dragon Naturally Speaking**—This program is perfect for higher-quality speech recognition.
- **Microsoft Office 2003**—The student uses this to prepare documents, email, presentations, and spreadsheets.
- **Microsoft OneNote**—This program is great for creating free-form notes and for brainstorming.
- **Adobe Photoshop Elements**—This program is used for photo manipulation.
- **Microsoft Visio**—This program is ideal for creating diagrams.
- **Windows Journal**—This program is ideal for taking notes and sketching ideas.
- **Microsoft NetMeeting**—The student uses this program for online meetings and video chats.

Value Proposition

Many students find that they need a combination of paper and computer in class because in addition to taking textual notes, they also need to sketch ideas, graphs, and the like. The Tablet PC allows the student to take notes using handwriting or the keyboard, as she chooses, and still sketch by using the pen interface. Now all her notes are digital.

Day in the Life

The student gets up, checks her email, and gets ready for the day. She turns on her camera and puts on her headset and calls her friend from high school over the Internet, who goes to school in another state. It's his birthday. They can see and hear each other through the video chat. She wishes him happy birthday and eventually disconnects.

She grabs her backpack, stuffs the Tablet PC into it, and heads for class. Once in class, she pulls out her Tablet PC and gets ready to take notes with Microsoft OneNote. OneNote enables her to enter text free-form and later organize the thoughts and sketches any way she wants. She prefers this mode of note-taking over Word, because it gives her more freedom to tie related thoughts together and to sketch ideas in real time. Plus, when she connects her zoom microphone to her Tablet PC, she can capture the lecture at the same time. Microsoft OneNote allows her to create a time-based record of the classroom, integrating the audio discussion with the notes she takes. This allows her to check her notes later to ensure she has the information correct.

When class is over, the student walks to her next class, and decides to take some pictures of a group of friends she meets along the way. By the time the day is over, the pictures are edited, annotated, and sent to each of her friends by using Photoshop Elements and email.

After the school day is over in the late afternoon, the student checks her TabletPlanner schedule and task list and knocks out her top two priorities for the day—a take-home quiz and an outline for an upcoming paper. Then she begins writing her paper by dictating it to her Tablet PC using the headset. She can capture many of her ideas without ever having to use a keyboard. Although she types quickly, she speaks even faster, and her speech-recognition software allows her to speak rapidly. After an hour of dictating, she has a good portion of her paper done.

Summary of Benefits

Features	Benefits
Pen input	Allows for natural note taking
Wireless networking	Is compatible with many college infrastructures
Speech input	Enables fast text input
Digital camera	Captures college life
Web Camera	Can be used for video chats
Headset	Can be used for speech recognition and chats
Zoom microphone	Captures lectures in OneNote
FranklinCovey TabletPlanner	Helps the student stay on top of school-related deliverables and events
Digital document readers	Keeps all reading materials in one place
Microsoft Office 2003	Aids in the creation of papers and other documentation
Microsoft OneNote	Provides a free-form environment for capturing notes, ideas, and lectures
Microsoft NetMeeting	Enables online video chats and meetings

The Family

Although not just an individual, this role will help you understand how each person in the family can benefit from a Tablet PC.

Toolkit

- **Slate style Tablet PC**—This Tablet PC design is great for mobility around the house.
- **Pocket PC**—This device allows for highly portable data.
- **Logitech QuickCam for Notebooks**—Use this for video chats.
- **Logitech Cordless Freedom Headset**—This headset can be used for online voice chatting and video conferencing.
- **Microsoft Office 2003**—Each member of the family can use this to prepare documents and email.
- **FranklinCovey TabletPlanner**—This program is used for time and task management.
- **Windows Messenger**—This program can be used for online chats.

■ **Zinio Reader**—Families can use this program to read electronic periodicals.

■ **MasterCook**—This menu-planning software can help keep the pantry and fridge stocked.

Value Proposition

The Tablet PC enables around-the-house information access when coupled with a wireless network. The Tablet PC's versatility allows it to be used as easily for menu planning and recipes as for writing term papers and surfing the Web wirelessly.

Day in the Life

When everyone comes downstairs for breakfast, the Tablet PC is poised on the kitchen counter, and each member of the family uses it to check his or her schedule for the day. The teenage son reminds his parents that he will need a ride to his friend's house that night, but that the time has changed. He makes a quick change in TabletPlanner.

After everyone checks their schedules, the father picks up the Tablet PC and clicks on the link for today's paper, which was automatically downloaded that morning. He notices an article about his favorite stock, and decides to buy more later that morning. He sets a reminder to do so over lunch.

After the father, the teenage son, and the middle school girl go to work and school, the mother retrieves the Tablet PC and checks her email. She carries the Tablet PC to the den, where she docks it in the docking station, providing a keyboard for easier input. After corresponding briefly with friends, she opens MasterCook and plans the week's meals. When she finishes, she transfers the grocery list to her Pocket PC. The mother then goes to her small business's Web site and is pleased to see several orders for her product. She shoots off an email to her supplier and gets a quick confirmation that the products will ship that day. Done with the morning's duties, the mother leaves the Tablet PC behind and heads for the grocery, Pocket PC in hand.

When the kids come home that afternoon, the teenage son gets on the Tablet PC to play a game online with some friends for an hour. Then the middle school girl takes the Tablet PC to her room, where she connects the Logitech QuickCam for Notebooks and fires up Windows Messenger for an online chat with her friend. Because they can both see what the other is doing, their endless phone call is like having a best friend in the next room.

Eventually, the video conference ends and she takes the Tablet PC back down to the den, where she docks it and gets ready to write a paper that was assigned a week ago (and that she has only one more night to complete). But then the mother asks for the Tablet PC, because she needs it for a recipe and for a chat with her mother.

The mother stands the Tablet PC on the counter, Web cam still attached, and opens her recipe for the evening meal. While she does so, she also launches a chat session with her mother, connecting via video as usual. After confirming the instructions for her husband's favorite recipe, the mother talks to her mother while she cooks, the Logitech Cordless Freedom wireless headset providing freedom during her cooking.

After dinner, the father takes his son to his friend's house, while the middle school girl finishes her paper in record time, researching her topic online.

The day ends, and the Tablet PC is put back in its docking station to rest for the night after a full day of helping the family. At 6:00 am the next morning, the Tablet PC wakes with the rest of the family, ready to provide information and communication services to all.

Summary of Benefits

Features	Benefits
Web camera	Enables users to connect to others virtually
Cordless headset	Enables users to roam free while chatting
Wireless networking	Provides access to information throughout the house
Microsoft Office 2003	Aids in creating documents
FranklinCovey TabletPlanner	Keeps life organized
Digital document readers	Keeps all reading materials in one place
Menu planning software	Organizes recipes

Wrap-up

You have seen the way many different people use their Tablet PCs to perform work and play, and to change the way they interact with the computer. This chapter should have provided a view of how the Tablet PC can work for you. Certainly, this is just a brief glimpse of how the Tablet PC can be used for a range of people. There are countless more roles and responsibilities for which the Tablet PC can be useful.

While you were reading through these examples, you may have taken notes and highlighted the ways you think you can use the Tablet PC, and I encourage you to think of even more ways you could use a Tablet PC. Take 30 minutes and write down the things you think you could do differently using a Tablet PC instead of a traditional computer.

Imagine you have a Tablet PC in front of you. Then ask yourself the following:

- How does it feel to use a pen?
- What ways can you use the pen to make your life easier and more productive?
- Will you use voice recognition? If so, how?
- What other devices will you need to interact with? What are their requirements, and what will you have to plan for in your Tablet PC purchase?
- Will you use the wireless networking to work in different places but still have access to information?
- Will others use your Tablet PC?
- What is the most important feature of the Tablet PC for you?
- Will it really help you?
- What do others think of your Tablet PC?

Think through these questions and ask more of your own. Does the Tablet PC look like a good fit for you? If so, grab one and meet me back here in Chapter 4, "Tablet PC Hardware Configuration," where we will get into setting the Tablet PC up for your way of doing things.

THE ABSOLUTE MINIMUM

Here are the key points to take away from this chapter:

- Different people have different needs and use their Tablet PCs in different ways.
- Think through how you want to use your Tablet PC, and get the right hardware and software to help you accomplish that goal.

PART

Configuring and Using Your Tablet PC

4

TABLET PC HARDWARE CONFIGURATION

Because there are numerous Tablet PC configurations, this chapter

explores the various configuration options in generic terms that apply

to all Tablet PCs. Tablet PCs don't come with CD and floppy drives

built in; not all have keyboards; and many items will need to be pur-

chased separately. There are numerous differences between models.

Each Tablet PC has the same features as a primary computer, but with

the addition of a few extra hardware buttons and usability enhance-

ments, which I'll discuss in this chapter.

Hardware Buttons

Most Tablet PCs have at least four hardware buttons: the Security button, the Enter button, and the Up/Down buttons. Some also have buttons for switching the screen from portrait to landscape, for function switching (which you use when you want to modify how the other buttons work, much like the Alt and Ctrl keys on the keyboard do), and more.

Power Button

Every machine must have a power button. On some, the power button is in fact a slider switch, and on others it's simply a depressible button. Understand what this button does. Depending on your configuration, it could power the system on and off, could put the computer in Standby mode, or could send the computer into Hibernate mode.

Standby mode shuts down everything but keeps enough power in the system to maintain the power to the memory, so that you can quickly resume where you left off. If you are going to be away from your Tablet PC for a longer period of time, you may want to use Hibernate mode, which stores all settings and current memory to the hard drive, and shuts down completely, saving battery life.

You can change the action associated with pressing the power button in Windows XP by tapping the **Start** button, tapping **Control Panel**, **Power Options**; and then choosing the **Advanced** tab in the dialog box that appears.

note

Each Tablet PC is unique in its use of buttons. I will discuss the common buttons here, but you should be aware that your Tablet PC may have something different.

tip

Some Tablet PCs have a lock for the power button so that you don't accidentally turn off the machine. I recommend locking the power button if you're working in slate mode, so that you don't accidentally power down.

Hibernate mode should be enabled by default on Tablet PCs, but if it's not, you can enable it by tapping the **Start** button, **Control Panel**, **Power Options**, and then choosing the **Hibernate** tab in the dialog box that appears. You can then check the box next to Enable Hibernation. If your Tablet PC uses another utility for power management, refer to your user's manual or online help to find out how to set it.

In Figure 4.1 (accessed from Power Options in Control Panel), notice that you can choose between Stand by, Shut down, and Hibernate for several actions. You can set this up however you want to; chances are, though, that you will probably use Standby mode more than Hibernate mode. Standby takes less time to return to operation, and still does a great job of minimizing power consumption.

FIGURE 4.1

Setting the power buttons for optimal usability.

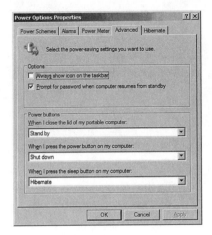

Note that on some Tablet PCs, the Power Options control panel is replaced by a manufacturer-specific utility, as shown in Figure 4.2. Notice the differences between Figures 4.1 and 4.2. Figure 4.1 is what most Windows XP users see, whereas Figure 4.2 is what the power options look like on my Toshiba Portégé 3500.

FIGURE 4.2

The Power Options control panel on some machines (here, the Toshiba Portégé 3500) has different options from the basic Power Options control panel.

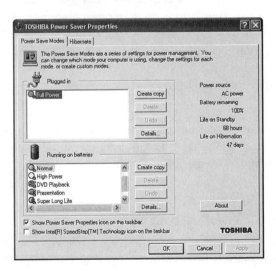

Windows Security Button

If your Tablet PC does not have a keyboard, it must have a Security button, which emulates the Ctrl+Alt+Delete Secure Attention Sequence, or SAS. Press this button during login to type your password, and press it during normal operation to see the Task Manager and shut-down options.

View Mode Button

If your Tablet PC has a View Mode button, you can click it to switch the Tablet PC screen from portrait to landscape mode. Some manufacturers let you customize this button for your preferences. If yours can be customized, follow the manufacturer's instructions to do so and make it work in your preferred orientation.

Navigation Buttons

Most Tablet PCs have navigation buttons for reading documents. The buttons usually include Up, Down, and Enter buttons that enable more natural reading for applications like Microsoft Reader. You can also use these buttons to scroll through a PDF or Word document, a spreadsheet, a Web page displayed in Internet Explorer, and so on.

Function Button

Your Tablet PC may not be equipped with a Function button. If it is, however, you should know that the Function button does not do anything on its own, but rather changes the function of the other buttons to their alternate mode (much like pressing the Ctrl or Alt keys on your keyboard affects how other keyboard keys behave). Consult your owner's manual or online documentation for more information if your Tablet PC has a Function button.

Pen-Based Buttons

Some manufacturers include other buttons that you can access by pressing them with the pen tip. The functions of these buttons vary by manufacturer. You should refer to the manufacturer's instructions for more information about how to use them.

Changing the Function of Your Buttons

Some people might want to use the buttons on their Tablet PCs in a different way from the buttons' default modes. For example, you might want one of your navigation buttons to open a particular application that you use frequently.

To change the way a particular button behaves, open the Pen and Tablet Settings dialog box in the Control Panel (tap the **Start** button, tap **Control Panel**, and tap **Tablet and Pen Settings**). As shown in Figure 4.3, the Tablet Buttons tab of the Tablet Settings dialog box allows you to change the function of the buttons on your Tablet PC. The number and location of buttons available to set will vary by Tablet PC. The device shown in Figure 4.3 shows the Tablet Buttons tab that is displayed by the Toshiba Portégé 3500, which is the tablet I use.

You can leave the settings alone and accept the default functions of the buttons, or you can customize them to suit your needs. To customize a button, select the button you want to change from the tablet button list and tap the **Change** button. The Change Tablet Button Actions dialog box opens; select the action you would like the button to perform, as shown in Figure 4.4, and tap the **OK** button.

> # caution
>
> The buttons on your Tablet PC are set up the way they are by default for a reason. Most manufacturers conduct usability studies to determine the best use for each button. Change the button functions only if you're sure you want to use them differently.

FIGURE 4.3

The Tablet Buttons tab lets you change the function of your buttons.

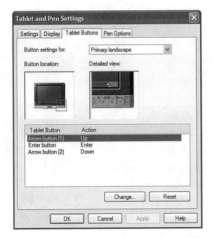

For example, you could set one of your buttons to automatically launch Windows Journal or Microsoft Word. Remember, though, that the buttons are helpful for navigating documents when you're using a pen, so decide which function would best suit your needs before changing the button functions. Of course, you can always change the buttons back to their original function by tapping the **Reset** button in the Tablet and Pen Settings dialog box.

FIGURE 4.4

You can change the function of each of your Tablet PC buttons by tapping the Change button.

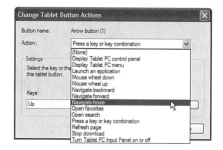

Input Options

The Tablet PC gives you more options for input than any other mainstream computer. In addition to the traditional keyboard and mouse, you can use voice and pen input. There are also many complementary devices that can extend the functionality of your Tablet PC, which I discuss in Part 7, "Extending Your Tablet PC."

Keyboard

Of course everyone understands how to use a keyboard, but doing so is optional for the Tablet PC. That said, few people can escape using their keyboards entirely, so be prepared to connect and disconnect one unless you have a convertible Tablet PC.

If you do use a keyboard with your Tablet PC, it will be USB-based, as opposed to using the round PS/2 connector that you may be used to. USB offers more flexibility for the keyboard, as well as auto-detecting the connection state (that is, detecting whether the keyboard is plugged in or not). Some USB keyboards even act as USB hubs, allowing other USB devices to connect to the computer through the keyboard. This may be a great option for you if you often leave your Tablet PC docked or somewhat distant from your keyboard.

note

Your old PS/2 style keyboard probably won't work with your Tablet PC. Most Tablet PCs are legacy-free, requiring you to get a USB keyboard.

Some Tablet PCs have docking stations that can have a keyboard constantly attached, so that as soon as you dock your Tablet PC, you'll have access to the keyboard.

Bluetooth keyboards are now available to eliminate the need for wires. You can use this keyboard with a Bluetooth mouse and a wireless network connection, and you'll have a wireless configuration on your desk. Just note that Bluetooth and Wi-Fi don't always work together perfectly. For more information about Wi-Fi and Bluetooth, refer to Chapter 17.

Mouse

The Tablet PC does not have the heavy dependence on the mouse that other Windows machines do. For most users, however, a mouse is still a necessity when working with a keyboard, and especially when the Tablet PC is docked or in use as the primary display.

Mice come in different configurations, have different numbers of buttons, come with or without scroll wheel, and so on. My favorite—and probably yours too—is the optical mouse. This device has no ball to get fouled up, and works on most surfaces better than a ball-based mouse does. If you have a glass-top or shiny work surface, however, the optical mouse is not for you unless you place it on a mouse pad or some other opaque surface. The optical mouse is perfect for the Tablet PC, though, because it allows for more portability. You can use it on airline tray tables just as effectively as on your mouse pad at home. And you never get the "stickies" that can result from the rollers inside the ball-based mouse getting gunked up with dirt, lint, and other nasties.

One more note on mice: Bluetooth-based mice are now available. This eliminates the need for cords, and even eliminates the mouse "base station" that's required for traditional wireless mice. The Bluetooth mouse can help keep you wire-free and ulti-mately mobile. Note, however, that your tablet may not have shipped with Bluetooth built-in, so you may need a Bluetooth adapter to use this feature. Some adapters are extremely small USB-based devices that are no bigger than your thumb.

Headset

With the Tablet PC, you have voice recognition and control ability. This is a phe-nomenal boon to many people. Being able to control your Tablet PC and applica-tions through voice command allows you to speak commands while you use your keyboard, mouse or pen, increasing your productivity. You can also dictate to your word processor. Most people use a headset to dictate or issue voice commands. An example of a headset is shown in Figure 4.5.

This headset connects to the headset/microphone plugs on the Tablet PC. There are two connectors for two-way communication with your Tablet PC.

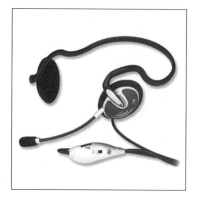

Headsets can be useful, but a bad headset can be worse than no headset at all. If you're interested in using your Tablet PC's voice recognition and control features, a noise-canceling headset is what you need. These types of headsets filter out ambient noise and give your Tablet PC the best chance at recognizing your words. If the computer can't understand you, it will frustrate you to no end as you repeat and correct your dictation or commands in a virtually endless loop.

tip

Get a noise-canceling headset to reduce misunderstandings between you and your computer.

Pen/Stylus

The pen is the new input device of choice for many activities dealing with your Tablet PC. You can write with it, input text, draw, use it as a mouse, and more. Since you will be using it quite a bit, it makes sense to have a pen that fits you well. Some of the pens that come with Tablet PCs are uncomfortable or too basic and should be used only if you can't find a better pen.

Remember that you cannot get just any pen for your Tablet PC, though. Some Tablet PC manufacturers use the Wacom electromagnetic digitizer, which does not require batteries in the pen. Some other manufacturers use other means, and you may need to get a pen that is self-powered.

Check with your Tablet PC manufacturer to see what kind of pen you can use with your Tablet PC. There are numerous pens available, including some made by traditional pen manufacturers such as Cross; a joint effort between Wacom and Cross has yielded the creation of the two pens shown in Figure 4.6.

FIGURE 4.6

Cross and Wacom have joined forces to create functional and stylish tablet pens.

Just as there are different types of pens, there are also pens with different capabilities. Some pens are pressure sensitive, some pens have erasers on the end (like a pencil), some have clips for easy storage in a shirt pocket, and some pens have buttons on the barrel. Some pens have all these options, and some have none. Find a pen that fits your hand, your preferences, and your style of working. If you have to fight with your pen, you will not enjoy the Tablet PC experience nearly as much.

tip

Get an extra pen in case you lose the one that came with your Tablet PC. Without your pen, you will have to use the track pad or a mouse for navigation.

Fortunately, some manufacturers understand the pen feel issue, and provide their Tablet PCs with a good-quality pen to start with. Others try to save money, including a pen that you may want to use only as a last resort. The Acers that I've seen actually ship with two pens—a small one that fits in the tiny slot in the system, and a larger, more comfortable one that includes a side switch and eraser. I would use the small one only if I had no other choice.

Data Communications Options

The Tablet PC is one of the most mobile primary PC platforms available. Most Tablet PCs have built-in data communications capabilities, including Wi-Fi (wireless

Ethernet 802.11), infrared, and even Bluetooth. Following is a discussion of how each of these capabilities can help you.

If wireless data communications don't work well for you for one reason or another, there are other options such as USB flash drives, which are discussed in Chapter 17.

Wireless Ethernet

Wireless Ethernet lets you use the Internet and other network services without using wires. You probably have a network cable at your office (or used to), which provides access to servers and the Internet. With wireless Ethernet, you no longer need the cable.

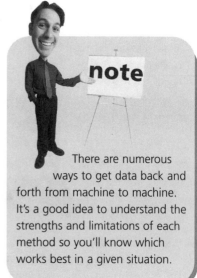

There are numerous ways to get data back and forth from machine to machine. It's a good idea to understand the strengths and limitations of each method so you'll know which works best in a given situation.

The most common implementation of wireless Ethernet is 802.11b, also called Wi-Fi. This is 11 Mbps, which is slightly faster than the traditional 10 Mbps Ethernet connections, and quite a bit slower than the 100 Mbps "Fast" Ethernet and the 1,000 Mbps "Gigabit" Ethernet speeds. However, Wi-Fi does not require wires.

As with any kind of radio-based communication device, obstacles such as walls and large objects can reduce transmission quality. If transmission quality is impaired, the data transmission rate can drop down to 2 Mbps or less (or could even be dropped totally), so a good wireless infrastructure is helpful in keeping your Tablet PC connected. Wi-Fi transmission quality (reception) can be affected by other radio-based devices that transmit at the same frequency.

Some cordless phones, microwave ovens, and baby monitors operate at the 2.4 GHz frequency range, which conflicts with Wi-Fi and can cause trouble for the Tablet PC's Wi-Fi reception. Keep this in mind if you have problems connecting to a Wi-Fi network.

Even with all these limitations, Wi-Fi is still an enabling technology. With it, you can run a meeting and have up-to-the-second data streaming onto your Tablet PC—without wires. Old-style meetings with laptops, cables, a network hub, and tons of power cords will hopefully become a thing of the past. As battery life improves, a full-day meeting with no wires and access to everything will be possible. In fact, a few manufacturers sell Tablet PCs that can run eight hours on a single charge.

Wi-Fi is available all around you. Airports, coffee shops, convention halls, office buildings, homes, and other places are ready for wireless connectivity. Some places require payment for using their network, others don't. With Windows XP Tablet PC Edition, you have a great platform that will automatically detect wireless networks around you and will help you get connected.

Learn how to connect to Wi-Fi networks so that you can do it quickly. You will inevitably visit somewhere when you need to have access to information and will need to know how to connect. Try connecting at the office, at the airport, in a coffee shop, and at your techie friend's fully wireless house. Better to tackle the learning curve when it's not necessary than when it is. Read Chapter 10, "Wireless Networking," for even more details about how to use wireless networking on your Tablet PC.

> **caution**
>
> Both Wi-Fi and Bluetooth can be negatively affected by other devices, such as microwave ovens, baby monitors, cordless phones, walkie-talkies, and other items that use the unregulated 2.4 GHz band.

Infrared

There are a couple flavors of infrared: slow and fast. Fast operates at 4 Mbps, and slow is just plain slow. You'll find that numerous infrared devices are available, including printers and PDAs. Infrared is a good choice when you can point two devices at each other and leave them that way until all the data is transferred.

Infrared requires that the transmitter/receiver of one device is in the line of sight of the other device's transmitter/receiver. Know where your infrared transmitter/receiver is located on your Tablet PC. It is usually a smooth oval that is reddish-black and shiny. Your Tablet PC manual will tell you where it is. To transfer data via infrared, you will need to have your other IR device pointed directly at this port.

One of the benefits of infrared is that it is one of the oldest and more predominant wireless technologies. It's been in laptops for years. I would use infrared as a last resort, because other data-transfer methods are often faster. Even so, infrared is good in many situations, such as an ad-hoc sharing of contact information with a PDA.

Bluetooth

Bluetooth is an excellent technology for Personal Area Networks (PANs). A PAN is the 5-meter radius circle around you that lets you connect everything within your vicinity. Bluetooth-enabled computers can communicate with Bluetooth-enabled phones, mice, keyboards, printers, and the like. The range is not as great as Wi-Fi, but it is great for short-distance communication.

If you decide to use Bluetooth, learn its strengths and weaknesses. Play around with its range and try to make it stop working (move your Bluetooth mouse until it is out of range). This will give you a feel for where you can have your components/devices in relation to your Tablet PC for effective communication. Also make sure you know how to force a connection between devices. Most Bluetooth devices automatically sense other Bluetooth components, but you will want or be able to turn the connection on or off. In addition, the first time you connect Bluetooth devices, you will probably need to know the security code of the other device. This prevents others from gaining access to your Bluetooth-enabled device without your consent.

> **caution**
>
> Bluetooth can interfere with Wi-Fi, so understand the limitations of your machine. Some systems require you to switch between Wi-Fi and Bluetooth because they both use the same antenna. Other systems enable both to work together. Test your system to be sure you can have both working at the same time.

Bluetooth can keep you cordless, yet enable you to get the most interconnectivity out of your devices. For more details on Bluetooth, see Bluetooth in Chapter 17, "Hardware Options."

Now that you've learned a bit about configuring your hardware, you're off to Chapter 5, "Windows XP Tablet PC Edition Configuration," to learn more about software configuration and making the Windows XP interface work best for you.

THE ABSOLUTE MINIMUM

This chapter should have helped you understand the hardware-configuration options for your Tablet PC. Here are the key points to keep in mind from this chapter:

- Set up the hardware buttons to meet your particular needs and method of using the Tablet PC.

- Set the power options to work the way you want: power, battery conservation, or a balance of the two.

- Understand the many ways you can interface with your Tablet PC: keyboard, mouse, pen, and voice.

- Understand the different data-transfer methods you have available to you and how each can best be used.

5

WINDOWS XP TABLET PC EDITION CONFIGURATION

Setting up your computer to suit your individual preferences is a simple and quick process, and can help you enjoy the Tablet PC experience even more. Following are several configuration settings you can change to better meet your needs and preferences.

You can access many of the items in this chapter from the Control Panel window, which you can open by tapping **Start**, and then tapping **Control Panel**.

Basic Interface Settings

Changing the basic interface settings may enable you to use the pen and Windows interface more easily; specifically, you can adjust these settings to specify whether you are right- or left- handed, and to note the way you hold the pen. To adjust these settings, tap on **Start**, **Control Panel**, and select **Tablet and Pen Settings** to open the Tablet and Pen Settings dialog box. You can also tap on the **Tablet and Pen Settings** button in the system tray, as shown in Figure 5.1.

Tablet and Pen Settings shortcut

Left- or Right- Handed?

Handedness is term used to say whether you are right- or left- handed. If you write with your right hand, you may want menus to open to the left so they don't appear under your hand, for example. Likewise, if you're left-handed, you might prefer for menus to open to the right.

You can specify handedness in the Tablet and Pen Settings dialog box, as shown in Figure 5.2; there, you tell your Tablet PC whether to expect right-handed or left-handed writing from you. This improves the handwriting-recognition accuracy. Right-handed is the default setting, which should not be changed unless you are left-handed.

tip

Tell your Tablet PC which hand you write with so it can read your handwriting better. You can also change the menu location so that menus don't appear under your hand when using the pen.

Menu Location

The Menu location setting, shown in Figure 5.2, can be set to your preference so that when menus appear, they won't be hidden by your hand. If you choose Left-handed, the menus appear to the right of your cursor, which is the way you're probably used to seeing menus in Windows on other machines. Otherwise, Windows will assume you are right-handed, and that you want the menus to appear to the left of your cursor, where they will be out of the way of your right hand when you select something. When you're using the pen, this setting really makes a difference; you don't have to pick up your hand to see what to tap next.

FIGURE 5.2

The Settings tab of the Tablet and Pen Settings dialog box allows you to customize the tablet interface for your needs.

Calibration

The Calibration setting aligns your pen and digitizer (the part of the screen that senses your pen) so that the cursor is right under your pen, instead of an inch away. To calibrate your Tablet PC, tap on the **Calibrate** button for both the landscape and the portrait orientations; when you tap the Calibrate button, you'll be instructed to tap the crosshair that appears on your screen, as shown in Figure 5.3. This will synchronize the position of your pen and the digitizer so that Windows will know where you are on the screen when you tap. This setting is usually fine as soon as you turn on your Tablet PC, but change it if you want to be sure or if you have problems with making marks that aren't quite under your pen. Adjusting the Calibration setting can increase your accuracy with selecting items, and can improve your Tablet PC's handwriting recognition. (If your pen is offset from the marks it makes, it can lead to funky handwriting.)

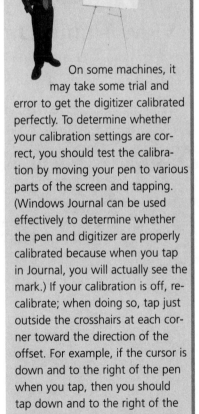

On some machines, it may take some trial and error to get the digitizer calibrated perfectly. To determine whether your calibration settings are correct, you should test the calibration by moving your pen to various parts of the screen and tapping. (Windows Journal can be used effectively to determine whether the pen and digitizer are properly calibrated because when you tap in Journal, you will actually see the mark.) If your calibration is off, re-calibrate; when doing so, tap just outside the crosshairs at each corner toward the direction of the offset. For example, if the cursor is down and to the right of the pen when you tap, then you should tap down and to the right of the crosshair when you re-calibrate the digitizer.

FIGURE 5.3

The Calibration screen lets you get pen-point accuracy with your digitizing pen.

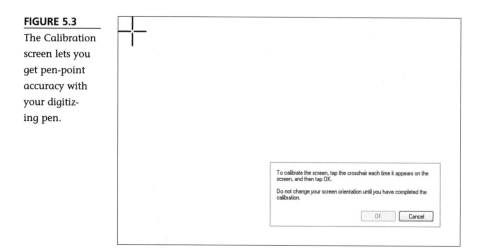

To calibrate the screen, tap the crosshair each time it appears on the screen, and then tap OK.

Do not change your screen orientation until you have completed the calibration.

OK   Cancel

View Things Differently: Screen Settings

Changing screen settings can enable you to use your Tablet PC more effectively. Changing the screen-orientation setting lets you rotate the contents of your Tablet PC's screen so you can more easily accomplish the task at hand, while changing the brightness setting affects your ability to see the screen at all. These settings are found in the Tablet and Pen Settings dialog box, under the Display tab.

Portrait or Landscape?

One of the great things about the Tablet PC is that you can rotate the screen contents to different orientations. For example, if I'm taking hand-written notes, I usually like to have my Tablet PC in portrait mode. If I'm typing, however, I pretty much have to use landscape mode unless I use an external keyboard.

Under the Display tab on the Tablet and Pen Settings dialog box, you can adjust your current screen orientation by changing the Orientation setting, as shown in Figure 5.4.

You can also set the Primary and Secondary positions that Windows uses when you change screen orientations. Tap on the Change button shown in Figure 5.4 to set the Orientation Sequence Settings shown in Figure 5.5. For convertibles, it's a good idea to choose Primary landscape for the first orientation because you will often use the built-in keyboard. For slates, Primary portrait is usually the chosen orientation.

FIGURE 5.4

You can set the screen orientation and brightness from the Display tab in the Tablet and Pen Settings dialog box.

FIGURE 5.5

You can change the orientation sequence so that your Tablet PC follows a particular order when you change the orientation.

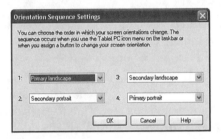

The Primary portrait orientation is the portrait orientation that Windows will mostly use unless you specifically select the Secondary portrait orientation option. Ditto with the landscape orientations. You can use the Tablet and Pen Settings system tray icon to change orientations. Just single-tap it and you will see an option to change screen orientation. Some Tablet PCs also come equipped with a Screen Orientation Change button that you can press to switch orientations.

Play around with the orientation and sequence settings to find one you like; as you do, think about how you will want to use your Tablet PC most of the time. For example, if you often connect to other devices using infrared and your infrared receiver is usually pointed toward you, that could be difficult to deal with. In that case, you can adjust the orientation so that when you use your Tablet PC, its IR port points to the device you use most often.

Brightness

Changing the screen's Brightness settings will enable you to see the screen better, or to conserve the battery—for example, during a long trip or meeting. You can change the battery-saving capabilities of your Tablet PC by changing the Screen brightness settings under the Display tab. You choose how bright or dark you want the screen to be in both plugged-in and battery-operated modes. This can help save batteries if you can live with a darker screen.

Other Settings and Options

There are numerous additional settings you can change on your Tablet PC. Following are a few that you can use to adjust your Tablet PC to meet your particular needs. As with the settings you've already explored, you can access these settings by opening the Tablet and Pen Settings dialog box. To open this dialog box, tap on **Start**, **Control Panel**, and select **Tablet and Pen Settings**; alternatively, tap on the **Tablet and Pen Settings** button in the system tray.

note

On some machines, rotating the screen contents of your Tablet PC will create a digitizer calibration problem. When you calibrate your digitizer for a particular sequence and orientation, it may negatively affect the calibration in the opposite (180°) orientation. It's a good idea to use your Tablet PC for a while to determine the landscape and portrait orientations you will use most often, and then set the calibration for each. This will prevent you from having to re-calibrate the digitizer each time you change orientations.

Pen Options

As you learned in Chapter 1, "Introducing the Tablet PC," the Pen Options tab on the Tablet and Pen Settings dialog box, shown in Figure 5.6, enables you to adjust how your pen behaves. (Notice that Press and hold on this screen represents Right-click.)

If your pen has a barrel button/switch, you can choose whether to enable that button for right-clicking/tapping and whether to use your pen's eraser (if equipped) to erase. If you use the erase feature, just turning your pen over will turn on the erase function of several applications, including Windows Journal. If you don't want to use your pen button (assuming, of course, that you have one) for right-clicking/tapping, or if you want to disable the eraser at the top of your pen (if available), simply deselect the corresponding checkboxes.

FIGURE 5.6

The Pen Options tab lets you change the way your pen inter- acts with your Tablet PC.

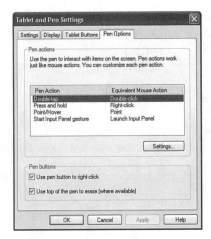

Most people accept the default pen settings, but if you want to customize how your pen operates, then by all means change the actions associated with the pen's vari- ous buttons. In addition, each of the available pen actions has settings that can be changed, such as the speed or spatial tolerance of a double-tap, or the duration of the press and hold action.

Double-Tap

To change the double-tap characteristics of your pen, tap **Double-tap** in the Pen Action list in the Tablet and Pen Settings dialog box's Pen Options tab, and then tap the **Settings** button. In the dialog box that appears (shown in Figure 5.7), you can set the Double-tap speed (that is, how quickly you have to double-tap in order for the system to recognize the action as a double-tap rather than two separate single- taps) and the Double-tap spatial tolerance (which determines how close together on the screen the two taps need to be), both of which can affect how precise you need to be when double-tapping, and by extension, how easy it is to do so.

If your hand shakes a little, you will probably want to make the spatial tolerance greater to accommodate a wider distance between the two taps.

Press and Hold

If you want to press and hold for only a short period of time before the right-tap action is activated, you can change the speed associated with this action. To do so, tap **Press and hold** in the Pen Action list in the Tablet and Pen Settings dialog box's Pen Options tab, and then tap the **Settings** button. The dialog box that appears lets you enable or disable Press and hold for right-tap, as well as change the speed and duration of the press-and-hold action. To adjust the speed with which the Press and hold action is activated, adjust the **Speed** slider to the desired delay. Changing the Duration setting will modify the length of time you have before the right-tap action is deactivated.

FIGURE 5.7

The Double-Tap Settings dialog box lets you change speed and spatial tolerance to make it easier to use the double-tap pen feature.

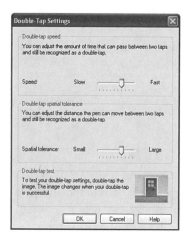

Point/Hover

You can adjust the amount of space your pen can move while still being recognized as hovering over a spot. You may want to adjust this is you are a heavy coffee drinker, or if your hand shakes. To change the spatial tolerance, tap **Point/Hover** in the Pen Action list in the Tablet and Pen Settings dialog box's Pen Options tab, and then tap the **Settings** button. In the dialog box that appears, move the **Spatial tolerance** slider to the right for a higher tolerance.

Start Input Panel Gesture

The Start Input Panel gesture is a rapid back-and-forth across-the-screen stroke with the pen while not touching the screen. This opens the Input Panel so that you don't have to tap the Input Panel icon in the Quick Launch Bar.

To modify the settings for launching the Input Panel, open **Tablet and Pen Settings**, tap on the **Pen Options** tab, tap **Start Input Panel** gesture in the Pen Action list in the Tablet and Pen Settings dialog box's Pen Options tab, and then tap the **Settings** button. In the dialog box that appears, check or uncheck the **Enable Start Input Panel gesture** check box to enable or disable the Start Input Panel gesture. You can also adjust the size of the gesture that is required to open the Input Panel. I suggest using the center setting or just to the right or left of center. Adjusting the slider all the way to the right will require a gesture that encompasses the width of the screen, and makes it difficult to use. Setting the slider all the way to the left makes it so that any tiny gesture may cause you to open the Input Panel inadvertently.

Power Options

To change power options on your Tablet PC, go to Control Panel, and then Power Options. The Power Options Properties dialog box, shown in Figure 5.8, enables you to define how your computer will respond to different power situations. For example, in the dialog box's Power Schemes tab, you can specify how much time should pass before the computer takes action to prevent further battery drain. Standby is a setting that allows for quick (less than 5 seconds) recovery, whereas hibernation saves data to disk and takes a bit longer to restore your system—though still much more quickly than a cold boot.

FIGURE 5.8

The Power Options Properties dialog box lets you change settings to optimize performance and/or power consumption.

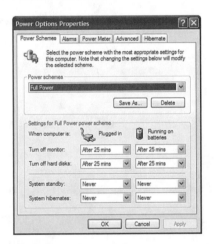

System standby requires very little power; the Tablet PC specifications require that standby mode last for at least 72 hours on a full battery. Hibernation mode takes no power, because it saves the system state to disk and then turns the power off. Hibernate mode will probably be set to Enabled when you get your Tablet PC, but you can check to make sure.

If you like, you can set alarms and battery status indicators if you want to be notified of an impending power outage by changing the settings under the Alarms tab.

Some machines use a different dialog box for these power settings. For example, my Toshiba Portégé 3500 has a different dialog box that lets me set multiple scenarios, such as Extra Long Life or Performance mode, each of which have their own battery-saving characteristics.

Wacom Tablet Properties

If you have a Wacom-based digitizer in your Tablet PC, you can download the Wacom Tablet PC driver to extend its functionality. To get this driver, go to http://www.wacom.com/tabletpcdriver.cfm, download the latest Penabled Tablet PC driver, and install it on your Tablet PC.

With this driver, you can change the feel of your pen/digitizer interface to further suit your needs, as shown in Figure 5.9. Play around with the different settings until you get what feels right for you.

caution

Some Tablet PCs, such as the Compaq/HP TC1000, do not use the Wacom digitizer. Do not install the driver on a machine that is not equipped with the Wacom digitizer.

FIGURE 5.9

The Wacom Pen Settings dialog box on the Toshiba Portege 3500.

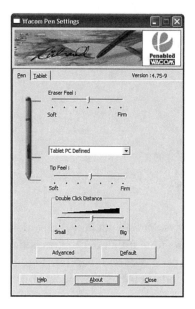

Start Menu Settings

The Start Menu is a critical part of your Windows XP experience. You will use it almost daily, so it makes sense to make it work for you by customizing its look and operation.

If you right-tap the **Start** menu button then choose **Properties**, you will see a dialog box (shown in Figure 5.10) that lets you change the way the Start menu looks. You can choose between Start menu (Windows XP style) and Classic Start menu (Windows 2000/9x style). For each option, there is a Customize button for changing basic settings, such as icon size and what appears on the Start menu.

FIGURE 5.10

The Taskbar and Start Menu Properties dialog box lets you change the overall appearance of the Windows XP Start menu.

You should familiarize yourself with each of the settings so you can better customize your Tablet PC environment. Leaving these settings in their default state is fine, and will probably work well for you, but if you like larger icons or want particular items on the Start menu (for example, My Computer or Printers), then select what you want. If you prefer the look of Windows 2000/9x over that of Windows XP, just choose **Classic Start menu** in the Properties dialog box.

Taskbar Settings

The taskbar is the bar that appears next to the Start menu at the bottom of the screen. It contains buttons for program shortcuts and for applications that are currently open.

On the dialog box that contains the Start menu settings, you'll find a Taskbar tab, as shown in Figure 5.11. This tab enables you to set taskbar properties such as showing the clock in the system tray, and auto-hiding the taskbar to free up a bit more screen real estate.

tip

I use the Quick Launch bar for quick access to my most-used applications. I size the Quick Launch area so that the applications I use all the time (Internet Explorer, My Computer, and so on) are displayed, and those that I use less frequently, but still often, are displayed only after I tap the expand button.

FIGURE 5.11

The items on the Taskbar tab let you change the appearance of the taskbar and make it easier to operate Windows XP.

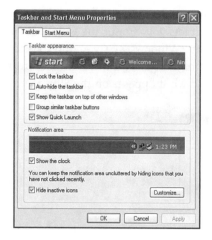

Shortcuts to Most-Used Items

I put shortcuts to my most-used applications in the Quick Launch area (the area next to the Start menu) so that I can get to them even if other applications are open. To use the Quick Launch bar, make sure that the Show Quick Launch check box on the Taskbar and Start Menu Properties dialog box's Taskbar tab is checked. You can then drag and drop applications to the Quick Launch area of the taskbar. If the taskbar is not locked (that is, if the Lock the taskbar check box on the Taskbar tab is unchecked), you can change the size of the Quick Launch area to see more or fewer shortcuts.

One of the best things you can do to improve productivity is to create shortcuts to your most-used information on your desktop and Quick Launch bar. Figure 5.12 shows the shortcuts I have created on my desktop for easy access.

FIGURE 5.12

I put shortcuts on my desktop for quicker access to frequently used items.

To create a shortcut to your desktop, you can use one of two methods:

- Right-tap the desktop and choose **New**, **Shortcut**. The Create Shortcut dialog box, shown in Figure 5.13, opens; in it, you can enter the filename of the file you want to access quickly or you can browse for it.

FIGURE 5.13

The Create Shortcut dialog box lets you search for a program or file from which to create a shortcut item.

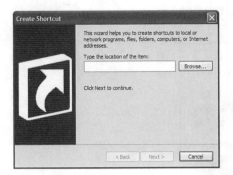

- Open a Windows Explorer or My Computer window that shows the file you want to access quickly. Then, while pressing the Ctrl and Shift keys, drag the file to the desktop. As you drag, you'll see a white box with an arrow inside; this indicates that the file you are dragging is a shortcut. Be careful as you drag, though; if you don't hold down the Ctrl and Shift keys when dragging the file, you might inadvertently copy or move the file to the desktop rather than creating a shortcut to it, which could cause you to lose track of your primary file.

Now when you want to access that file or application, you can simply double-tap on its desktop shortcut to launch it.

Overall Display Properties

This section covers several major display settings for Windows XP. These settings, such as Themes and Appearance, determine the overall look and feel of Windows XP. All these settings are accessible from the Display Properties dialog box, shown in Figure 5.14. To access the Display Properties dialog box, right-tap the desktop and choose Properties. Alternatively, choose Display from the Control Panel window.

tip

The difference between shortcuts on the desktop and shortcuts in the Quick Launch area is that those on the Quick Launch area can be accessed even while other applications are open and hiding the desktop. Shortcuts on the desktop require you to minimize other applications first so that you can tap the icons. You can also use the Start menu to access shortcuts, but I find this takes longer than using Quick Launch or Desktop shortcuts.

Themes

Themes are groups of visual settings that change the desktop, screensaver, and icons
of Windows XP applications to share similar col-
ors and graphics. You get only a few themes
with your Tablet PC, but you can purchase or
create additional themes—for example, an
Aquarium theme. Consider checking out Plus!
for Windows XP; it includes many additional
themes,such as Aquarium, Space, Nature, and
Da Vinci. There are also third-party themes
available, such as ones that relate to golf. To
find these themes, search for the phrase "desktop
themes" in your favorite Internet search engine.
Some are free, some are not.

> **tip**
>
> Since many Tablet PCs
> have slower processors than
> newer laptops, it may help
> to disable themes and use
> the Classic look. Test it to see
> if it helps your system per-
> formance noticeably.

Changing the Look of Your Desktop

Do you have a favorite photo of your spouse and kids, or of your awesome car? Or
maybe you like to relax to the view of a waterfall. Whatever your favorite image,
you can place it directly on your Tablet PC's desktop, enabling you to see it whenever you want. You can also change the default colors of your Tablet PC and other
settings, which will all be covered in the next sections.

Adding an Image to Your Desktop

To change your desktop's background to include an image you like, first make sure you have a digital version of the image. For example, you might use a scanner to scan a photo print, or transfer an image from your digital camera to your Tablet PC. (If you don't have a personal photo you want to use, fear not; Windows XP offers some stock images to choose from.) Then, right-tap the desktop and choose **Properties**, or choose **Display from the Control Panel** window. The Display Properties dialog box, shown in Figure 5.15, opens; tap the Desktop tab. Click an item in the Background list to preview it in the dialog box. If the image you want to use isn't listed, click the **Browse** button, locate the image you want, and tap it to select it.

FIGURE 5.15

The settings on the Desktop tab let you change the desktop's appearance to suit you.

In the Position drop-down list, Windows gives you a few options for placing the background image you select:

- Choose **Stretch** to make the image completely fill the screen.
- Choose **Center** to center the image on the screen. If the image is smaller than the screen, you'll see a border around the image. (To change the color of this border, choose a color from the Color drop-down list in the Desktop tab.)
- Choose **Tile** to repeat, or tile, the image on your screen. Tiling is great for small images or patterns.

Changing the Background Color

If you don't want to place an image on your desktop, you can always change the background color to spice things up a bit. To do so, simply choose a color from the Color drop-down list on the Desktop tab.

Changing Other Desktop Settings

To adjust additional settings, such as which icons show up on your desktop and what they look like, or to configure Windows to clean up your desktop on a set schedule, tap on the **Customize Desktop** button to open the Desktop Items dialog box, shown in Figure 5.16. You can include particular desktop icons, such as My Computer, and you can also enable the Desktop Cleanup Wizard.

FIGURE 5.16

Click the Customize Desktop button to open a dialog box that lets you change additional properties, such as which applications appear on your desktop.

Adding Web Content to Your Desktop

The Web tab on the Desktop Items dialog box, shown in Figure 5.17, enables you to put Web content on your desktop (this feature is known as Active Desktop). Doing so can help keep you abreast of information. This feature can be customized in numerous ways. For example, you can display today's weather, stock tickers, and search engines directly on your desktop by including the appropriate Web pages.

It all depends on the Web site that you put on your desktop. You can have multiple Web pages arranged on your desktop if you'd like. If you know how to create Web pages, you can even customize your desktop to have links to your favorite Web sites, network places, and files. You can use a Web page or pages as your desktop to keep you abreast of whatever information you want.

Screen Saver

Most people are familiar with screen savers. In fact, I'm sure you've been captivated by one or two in particular, and you just sit at your computer doing nothing until it pops up. (In that case, you might want to consider disabling your screen saver, since you probably want to get SOMETHING done.)

FIGURE 5.17

The settings on the Web tab let you set the desktop to use a Web page for your background, which can provide quick links to frequently used sites as well as active content.

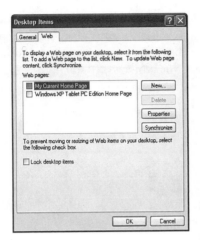

To change—or disable—your screen saver, right-tap the desktop and choose **Properties**, or choose **Display from the Control Panel** window. The Display Properties dialog box opens; tap the **Screen Saver** tab (see Figure 5.18). You can disable the screensaver by setting it to (None). In addition to enabling you to change or disable your screen saver, the Screen Saver tab allows you to set additional options, such as requiring a password when the system resumes from the screen saver, and how long the Tablet PC should be idle before launching the screen saver.

FIGURE 5.18

The settings on the Screen Saver tab let you change the screen saver and its characteristics.

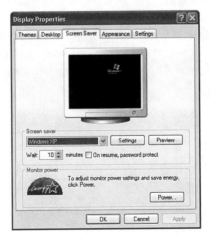

Appearance

Appearance refers to settings such as the colors of windows and dialogs, the fonts used by Windows XP, and more. To change your Tablet PC's appearance settings, right-tap the desktop and choose **Properties**, or choose **Display from the Control Panel** window. The Display Properties dialog box opens; tap the **Appearance** tab (see Figure 5.19). There, you can adjust big look-and-feel settings such as Windows and buttons (Classic or Windows XP style), the Color scheme, and Font size. Try each of the settings to determine what you like most; preview your selections in the top half of the dialog box.

FIGURE 5.19

The settings on the Appearance tab let you change the overall appearance of Windows XP.

To set transition effects for menus, and to specify whether you want to use font smoothing, click the **Effects** button on the Appearance tab. Doing so opens the Effects dialog box, shown in Figure 5.20. You can change numerous settings here; play around with them to make things look the way you want. To learn more about a particular feature, select it and press **F1**, or right-tap the setting and then tap **What's This?**.

FIGURE 5.20

The Effects dialog box lets you change the finer points of appearance in Windows XP, such as screen font smoothing and menu effects.

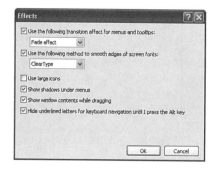

I recommend using the Clear Type setting, because it makes text easier to read. (If you plan to read e-books on your Tablet PC, Clear Type will make your eyes happier.) Because of the way LCD screens are made, however, Clear Type works in only one orientation—either portrait or landscape—so try it in each mode to determine which way looks best on your Tablet PC. New technologies are available that get rid of this single-direction problem, but they will not be in many Tablet PCs for some time to come.

Settings

To change your display's screen resolution (that is, how much information you can see onscreen at once), color depth (the number of colors you can see onscreen), and whether you want to extend your Tablet PC's desktop to an additional screen, right-tap the desktop and choose **Properties**, or choose **Display from the Control Panel**. Then tap the **Settings** tab (see Figure 5.21).

FIGURE 5.21

The Settings tab allows you to change your display size, whether you have an external display, and the color depth of your display(s).

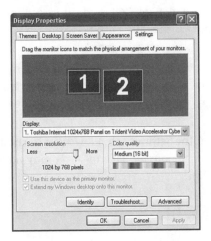

With Tablet PCs, the screen resolution is almost always maxed out at 1024×768. If your Tablet PC supports it, you can attach another display to your Tablet PC. That display can either mirror your Tablet PC display or extend the desktop to the additional screen. I usually use two screens to maximize my screen real estate; that way, I can have applications open on both displays. For example, Figure 5.22 shows what my two displays look like together while I'm writing this passage.

FIGURE 5.22

This is what my two displays look like as I'm writing this section. Double the screen real estate with a second display.

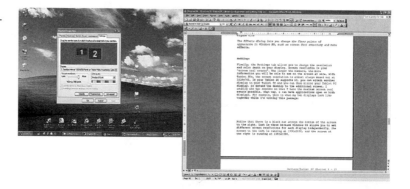

Notice that there is white space across the bottom of the screen to the left. That is there because Windows XP allows you to set different screen resolutions for each display independently. Screen resolution is your "screen real estate." The larger the numbers, the more information you will be able to see on the screen at once. In this case, the screen to the left is running at 1024×768, and the screen at the right is running at 1280×1024. The white space is the difference between the vertical sizes of the screens.

Color quality (also called color depth) determines how many colors you can see on the screen. The more the better, but some video controllers are not fast enough to keep up at the highest settings. Fortunately, this is probably not the case with your Tablet PC.

Tapping the **Advanced** button on the Settings tab allows you to change additional settings that are specific to your video adapter. Like me, you may have a vendor-specific set of tools (see Figure 5.23).

FIGURE 5.23

This is how the Display, Settings, Advanced dialog box looks on my Toshiba Portégé 3500.

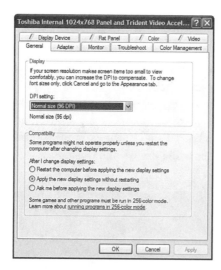

Unfortunately, I can't offer much guidance here, because there is no way for me to know what you have on your Tablet PC. For more information about settings specific to your Tablet PC, consult your user's guide.

THE ABSOLUTE MINIMUM

Here are the key points to take away from this chapter:

- Set up your Tablet PC to recognize your handwriting better by telling it whether you are right- or left-handed.
- If your pen and the cursor don't match up exactly on the screen, calibrate your tablet's digitizer.
- Change your pen and power options to support the way you work with your Tablet PC.
- Use shortcuts on the desktop and the Quick Launch bar to work more efficiently.
- For personal satisfaction, you can change the themes, desktop, screen saver, and appearance of Windows XP.

PART III

Using Included Applications

6

Using Windows Journal

Windows Journal is the cornerstone application of the Tablet PC. In addition to enabling you to take notes at the same speed as you would with a pen and paper, Windows Journal also offers more flexibility. For example, using Windows Journal, you can insert space between ideas and choose from an almost limitless set of drawing tools. In addition, you can create templates and forms using Windows Journal.

Notice in Figure 6.1 that you can write directly inside the application. With the exception of making paper airplanes, whatever you would normally do with a paper notebook—write, doodle, take notes—you can do in the Windows Journal. And then some.

Since Windows Journal is specifically a Tablet PC application, there is a Windows Journal Viewer available for those who are not enlightened enough to use Tablet PCs yet. I show you how to get it at the end of this chapter.

FIGURE 6.1

You can use Windows Journal to do almost anything you would do on a piece of paper.

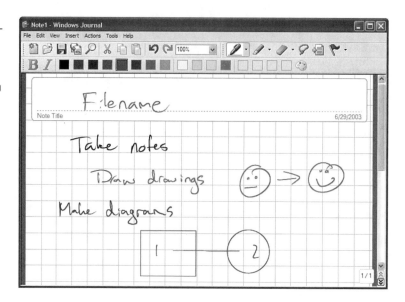

Start with the Windows Journal Tutorial

The Windows Journal tutorial is a good place to start learning about the capabilities and uses of Windows Journal. To start the Windows Journal tutorial, open Windows Journal, and then tap on **Help**, **Journal Tutorial**. This launches a multimedia presentation that covers the basics of using Windows Journal. When you're finished with the tutorial, return to this book; I will use this chapter to reinforce some of the tutorial's main points, and take you deeper.

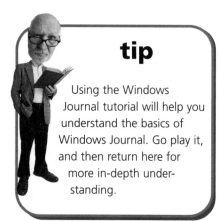

tip

Using the Windows Journal tutorial will help you understand the basics of Windows Journal. Go play it, and then return here for more in-depth understanding.

Windows Journal Basics

The rest of this chapter is devoted to the basics of Windows Journal, which you'll want to absorb before moving on to Chapter 7, "Advanced Windows Journal." This chapter discusses the Windows Journal interface, as well as working with your handwritten notes and sharing your notes with others.

The Interface

Figure 6.2 shows the different sections of the Windows Journal interface.

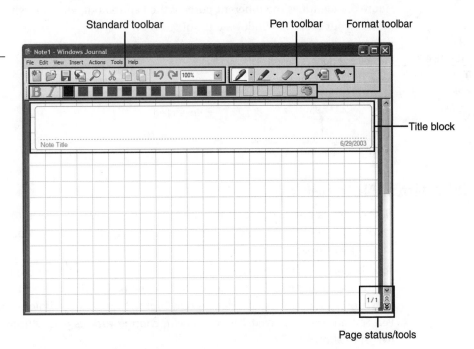

These sections include the following:

- ■ **Standard toolbar**—This toolbar contains several basic tools: New Note, View Recent Notes, Save, Import, Find, and so on.

- ■ **Format toolbar**—Use this toolbar to change the color of your pen strokes, as well as specify whether they appear bold or italic. Note that bold and italic may only be applied once something is written or drawn, and not as a modifier before the pen is used.

- ■ **Pen toolbar**—This toolbar enables you to select the type of pen you write with, as well as the highlighter style, eraser size and style, and other tools.

- ■ **Page status/tools**—This area of the Journal window tells you what page you're currently viewing, and lets you add pages as well as go back and forth between pages.

- ■ **Title block**—Here is where you write the filename that you want your note saved as. Windows Journal automatically uses the note title as the filename. If you do not write a title, Windows Journal uses the first line of text as your title.

■ **Blank page**—This is the main surface for you to write and draw on. I will show you in Chapter 7 how to change the look of the page to suit your needs.

Figure 6.3 identifies the different parts of the Pen toolbar, which is where you select most of your tools in Windows Journal.

FIGURE 6.3

The tools available on the Pen toolbar.

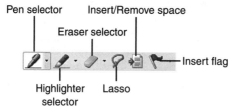

Pen selector   Insert/Remove space

Eraser selector

Insert flag

Highlighter   Lasso
selector

Take Note: Note-Taking

Note-taking is now natural on the Tablet PC. You can use your pen to write, draw, scribble, highlight, and erase notes. You can change the color of your pen by just tapping on the pen color you want.

You change your pen style by opening the Pen drop-down list on the Pen toolbar (see Figure 6.4). If you want to further customize the pen settings, select the **Pen Settings** option; this opens the Pen and Highlighter Settings dialog box with the Pen Settings tab displayed. There, you can change various pen settings to meet your needs, as shown in Figure 6.5.

FIGURE 6.4

The options available from the Pen drop-down list.

FIGURE 6.5

The Pen and Highlighter Settings dialog box lets you select the characteristics of your pen.

In the Pen and Highlighter Settings dialog box, you can change the color, thickness, and tip style of the pen, as well as whether it is pressure sensitive. Pressure sensitivity makes notes look more natural, because the harder you press, the thicker the line is (up to the pen's maximum thickness as set in this dialog box). Note that some Tablet PCs do not have pressure-sensitive pens, so this may not be an option for you.

After you've written some notes, you can highlight them using Journal's Highlighter tool. You can customize the Highlighter tool by opening the Highlighter drop-down list and either choosing the style you want to use or selecting the **Highlighter Settings** option. Performing the latter again opens the Pen and Highlighter Settings dialog box, but this time with the Highlighter Settings tab revealed, as shown in Figure 6.6.

FIGURE 6.6

The Pen and Highlighter Settings dialog box lets you change the Highlighter tool's qualities.

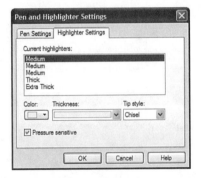

As you use Windows Journal, realize that you can do anything you want with the pen—write, draw, change pen color and type, select text, and so on.

Adding "Paper"

With paper notebooks, if you didn't leave enough space for notes on a particular topic, you need to start a new page. Not so with Windows Journal. With Windows Journal, you simply insert space as needed. To do so, you use the Insert/Remove Space tool; Figure 6.7 shows the Insert/Remove Space tool as it appears when you start to insert a space.

Look at the differences between the screens in Figures 6.7 and 6.8. Notice the additional space and text below Heading 1, Point 2. I made room for the addition of Point 3 and Point 4 by using the Insert/Remove Space tool.

FIGURE 6.7

Use the Insert/Remove Space tool to add more space between items.

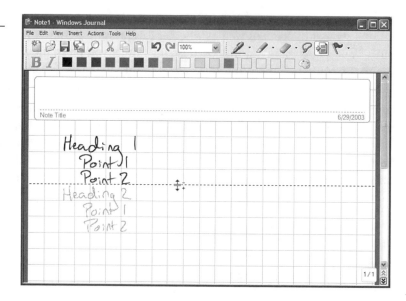

FIGURE 6.8

Notice the additional points in this figure.

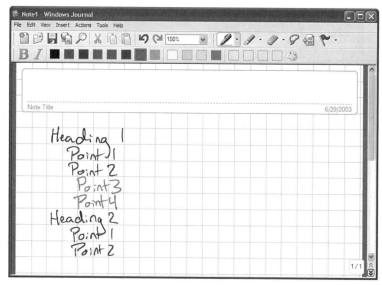

To insert space in your note, do the following:

1. Click the **Insert/Remove space** button (between the Lasso and Insert Flag buttons) on the Pen toolbar.

2. Tap the note where you want to insert space.

3. Drag the pen down the page as far as you need for additional space.

If you insert enough space, some elements on your page will move to the next page. You can get to those elements by tapping the Next button below the vertical scrollbar in the bottom-right corner of the Windows Journal window.

You can also remove space in your note by dragging up instead of down in step 3. When you remove space, the space to be removed as you drag your pen becomes darker. Windows Journal will not let you remove space other than blank space, which protects you from accidentally (or purposefully) deleting items.

Formatting Ink

Once you write or draw on the page, you have several options for formatting the ink. To select the ink you want to format, use the right-tap capability of your pen (either pressing and holding, or using the barrel button on your pen), then drag around the ink you want to select, as shown in Figure 6.9.

FIGURE 6.9

Right-tap and drag around the ink you want to select.

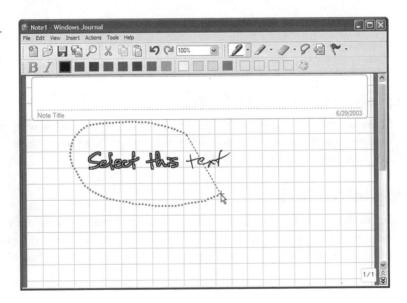

Once you have selected the ink, you can change its color by selecting any of the color swatches on the toolbar. If you want more color options, select the **More Colors** button on the toolbar (the one that looks like a painter's palette to the right of the color swatches) to define custom colors.

With the ink selected, you can also tap the **Bold** and **Italic** buttons on the toolbar. This does exactly what you would expect.

Notice in Figure 6.10 that after you select the ink, you see a context-sensitive menu that lets you choose additional options to perform on the ink. If you choose the **Format Ink** menu item, you can choose stroke thickness, color, bold and italic formatting, and pen style, just as you can from the Format toolbar.

FIGURE 6.10

A context-sensitive menu opens when you select ink. The one here may show more than yours, as I have the Show extended short-cut menus option enabled (Tools, Options, View).

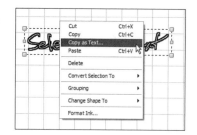

Making Sense Out of Scribble

There are many things you can do with the text you've hand-written. You can convert ink to text, change shapes to more definite forms (squares, circles, lines), erase ink, and even search for ink in documents.

Converting Ink to Text

To convert ink to text, select the ink you want to convert, just as you would if you wanted to change the formatting. After you make the selection, the menu you saw in Figure 6.10 appears. Choose **Copy as Text** to open a dialog box like the one shown in Figure 6.11.

FIGURE 6.11

The Copy as Text dialog box opens to confirm spelling.

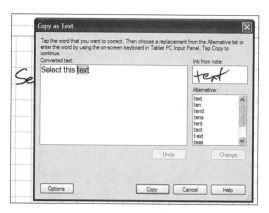

Notice that Windows Journal doesn't quite like my handwriting. Specifically, it questions my rendering of the word text, and provides options for words to replace it. I can choose another word, or I can choose to use Journal's best guess, which in this case is correct.

After Windows Journal has cleared up any spelling issues, tap the **Copy** button. Then, right-tap in the note space and choose **Paste**. Figure 6.12 shows the text box that was inserted into Windows Journal at the spot I right-tapped.

FIGURE 6.12

The text box was created using the Copy to Text option.

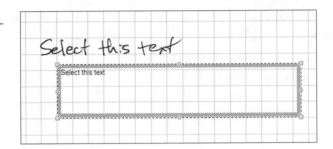

Another way to convert ink is to select it as before, but open the Actions menu and choose **Convert Handwriting to Text**. This opens the same dialog box you saw in Figure 6.12. In this operation, however, after you close the dialog box, another will appear to ask what you want to do with the converted text (see Figure 6.13).

FIGURE 6.13

The Text Correction dialog box asks how you want to treat the text you just converted.

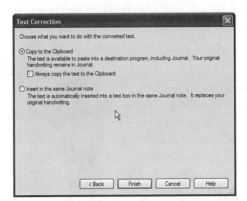

The Copy to Clipboard option does the same thing as the Copy to Text option in the right-tap menu. The Insert in the same Journal note option replaces the original ink with the text.

If you choose the Clipboard route, you can then paste the text into any other Windows-based application that is Clipboard-aware.

Changing Shapes for More Clarity

Sometimes when I'm drawing, my circles look more like turtles. If you have to communicate using graphics as well as text, Windows Journal has a feature that lets you convert poorly drawn circles, lines, and squares into the shapes you meant to draw.

Unfortunately, it does not convert triangles, as does Corel Grafigo, but if you're a square-and-circle kind of person, it will help you out.

To convert a shape, do the following:

1. Tap **Tools**, **Options**, **View** and check the **Show extended shortcut menus** checkbox. This turns on extra shortcut menu items.
2. Click the **Lasso** button on the Pen toolbar.
3. Select the shape you want to convert.
4. Right-tap the shape and choose **Change Shape to**.
5. Choose either **Square**, **Circle/Ellipse**, or **Line**.

As an alternate method, you can replace steps 4 and 5 above with this step 4:

4. Tap **Actions**, **Change Shape to**, and then select either **Square**, **Circle/Ellipse**, or **Line**.

Now, thanks to Windows Journal, you don't have to be as concerned about your artistic abilities. Your message will come across loud and clear. And once you've changed the shape, you can stretch it in any direction you want by selecting the shape and then dragging the sizing handles that appear on it.

Erasing Stuff

If you put it down, you have to be able to pick it up. Windows Journal offers a flexible Eraser feature that lets you choose the style of eraser you want to use. You can choose a stroke eraser or a regular wipe-type eraser.

The stroke eraser will erase an entire stroke, such as a line, squiggle, or anything else that was created with a single stroke of the pen. The wipe eraser will erase everything in its path, cutting through strokes and leaving the page beneath clean.

tip

Use the Stroke Eraser tool for faster and more complete erasing.

The wipe eraser comes in three sizes—small, medium, and large—all of which erase the pixels themselves without respect to the full stroke. This lets you chop up your ink strokes or cut a path through a line of text.

I usually use the Stroke Eraser tool as my default because it helps me erase faster and more thoroughly (not that I ever make mistakes). If your Tablet PC supports a pen with an eraser on the end (like the Wacom pens mentioned earlier in the book), you can just flip your pen over to activate the Eraser feature. If not, you will need to tap the Eraser button on the Pen toolbar.

Searching for Ink in Documents

One of the really cool things about ink is that it enables you to run searches on your handwritten notes, just as you can in word-processing programs such as Microsoft Word. Ink is searchable because it is not treated as mere graphics. The strokes are interpreted as handwriting even when no conversion to text has taken place. For a quick example of this, just write something in the Note Title block and then save the file. You'll notice that it automatically recognizes the text and recommends the note title as the filename (assuming your handwriting is acceptable to Windows Journal).

tip

You can search for ink in documents even if you haven't converted the handwriting to text.

If you have several pages of notes, or even several notes files, you can search for text that you either typed or wrote. This provides more flexibility with your ink-based notes than you get with paper notes.

Figure 6.14 shows what happened when I searched for "select" in my note file.

FIGURE 6.14

Searching for text inside a document will also find ink text.

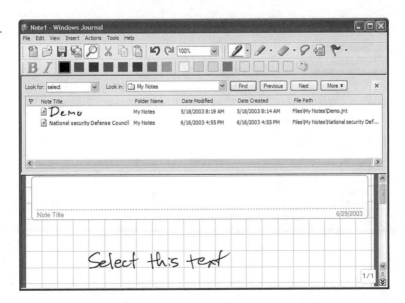

In Figure 6.15, I have saved the file as Demo.jnt, and then searched within the file system for the word "select" within the files in the My Notes folder.

FIGURE 6.15

Click on the magnifying glass in the file system to search for documents. Then select advanced search options to search for text inside files.

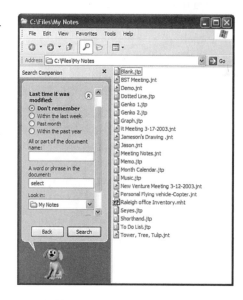

Figure 6.16 shows the results of the search—success! And that was after I took out the text box, leaving only the ink.

FIGURE 6.16

When I searched for the word "select" within the My Notes folder, Windows XP found the Demo.jnt file, which only contained the ink version of the word.

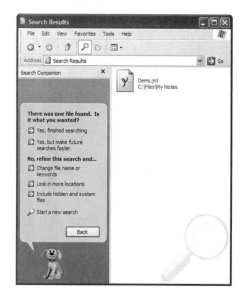

To search for content, just tap the **Search** button (the one with a magnifying glass on it) in Windows Journal's Standard toolbar or in the file system. This opens a search box, which you saw in Figure 6.14. Then, simply enter the word(s) you want to find and tap the **Find** or **Search** button.

Using the Thumbnail View PowerToy

A great way to improve your ability to find your Journal notes in the file system is to use the Thumbnail View PowerToy. PowerToys are applications that Microsoft's developers have created to make computing easier, or to have a little fun. You can download the Thumbnail View PowerToy from http://www.microsoft.com/windowsxp/tabletpc/downloads/powertoys.asp. After installing Thumbnail View, you will see your Journal notes pages in a thumbnail preview similar to that in Figure 6.17.

> **tip**
>
> Even Microsoft SharePoint Portal Server can search on ink. This allows others on your SharePoint intranet to search inside any notes you post on the intranet for text and handwriting.

FIGURE 6.17

The Thumbnail View PowerToy can help you find notes quickly if you know what the first page looks like.

As you can see, this can help you find a notes page visually. This is a useful tool especially if many of your notes are sketches.

Sharing Your Notes with Others

Inevitably, you will want to share your super-cool notes and sketches with others. Doing so is not quite as straightforward as sharing paper, but it's a lot handier for working in a team. There are several methods for sharing your notes, as I will discuss here.

The Windows Journal Viewer

If you want to share your Windows Journal notes with others who do not have a Tablet PC, they can download the Microsoft Windows Journal Viewer. Simply tell them to visit http://www.microsoft.com/windowsxp/tabletpc/ downloads/default.asp where there should be a link to the viewer.

The viewer is similar to Excel and Word viewers, in that the person can see the content of the file, but not edit it. This allows you to take notes in your own handwriting, and yet use the Internet, email, or your local network to share your notes with others.

tip

People you work with who don't have a Tablet PC can download the Windows Journal Viewer in order to view your notes.

Exporting Notes

Windows Journal also allows you to export notes into two formats: Web Archive format (.mht), and Tagged Image File format (.tif).

MHT Format

Web Archive format is readable by Internet Explorer, which means that saving your notes in this format allows anyone with a Windows-based machine to view the notes.

In addition to Internet Explorer, MHT files can be viewed in Office XP and 2003, and in Office 2000 with the Web Archive add-in. You can get the add-in at http://office.microsoft.com/ downloads/2000/webarchive.aspx.

tip

MHT format is probably the easiest for others to use, because most people have Internet Explorer. Always check with the person you're trying to share files with to determine his or her preference.

Realize that although Internet Explorer accounts for the majority of browsers in the world, it is not on everyone's machine. Just make sure that if you're saving the file in MHT format that your intended audience has the capability to open the file. Figure 6.18 shows how the MHT file looks in Internet Explorer.

FIGURE 6.18

In Internet Explorer, the MHT file appears just like the Windows Journal file, and even has a navigation pane.

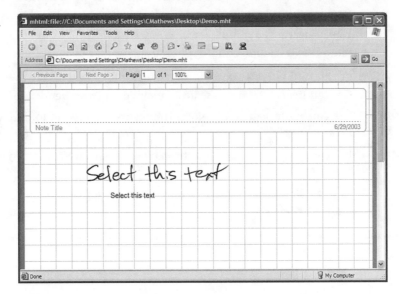

TIF Format

An industry standard, TIF files can be viewed in numerous applications, including Microsoft Office applications and almost all image-editing programs. This is more of a cross-platform solution than the MHT file, but for many, it is not as easy to view. Microsoft Office Document Imaging does a good job displaying TIF files, and even keeps the multiple pages separate. Again, determine the needs of the recipient before deciding which method to use.

THE ABSOLUTE MINIMUM

Here are the key points to take away from this chapter:

- View the Windows Journal tutorial. It has some good pointers, and lays the foundation for learning more.

- You'll never run out of paper in Windows Journal. Just tap the **Next Page** button, and you have more space to scrawl and doodle.

- If you want to insert space between notes, use the Insert/Remove Space tool.

- Convert ink to text if you want to include it in another document.

- You can easily search for ink in documents if you want to find handwritten notes.

- Have your workgroup install the Windows Journal Viewer if they don't have Tablet PCs.

- Export notes in MHT or TIF format so others can view them without Windows Journal or a viewer.

7

ADVANCED WINDOWS JOURNAL

In this chapter, you'll take a look at the more advanced features of Windows Journal that let you really start gaining productivity from the application. This will build upon your basic knowledge of Windows Journal.

Beyond the Pen

Windows Journal is great for drawing and writing using a pen. But it can do more. You can add elements to your notes, such as text and graphics, and you can easily rearrange your thoughts if your notes were a bit scrambled on the way in.

Adding Text, Graphics, and Flags

To add a text box or picture to your note, just tap **Insert** and then choose either **Text Box** or **Picture**.

If you choose Text Box, you will then see a crosshair cursor that you will use to tap where you want the text box inserted. You can either tap to insert the text box, or you can drag to create a text box of a specific size. You can now type or enter text directly into the text box.

If you choose to insert a picture, you will then see a dialog box that lets you choose the picture you want to insert. Once you select the image, you will see it in Windows Journal. You can then annotate the image and the note, as in Figure 7.1.

tip

Inserting a text box allows you to type in your Windows Journal notes.

FIGURE 7.1

This is a picture I inserted into Windows Journal so that I could make notes about it. (Yes, I really was the cow.)

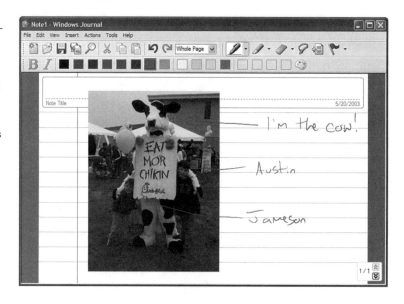

To add a flag to your note, go through the same process—tap **Insert**, **Flag**, and then choose the color of the flag you want to insert. You can insert any number of flags into your note. Flags can be useful as placeholders and as bookmarks. Figure 7.2 shows how you can search for flags in your notes. This is a great way to jump to specific points in long notes. Notice, too, that you can search through more than just your current note. By tapping the **More** button in the search pane, you can select **Look for Flags**, as well as change the breadth of your search to include notes throughout your hard drive.

tip

If you add a text box or image to your note, you will have a hard time selecting it if you're in Pen mode. In fact, you will have to right-tap the text box or graphic to select it. Seems weird, but this is because by default, you can write over the same spot on the page as much as you want, so ink takes precedence over the object.

FIGURE 7.2

In addition to searching for notes, you can also search for flags and set the context of the search to include multiple notes.

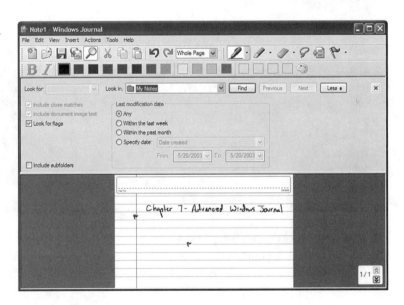

Reorganizing Your Thoughts

Once you have created notes, you can easily rearrange your thoughts. Just select the line or lines of notes you want to move (either by using the Lasso tool or by right-tapping), and drag the item to where you want it. With a few quick moves, you can rearrange the order of your ideas, as I have done in the two notes shown in Figures 7.3 and 7.4.

From Figure 7.3, I took the ideas and moved them around. Figure 7.4 shows the rearranged thoughts.

tip

Inserting a flag in your notes can help you identify key parts of your notes. These could be used in place of an asterisk—for example, to identify critical ideas.

FIGURE 7.3

This is the order of my notes before I rearranged them.

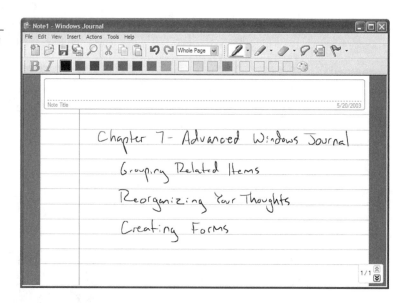

You can also move text boxes, pictures, flags, and figures. All items in Windows Journal are treated as objects, so it is easy to select and rearrange them. Just use the Lasso tool to select an item, or right-tap the object, and then move it where you want it.

Grouping Related Items

In addition to rearranging items, you can fix the relationship between items—for example, if you have a complex drawing or a series of notes that you want to move to another page, but that you want to keep together.

FIGURE 7.4

This is what it
looked like after
I swapped two
of the ideas.

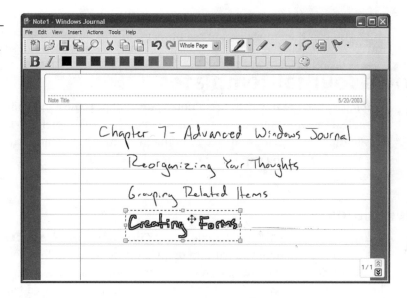

To group items, select everything that is related, and then tap **Actions**, **Group**, as
shown in Figure 7.5. Unfortunately, you can only select a connected group of objects,
so selecting individual items that are all over the place will result in one large selection box instead of lots of individually selected objects. To resolve this, move related
items together before selecting group.

FIGURE 7.5

You can group
related items so
that they stay
together.

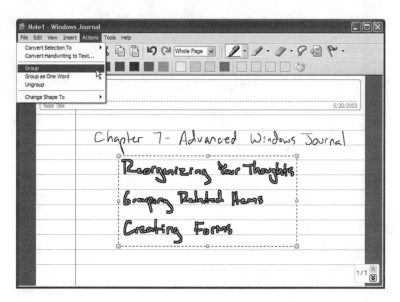

Now, instead of being able to select individual notes, you can select the entire group, which you can then move as you see fit.

Windows Journal Templates

Templates are a great way to use a note "paper" that is most appealing to you. For example, I prefer graph paper over lined paper; you might prefer to go without any lines at all. Windows Journal gives you the freedom to create note paper that suits your needs. And if you export the note, it will look exactly like your customized paper.

Using Templates

To create a new note using a template, tap **File**, **New Note from Template**, and then select the template you want to use. Unfortunately, Windows Journal does not let you preview the template, so you must open each one to see what it looks like. In Figure 7.6, you see my preferred grid paper, which is a customized template.

FIGURE 7.6

My customized graph template.

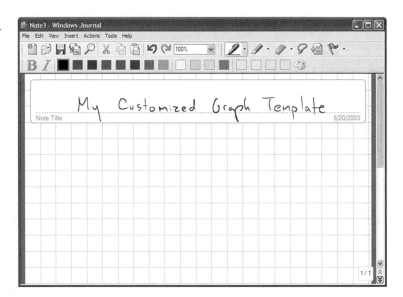

Setting the Default Template

If you have a template that you want to use most of the time, you can set it as your default template. To do this:

1. Tap **Tools**, **Options**, and select the **Note template radio** button on the Options dialog box. (The stationery button is the same as what is covered in the next section, "Creating Templates.")

2. Select the template you want to use by tapping the **Browse** button and choosing the template file name.

3. Tap the **OK** button to save the template as your default.

tip

Windows Journal templates can help you use the "stationery" that appeals most to you or your audience.

Formatting Notes and Creating Templates

To set the default page style, do the following:

1. Tap **File**, and then **Page Setup**.

2. Change the paper size, orientation, line styles, paper color, background image, and title area settings as desired.

3. After creating the page the way you want, tap the **Set as Default** button to save the settings as your default page style.

tip

Setting a default template ensures that all of your notes begin with the same look.

4. Save the blank notes page as a template so that you can easily use it later. Tap **File**, **Save As**, and then change the **Save As** type to **Windows Journal Template (*.jtp)**.

5. Enter a name for the template in the File name field.

6. Tap **Save**.

Figure 7.7 shows the settings I used to create my favorite graph paper. Notice that you can specify the horizontal and vertical line styles, spacing, and colors, as well as whether there is a margin rule. You can also select from the program's standard line options in the Line style drop-down.

FIGURE 7.7

The settings for
my customized
graph paper.

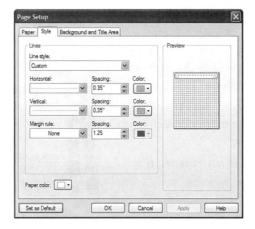

In addition to changing the style of the note or template, you can also use the Page Setup dialog box's Background and Title Area tab to change the background and title area options. For example, you can set a background image or form, change the transparency of the image, and choose to include or exclude the title area. Through these various selections, you can achieve interesting results, such as my psychedelic graph paper, shown in Figure 7.8.

FIGURE 7.8

My psychedelic
graph paper.

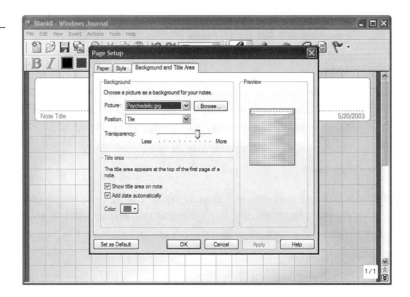

Be sure to choose the Windows Journal Template (*.jtp) option in the File type drop-down list, as shown in Figure 7.9. Otherwise, you will only save the notes page itself, and not be able to use it as a template.

FIGURE 7.9

I saved my psychedelic graph paper as a template so that I can easily reuse it.

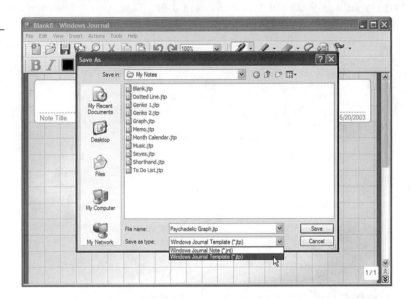

After you have created a template, you can use it to create new notes just as you would any other template: by opening the **File** menu, choosing **New Note from Template**, and then selecting the template you created.

Creating Forms

If you've ever visited a Web site that asked you to fill out your name and email address, then you've used a form. Forms offer a great way to capture specific pieces of information from multiple sources. With Windows Journal, you can create forms that accept handwritten capture areas. The downside to creating forms this way is that the data will not feed into a database automatically. Forms filled out like this will be better used for printing or for later reference, not as a front-end to a database.

That said, it is often useful to be able to use the Tablet PC the same way as a paper pad. Forms can then be emailed more easily than faxing or copying. Using a form like this can help you eliminate the paper forms that you would otherwise use. Since you can search on ink, this is still a step above paper. This could be a class notes form—something that you don't want to put in a database.

Creating forms is almost as easy as creating templates. With a form, you usually want to specify areas where you want input, such as the name and address of a person on a contact form, as shown in Figure 7.10. Although contact information like this would probably be better saved in a database, you can search for ink later, so this has some benefit if you want to keep things simple.

FIGURE 7.10

A form I created using text and graphics. Just fill it in.

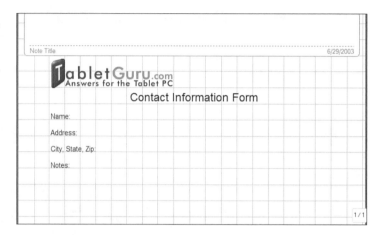

Creating Forms Inside Windows Journal

After you have created a note that includes any text and graphic areas you want (and you can certainly create a form using handwriting if you want), save the file as a template, as explained earlier. This time, though, since you have added objects to the notes page, you will be prompted to choose how you want the elements on your note treated, as shown in Figure 7.11. To use the note as a form, you will want to select the second option, **Save existing ink, pictures, and text boxes so they cannot be edited**. This will prevent the underlying text box or other elements from changing. Alternatively, you can choose to save the template so that those elements can be changed; if there is a standard piece of text you would normally use in your form that may change, this may be a good option.

Notice in Figure 7.12 that I have written information in a new note based on the previously saved form.

FIGURE 7.11

When you choose Save as Template with elements on the note, you will be prompted for how you want the objects treated.

FIGURE 7.12

You can write on forms saved as templates without disturbing the text or other elements underneath.

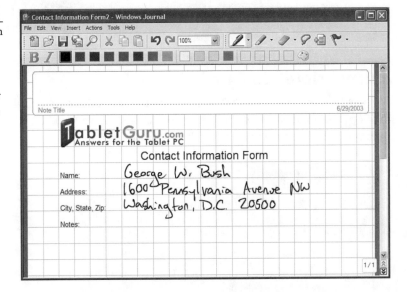

Importing Forms from Other Applications

You can also use other programs to create the form you will use, then print the document to the Journal Note Writer (as explained later in this chapter) to create a Journal note. You can then save the form from within Windows Journal as a template.

Outlook Integration

Windows Journal is a good tool for sharing information with others through Outlook. You can automatically insert meeting information into your notes, as well as easily send Windows Journal notes to others.

INSTALLING THE OFFICE XP PACK FOR TABLET PC

Even if you have Office 2003 (as of this writing), you can extend the functionality of Windows Journal (and of Office XP or Office 2003) by installing the Office XP Pack for Tablet PC (you can download the Pack from http://www.microsoft.com/office/tabletpc/). This gives you a few extra helpful features that don't come with your Tablet PC or with Office XP or 2003. The main additions are the integration with Outlook. For Example, if you use Outlook XP or 2003, the add-on enables you to import meeting information directly into your Journal notes, as shown in Figure 7.13.

note

This section covers Outlook only. For other applications, the integration will not be as automatic.

Sending Journal Notes as Email

It's easy to share your notes when you send them to others via email. With your note open in Journal, open the **File** menu, choose **Send to Mail Recipient**, and then select the file type to send, as shown in Figure 7.13.

FIGURE 7.13

Choose the format of the attachment you are sending to the recipient.

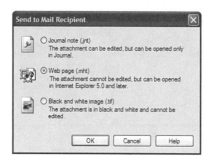

Once you select the format for the attachment and tap **OK**, Outlook will open, enabling you to send the note as an attachment. Figure 7.14 shows that the received email is viewed exactly like the original note, as you would expect based on what we learned about exporting at the end of Chapter 6.

Importing Outlook Meeting Information

To import meeting information, simply tap **Insert**, **Outlook Meeting Information** and choose the meeting that you want added into your notes (see Figure 7.15).

FIGURE 7.14

The email message's attachment looks exactly like the original note.

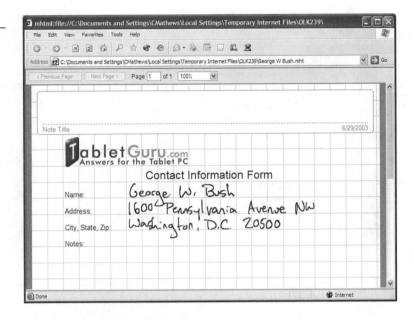

FIGURE 7.15

Choose the meeting you want to insert into your Windows Journal note.

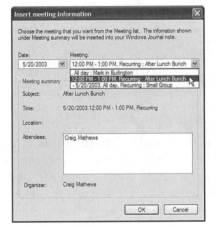

Figure 7.16 shows what the meeting information looks like when imported.

tip

You can import Outlook meeting information into your Journal notes only if you've installed the Office XP Pack for Tablet PC. For more information, refer to the sidebar titled "Installing the Office XP Pack for Tablet PC" earlier in this chapter.

FIGURE 7.16

The information
that Windows
Journal imports
from your
Outlook meeting
information.

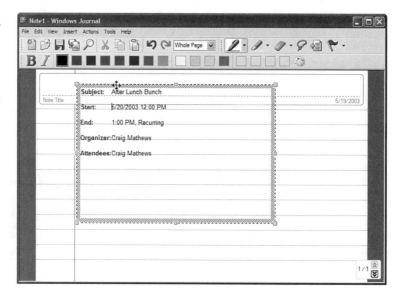

Once the meeting information is in your note, Windows Journal will use the contents of the subject line as the filename unless you type something else above the subject line in your note. (Windows Journal always takes the top-most item as the filename by default.)

Converting Selections to Outlook Items

If you've installed the Office XP Pack for Tablet PC on your Tablet PC (refer to the sidebar "Installing the Office XP Pack for Tablet PC" earlier in this chapter), you can convert selected notes to Outlook items, such as appointments, contacts, and tasks. To do this, first open the note that you want to convert. Then, tap **Actions**, **Convert Selection to**, and select what you want the note to become in Outlook (in this case, Outlook Appointment, as shown in Figure 7.17). The text is converted and saved in the notes part of the Outlook item, but you can easily drag and drop the content into the appropriate fields.

FIGURE 7.17

Convert text or
ink to an
Outlook item.

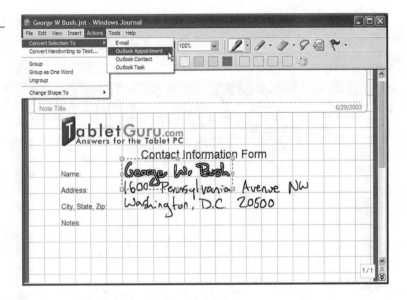

Working with Other Applications

If you want to use Windows Journal to mark up a document from another program,
you can. You can also copy anything you have in Windows Journal notes into
another application, such as copying a sketch of a house plan or an org chart into
Microsoft Paint.

Printing to the Journal Note Writer for Marking up Documents

The Journal Note Writer provides a way to mark-up a document outside its native
application. By using Windows Journal to annotate in ink, you can then save the
file in a way that others can easily view the annotations. (I only recommend this if
you do not have a version of Microsoft Office that supports ink. If you have Word XP
or 2003, you will be able to annotate directly in the application.)

To edit your document in this format, just print from your application to the Journal
Note Writer. This will not actually create a paper document. Instead, it creates a
Journal note from that application. Follow these steps to "print" your form to
Windows Journal:

1. Tap **Print** (or **File**, **Print**) from your application.

2. Choose **Journal Note Writer** as your printer.

3. Tap **OK** or **Print** to "print" to a Journal note file.

For example, if it's a Word document you want to edit, print that Word document to Journal Note Writer. Doing so opens Windows Journal with your document ready for editing, as shown in Figure 7.18.

FIGURE 7.18

After you print a document to Journal Note Writer, you can edit the document in Windows Journal.

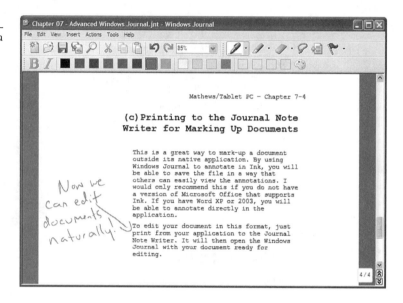

At this point, you can add anything you want to the document. Realize, though, that there is no way to transfer the document back to its native format. You will only have a Windows Journal note.

Using Windows Journal with Other Applications

As you just saw, you can import information into Windows Journal. But how do you get information out of Windows Journal and into another application?

If you're just copying notes, you can select the ink using the Lasso tool, choose **Copy as Text** from the pop-up menu, and then paste the recognized (converted) text into the other application (Figure 7.19 shows the results of such an operation into Word 2003).

You can also copy sketches from Windows Journal to other applications. To copy an ink sketch, just select it with the Lasso tool, choose **Copy** from the shortcut menu that appears, and then paste it into the other application. Figure 7.20 shows the results of copying a diagram from Windows Journal to Word 2003.

FIGURE 7.19

The results of copying and pasting from Windows Journal to Word 2003.

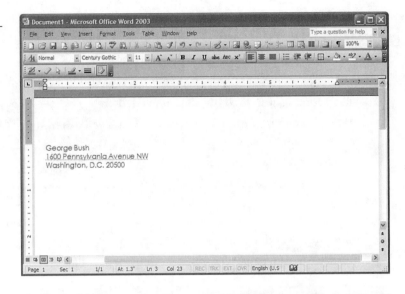

FIGURE 7.20

Copying diagrams from Windows Journal to other applications makes a lot of sense.

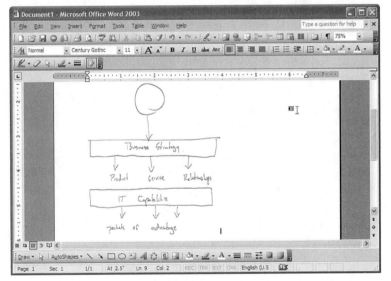

THE ABSOLUTE MINIMUM

Here are the key points to take away from this chapter:

- Add text, graphics, and flags to your notes to clarify your thoughts.

- Rearrange your notes and group related ideas to improve clarity.

- Use templates to make the "paper" look and work the way you want it, and to show your personality or your company's logo.

- Use forms to gather information in an organized way.

- Use Windows Journal with email to improve and personalize your communications.

- Install Office XP Pack for Tablet PC, even if you're running Office 2003. This will provide additional Outlook-integration options.

- Use the Journal Note Writer to mark up documents from other applications.

8

USING THE TABLET PC INPUT PANEL

The Input Panel is one of the core features of the Tablet PC. The panel allows you to enter handwritten text, turn on voice recognition, and use an on-screen keyboard. Understanding how to use the Input Panel is key to using the special input characteristics of the Tablet PC.

Input Panel Basics

With the Input Panel, you can use handwriting in any application. This section introduces you to the basics of opening the Input Panel and switching between modes.

Opening the Input Panel

One way to open the Input Panel is to make three or more quick strokes across the screen with your pen, but without actually touching the screen, as shown in Figure 8.1. This is called the Open Input Panel gesture. The strokes can be made in any direction, not just horizontally. The strokes can be relatively small, but you may want to practice the gesture to get a feel for what works. The strokes should overlap.

FIGURE 8.1

Open the Input Panel with the Open Input Panel gesture.

Another way to open the Input Panel is to tap the **Input Panel** button next to the Start menu button, as shown in Figure 8.2.

FIGURE 8.2

You can also tap the Input Panel button on the taskbar to open the Input Panel.

Understanding Input Panel Modes

The Input Panel has two primary modes:

- **Keyboard mode**—If you have particularly atrocious handwriting (like I do sometimes), or if you just need to enter a few characters, the keyboard, shown in Figure 8.3, can be more effective than the writing pad. To activate the keyboard, just tap the **Keyboard** tab in the bottom-right corner of the Input Panel.

- **Writing Pad mode**—The writing pad, shown in Figure 8.4, is how you enter handwritten text. With the writing pad, you can have the computer "read" your handwriting and convert it to text. To activate the writing pad, just tap the **Writing Pad** tab in the bottom-right corner of the Input Panel.

> **tip**
>
> Undock the Input Panel by opening the **Tools** menu, and then tapping on the **Dock** option to remove the check mark next to it.

FIGURE 8.3

The Input Panel keyboard allows you to tap out text.

FIGURE 8.4

The Input Panel writing pad lets you convert handwriting into text in virtually any application.

The rest of this chapter will focus on using the writing pad portion of the Input Panel. I'll assume you already know how to use a keyboard, and the Input Panel keyboard is nothing new as far as layout and functionality.

Using the Input Panel Writing Pad

Using the Input Panel in Writing Pad mode, you can use handwriting and gestures to speed up your data entry and to help you avoid using a keyboard—no matter what application you're working in. This section shows you how to effectively use the Input Panel writing pad, and how to get the most from your pen. As mentioned earlier, you can enable the writing pad by opening the **Input Panel** and tapping on the **Writing Pad** tab in the bottom-right corner.

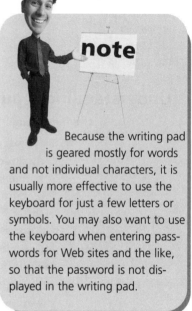

Because the writing pad is geared mostly for words and not individual characters, it is usually more effective to use the keyboard for just a few letters or symbols. You may also want to use the keyboard when entering passwords for Web sites and the like, so that the password is not displayed in the writing pad.

Using the Text Preview Pane

The Input Panel writing pad's text preview pane allows you to see the text you've written before it appears in the application you're working in. This enables you to ensure that the Tablet PC's handwriting-recognition feature has correctly interpreted your chicken scratches. For example, if you're using Word, you can use the Input Panel writing pad's text preview pane to edit your text (that was just recognized from your handwriting by Input Panel) before the text is placed in your document. Figures 8.5 and 8.6 show the effects of the Text Preview pane.

The great thing about the Input Panel is that it can be used with any Windows application, and even a command prompt. This allows you to operate without a keyboard in any situation.

FIGURE 8.5

The text written in the writing pad.

Notice in Figure 8.6 that the text written in the writing pad now appears in the Text Preview pane, letting you confirm its accuracy before sending it to your document or application.

FIGURE 8.6

The text as it appears in the Text Preview pane.

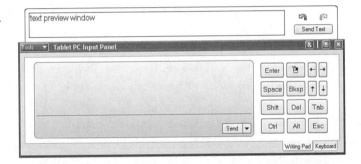

To enable the Text Preview pane, tap the **Tools** button in the upper-left corner of the Input Panel and choose **Text Preview** from the list of options that appears. To disable the Text Preview pane, simply deselect the same option.

When using the Text Preview pane, you also have the option of selecting alternate words—for example, if your Tablet PC misinterpreted a word that that you wrote longhand in the writing pad. To do this, simply tap or double-tap the word in question and click on the drop-down list that appears to see the alternate word choices, as shown in Figure 8.7.

tip

Using the text preview pane is a great way to ensure that your handwriting has been properly recognized. In addition, it enables you to select another word if your original writing was not recognized accurately.

FIGURE 8.7

Tap a word in
the Text Preview
pane to choose
alternate words.

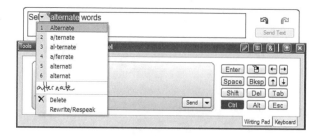

The list provided includes the computer's best guess of the top-ranking options for
the written word. If the word you want is not there, you can always choose the
Delete or Rewrite/Respeak option from the drop-down list and then try again.

Using Gestures

Gestures on the Tablet PC are shortcuts that you execute using your pen. For example, as you learned earlier in this chapter, scribbling several back-and-forth lines
across the screen will open the Input Panel.

Table 8.1 shows a list of the available gestures, and what they look like. Each gesture
starts at the dot and travels to the arrow in one fluid, non-stop movement.

TABLE 8.1   Available Gestures in the Writing Pad

Gesture Sample	Meaning	Comments
→	Backspace	Deletes the character to the left of the cursor, as does pressing the Backspace key.
—	Space	Inserts a space at the insertion point.
⌐	Enter	Inserts a carriage return at the cursor.
Γ	Tab	Inserts a tab.
≋	Scratch-out	Tells the recognizer to ignore the handwriting before it leaves the input area. Can be used over a letter, word, or several words. Must block out most of the item to be deleted.

Using the Input Panel Quick Keys

In addition to using the writing pad for handwriting, you can also use the quick keys next to the writing pad to move the cursor, delete text, and emulate the use of special keys, such as Enter and Tab.

The quick keys are helpful when you're not using a keyboard, because you often will need to insert a space or tab, or emulate pressing the Backspace, Enter, or Delete keys. Simply tap the keys to use them, just like with a keyboard.

The Shift, Ctrl, and Alt buttons are really best used with the keyboard, because letters entered from the writing pad will be entered into the destination application as plain text. But then, if you're using the Keyboard mode, you won't need the quick keys.

Setting Input Panel Options

There are numerous options you can set in the Input Panel that enable you to use the Input Panel more effectively. Some of these change the nature of the Input Panel itself, and others change how it does things behind the scenes. You change these options in the Options dialog box, which you can open by tapping the **Tools** button in the upper-left corner of the Input Panel and then tapping **Options**. This opens the Options dialog box.

Writing Pad Options

In the Writing Pad tab of the Options dialog box, shown in Figure 8.8, you can change the number of lines in the writing pad as well as the delay period before the writing pad submits your handwriting to your application.

FIGURE 8.8

The Writing Pad tab of the Options dialog box lets you change several settings.

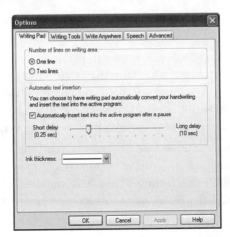

To change the number of lines in the writing pad, click either the **One line** or **Two lines** option button in the Number of lines on writing area box. Choosing the Two lines option enables you to write more text at a time in the same space, as shown in Figure 8.9. Using the Two lines option also seems to work faster because as you write on the next line, the previous line is recognized and converted to text.

tip

In general, thicker scrawls are harder to read. Use a finer pen thickness to increase legibility.

To set the delay period before the writing pad submits your handwriting to the open application, drag the slider bar to the desired delay. The delay you set can be as brief as 0.25 seconds or as long as 10 seconds. If you want the Input Panel to automatically insert text into your application after the delay, mark the check box above the slider; if you prefer to tap Send in order to insert the text, leave the check box unchecked.

FIGURE 8.9

Using the Two lines feature lets you enter twice as much text in the same space.

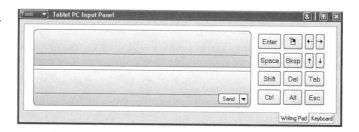

Finally, you can use the Ink thickness drop-down list in the Writing Pad tab to specify how thick the lines drawn by your pen appear in the writing pad.

Writing Tools Options

The Options dialog box's Writing Tools tab, shown in Figure 8.10, lets you choose whether or not to use a character recognizer with the Input Panel's writing pad, and if so, which one. The character recognizer can help you enter individual letters and symbols more accurately than with the writing pad alone. To enable the character recognizer, mark the **Show character recognizer on writing pad** check box.

Using a character recognizer is for those who are most comfortable with the Pocket PC or Palm PDAs. If you're familiar with one of these PDAs, it may be helpful, at least in the short term, to enable this feature. Figure 8.11 shows what it looks like when you have the Pocket PC letter recognizer enabled.

FIGURE 8.10

The Writing Tools dialog box is where you can choose to use the character recognizer and the quick keys.

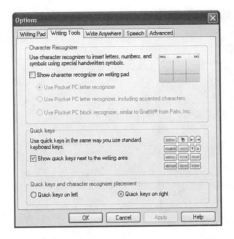

FIGURE 8.11

The character recognizer is enabled here.

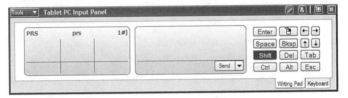

Quick keys is the other setting that you can change in the Option dialog box's Writing Tools tab. Quick keys are special buttons in the Input Panel that enable you to emulate the use of some of the main keys on the keyboard, such as the arrow keys, Enter, Tab, and others. If you don't want the quick keys to be displayed in the Input Panel Writing Pad tab, simply de-select the **Show quick keys next to the writing area** check box. You can also choose whether you want the quick keys to be placed on the left or right of the writing pad.

Write Anywhere Options

The next tab in the Options dialog is Write Anywhere. In addition to using the writing pad, you can enable the Write Anywhere feature, as shown in Figure 8.12, to convert most of your screen to a writing area that recognizes your handwriting. If you enable the Write Anywhere feature, you will no longer be limited to using the small writing pad available in the Input Panel.

FIGURE 8.12

The Write Anywhere tab of the Options dialog box lets you change the Write Anywhere settings.

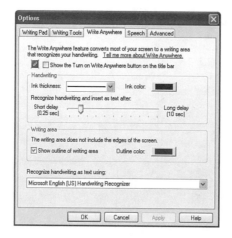

In addition to enabling the Write Anywhere feature, you can use the Options dialog box's Write Anywhere tab to change settings like Ink thickness, Ink color, and the text-insertion delay period. You can also choose to show the outline of the writing area so you'll know where you can write on the screen, and even set the color of the outline in order to see it better in certain applications. (Figure 8.13 shows what the outline looks like in Word.)

Notice that a line appears to guide your handwriting. This method of text input allows a much larger input area than the writing pad. Just realize you can't use your pen in the writing area without it marking, because the Write Anywhere feature assumes that all pen strokes are handwriting. In other words, you can't try to move the cursor, as this will create marks on the screen that the computer will try to recognize as handwriting.

tip

I recommend that you mark the **Show the Turn on Write Anywhere button on the title bar** check box at the top of the Write Anywhere tab; doing so adds a button to the Input Panel title bar that you can click to launch Write Anywhere.

Speech Options

You can use the Options dialog box's Speech tab to set some basic speech-input settings. Speech input is covered in the next chapter, but to give you a taste of what's to come, look at Figure 8.14 to see the basic Speech settings that can be changed. Note that you can use this tab to, among other things, specify whether the text preview pane should appear automatically when you begin to dictate, as well as whether sounds should be played when the microphone is turned on or off.

FIGURE 8.13

The Write Anywhere outline shows where you can write, and the guides help you keep your handwriting legible.

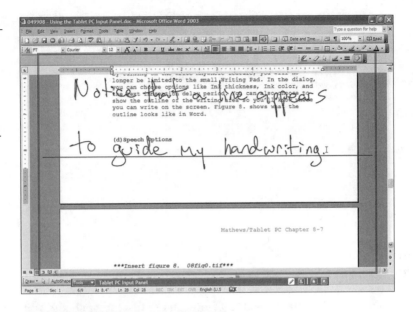

FIGURE 8.14

The Speech tab of the Options dialog box.

Advanced Options

The Advanced tab in the Input Panel's Options dialog box, shown in Figure 8.15, lets you specify how long the pen-input area should be displayed when it is not being used before it is hidden. To change the delay, mark the **When Input Panel is not docked, hide the pen input area after:** check box, and then drag the slider beneath the check

note

I cover speech input in more detail in Chapter 9, "Speech Recognition and Voice Control."

box to set the amount of time the system should wait. The delay can be as brief as half a second, or as long as 60 seconds.

FIGURE 8.15

The Advanced options dialog box lets you set pen input and title bar button options.

In addition to setting the delay, you can use this tab to choose which buttons—Hide/Show Input Area, Quick Keys Pad, and Symbols Pad—show up on the right side of the Input Panel's title bar. Displaying these buttons enables quicker access to the associated function.

Maximizing Handwriting Recognition

Having a pen and a digitizer is a great boon for computing. But if you can't get the computer to read your handwriting, it will be frustrating. Here are a few tips on improving handwriting recognition, and strategies for using the Input Panel.

Word and Letter Spacing

As you write in the Input Panel, make sure you have consistent spacing between letters and words. If you have varying spaces and character widths, your Tablet PC will have a more difficult time recognizing your writing. The main problem to avoid is running words together. Make sure you have space between words.

tip

Make sure you have adequate spacing between your words so that Input Panel can properly recognize your handwriting.

Style of Writing

Using a combination of upper- and lowercase letters works best. If you use all caps, your Tablet PC may have more trouble recognizing what you've written. Slanting is okay, but not if it's to the extreme. Cursive, believe it or not, is the most accurately recognized writing style.

Table 8.2 displays the results of several handwriting samples. Take a look at the styles of writing and notice which work best.

TABLE 8.2 Writing Samples and Their Resulting Text

Writing Pad Sample	Text Output	Comments
	STYLE of writing	Block capitals can work well if spacing and letter size are consistent.
	Styli, of visiting	Very close to the first sample, but the recognition is quite different.
	Style of writing	Recognition is good even on jumbled writing when the pen is barely lifted.
	Style of writing	Upper- and lowercase almost always works well.
	Style of woofing	Just a bit too crammed together on the last word.
	she obv sting	Lack of spacing caused this misrecognition.

TABLE 8.2 (continued)

Writing Pad Sample	Text Output	Comments
	Style of writing	Even mixed case gets converted to proper case.
	Style of writing	The recognizer works well enough to handle this scratch. Shows that cursive recognition is quite good.
	style Oban Gong	Again, inconsistent spacing causes problems.
	style of writing	Even small writing can be recognized accurately, but this is not recommended as less stroke information is available to the recognizer.
	Style of cursing	I can't even read this one. Good guess, Input Panel.
	Strobe of uniting	I had to try hard to make it NOT read my handwriting well.
	Sits off 15	Accuracy of acronym recognition is low. Use the keyboard for things like this.

Overall, handwriting recognition on the Tablet PC is really good. The intelligence that goes into recognition uses several factors, including putting the writing sample into context to determine the best fit for the text next to it. You will have some bumps to get over, but spending some time with the Tablet PC Input Panel will help you achieve higher handwriting recognition accuracy.

To maximize recognition, keep word and letter spacing consistent, use cursive, avoid stray marks, and write legibly. If others can't read it, your computer will probably not be able to either.

Dealing With Characters and Symbols

Often, when writing text, you will need to enter individual characters and symbols. One of the easiest ways to enter characters and symbols is to use the Input Panel keyboard or the Symbols pad.

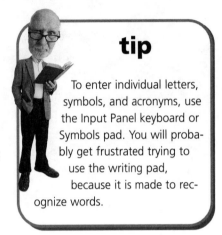

tip

To enter individual letters, symbols, and acronyms, use the Input Panel keyboard or Symbols pad. You will probably get frustrated trying to use the writing pad, because it is made to recognize words.

To open the Symbols Pad, click on the ampersand (**&**) button in the upper-right corner of the Input Panel. Using the Symbols pad to enter symbols is usually faster than trying to get the Input Panel to recognize your symbols. In fact, you may not be able to get it to recognize them anyway. For example, writing a plus sign (+) usually yields a 't'.

You can also enable the character recognizer in the Options dialog box to help you enter symbols and single words faster.

Get Help with the Online Tutorial

One way to learn more about the Tablet PC Input Panel is to use the online tutorial included with the application. As shown in Figure 8.16, you can view the tutorial by clicking the **Tools** button in the upper-left corner of the Input Panel, choosing **Help**, and then **Tutorial**.

FIGURE 8.16

The tutorial is another way to learn Input Panel basics.

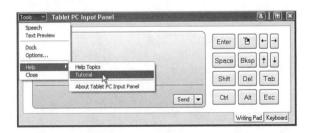

The tutorial is a multimedia presentation that introduces several of the features I just told you about. It's not comprehensive, but it is useful for getting someone started using the Input Panel, and for reinforcing what I showed you here.

THE ABSOLUTE MINIMUM

Here are the key points to take away from this chapter:

- Understand the differences between the Input Panel writing pad and keyboard, and the benefits of each.

- Use the text preview pane if you want to be able to edit the recognized text before inserting it into your application.

- Learn what style of writing works best for you with the handwriting recognizer.

- For maximum handwriting recognition, keep words separated, use lowercase letters predominantly, and use cursive.

- Use the Input Panel keyboard and/or the Symbols pad to insert just a few characters or symbols.

9

Speech Recognition And Voice Control

Speech recognition is a feature included in Windows XP Tablet PC Edition that allows you to use your voice to input text. Just to show you the power of this feature, I have dictated this entire chapter using speech recognition. Every word is dictated (but some minor editing was done manually, such as deleting or inserting spaces and lines).

How Does Speech Input Work?

You're probably wondering whether speech recognition is really ready for prime time. It is. Those last two sentences that you just read were spoken and not typed. Without any editing.

Speech recognition allows you to speak into a microphone and have the computer convert your spoken words into text. There is some training required, but it is not as cumbersome or time consuming as it was just a few years ago. In fact, I have not trained the speech recognition system for more than about 15 minutes, which was the original setup time. As I am dictating this chapter, I have to edit the words somewhat, but voice dictation is probably much faster than many peoples' typing.

Speech input also allows you to control your Tablet PC through the use of your voice. Using the Command feature of speech input, you can control applications by saying the names of the menus and commands that you want the computer to act on. So instead of dictating, you could be typing and have the computer format or take action while you're typing.

In order for speech recognition to work well, you need to have a good quality headset. A noise-canceling headset is a must; the microphone built into your Tablet PC is not usually acceptable for voice recognition. Once you have a good headset, hook it up to your Tablet PC. Be ready to spend 15 to 30 minutes training the system to recognize your voice. Then spend some more time getting used to functioning with the headset instead of a keyboard. A couple of hours should be sufficient to learn the main commands and get you used to using speech recognition. After that, you can be pretty effective.

I really did speak every word in this chapter. Just to show you the power of the speech-recognition capabilities of your Tablet PC, I wanted to show you that writing 4,000 words or so could be accomplished using speech recognition.

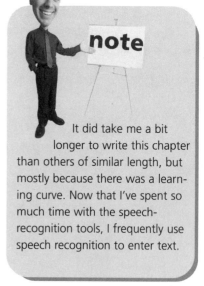

It did take me a bit longer to write this chapter than others of similar length, but mostly because there was a learning curve. Now that I've spent so much time with the speech-recognition tools, I frequently use speech recognition to enter text.

Selecting a Headset for Speech Input

The main thing that you want to look for in a headset is a noise-canceling feature. A noise-canceling headset will block out ambient noise and recognize your voice more clearly.

Consider this: I was sitting in an airport gate with a friend of mine when I first started to research the voice-recognition capabilities of the Tablet PC. I put on my headset and carried on a conversation with him. Only my part of the conversation was recorded. My new noise-canceling microphone didn't even pick him up, even though he was sitting right next to me.

Usually, a microphone will pick up a voice that is right next to it, which is why most headset microphones are positioned right next to the mouth. Excess sharp noises in the immediate area will probably cause some stray words to be "recognized."

You want to find a headset that is comfortable to wear for an extended period of time. I have been using Plantronics and Logitech headsets for the past month or so. The Logitech Internet Chat Headset is what I'm using as I dictate this chapter. It's a combination of a stereo headset with a flexible boom microphone. It's small, light-weight, and performs well in voice-recognition applications. It's also inexpensive and stylish, with several color options included. I like the stereo headset feature because I'm listening to music as I'm dictating this, and the music does not interfere or get recognized because it's only in my ears, and is not ambient sound.

tip

Set aside two or three hours to effectively learn some of the commands used in speech recognition, as well as how to dictate in your favorite applications. This time will pay off, as you'll be able to rant and rave and have the computer record your thoughts. If you're more effective talking through an issue, you may find that speech recognition is the perfect solution for you.

tip

A good quality headset is crucial for effective speech recognition. Find a noise-canceling headset that is comfortable to you. There are several options available, so look around.

I've not found a good headset with large ear enclosures that also works with voice recognition. I would imagine that an aviation headset such as a Dave Clark headset could work nicely, but it may not be good for discerning music listeners. I wish that the Bose QuietComfort headset was also made with a noise-canceling microphone. The "cans" are big enough to fit fully around the ear, and also include active noise reduction, which is great in noisy environments like an airplane or train.

The chapter on hardware accessories includes some headsets that I have tried and have found work well. It's totally up to you to decide which headset is most comfortable for you and meets your particular needs. Some people are fine with a headset that's stuck in the ear and is very small, while others may want a larger headset for extended comfort. Whichever way you go, make sure it is a noise-canceling headset. That is the most important aspect of your headset.

Open the Speech Input Panel

To begin using speech recognition, you need to turn on the speech tool, and provide some initial training.

To begin, open the **Tablet PC Input Panel**, open the **Tools** drop-down list, and select **Speech**, as shown in Figure 9.1.

When you select the Speech command, The Speech bar will appear, and you'll need to tap on the **Start Speech** button to set up speech recognition. The first time you run this, you will see a series of dialog boxes that ask you to configure your system for speech input. You will be asked to set up your headset and perform the initial voice training. The first dialog box that you will see is shown in Figure 9.2.

tip

This is where you need to be ready to spend at least 15 minutes with your computer to get it ready to accept your voice input.

FIGURE 9.1

Select Speech from the Tools drop-down list on the Input Panel.

FIGURE 9.2

The Speech Recognition Enrollment dialog box is the first step in training speech input.

As you continue through the Microphone Wizard, you will see several more dialog boxes, including the one in Figure 9.3. In Figure 9.3, notice how the headset is positioned on the person's head. The microphone should be close to your mouth but to the side so that excessive breathing will not affect speech input. (That's right—heavy breathing is not appreciated by your computer.)

FIGURE 9.3

Adjust the headset and microphone like this picture and continue to use the wizard to adjust the volume levels for proper speech recognition.

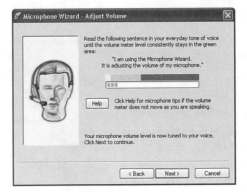

After you complete the wizard, you will see that the Input Panel looks like the one shown in Figure 9.4. Notice that you now have a Dictation button, a Command button, an area that shows the status of the speech recognition, and a Speech Tools section.

FIGURE 9.4

Now the Input Panel shows the Speech bar, enabling you to use speech tools.

Training the System

Once you're finished going through the wizard, it's a good idea to train your system to better recognize your voice. It's an easy process that doesn't take much time. To begin speech training, click on the **Speech Tools** down arrow and choose **Voice Training**. You'll see a dialog box that looks like in the one in Figure 9.5, where you choose which text to read for your voice-training session.

FIGURE 9.5

Choose the text you want to read for your voice-training session.

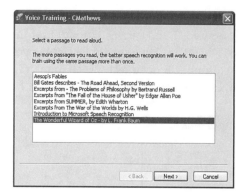

You will then see a dialog box like the one in Figure 9.6. This is where you read the text aloud, and the system learns how you speak.

When you're finished reading the text for the voice-training session, you will see the Updating Speech Profile dialog box, as shown in Figure 9.7. Your Tablet PC now knows how you speak and will be able to recognize your voice more accurately.

tip

Spend a little extra time to go through one of the additional voice training sessions. This will increase the accuracy of speech recognition.

FIGURE 9.6

Begin reading the text aloud so that the system will understand how you speak.

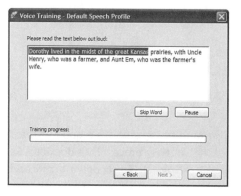

When you're finished with the training session, you will be asked if you want to provide more training. The more you train your system, the better it will be able to recognize your voice, yielding higher accuracy in speech-to-text conversion.

FIGURE 9.7

When you're finished reading the text, the Voice Training Wizard updates your speech profile.

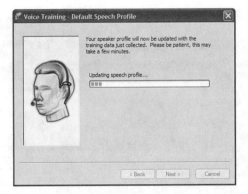

Now that you've finished the training, it's time to start using your speech-recognition capabilities. But first, let's use the Speech tutorial to get a better handle on the basics of speech recognition.

Use the Speech Tutorial to Get the Basics

As soon as you finish training the speech-recognition tool, you'll be asked if you want to run the Speech tutorial. I suggest that you run the tutorial, because it will help you get the basics down. When you run the Speech tutorial, you will see a screen that looks like the one shown in Figure 9.8.

FIGURE 9.8

Use the Speech tutorial to get acquainted with speech recognition quickly.

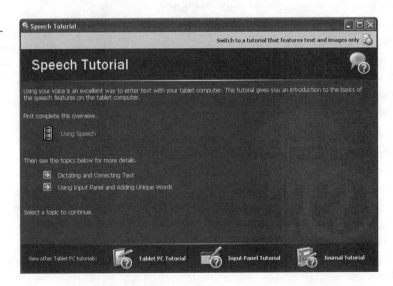

From this screen, tap on the **Using Speech** link to start the video tutorial. You'll see a screen like the one shown in Figure 9.9.

FIGURE 9.9

The Using Speech tutorial uses video to show you how to effectively use speech recognition.

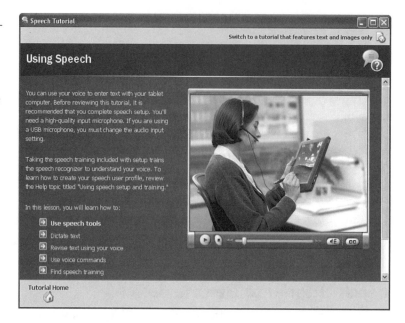

Using Voice Commands

The Command option of speech recognition enables the speaker to use voice commands to control the computer. Commands are application sensitive— that is, they differ from application to application. There are some basic commands that you can use in all applications, while others are for specific applications. This section will introduce you to the basics of voice commands.

tip

Use the Using Speech tutorial to quickly learn about speech recognition.

Controlling Speech Recognition

The first commands that you need to know are about how to control the speech-recognition system. Once you turn on speech recognition by tapping Dictation or Command, you will then be able to switch to either Dictation or Voice Command mode by saying either "dictation" or "voice command." You can also say "microphone" to turn off the microphone. But because the microphone will then be turned off, you must tap on either Dictation or Command to turn speech recognition back on.

What Can I Say?

"What can I say?" is one of the basic commands available to you in speech recognition. When you say "what can I say?" in Voice Command mode, a dialog box that looks like the one shown in Figure 9.10 will open.

Notice that several items are grayed out, such as Dictation into foreground application. This is because Voice Command mode and Dictation mode use different sets of commands and control words.

If you want to switch from Voice Command mode to Dictation mode, just say "dictation." You will then see a dialog box like the one shown in Figure 9.11.

> **tip**
>
> Use the "what can I say?" command to find out the appropriate commands for the given speech-recognition mode and software application.

FIGURE 9.10

The What Can I Say dialog box opens when you say "what can I say?" while in Voice Command mode.

FIGURE 9.11

The What Can I Say dialog box in Dictation mode has different options enabled. Here, Dictation into foreground application is expanded to show voice commands available in Dictation mode.

You can expand any of the sections in the What Can I Say dialog box to be able to see the specific commands that are available to you in the mode you are in.

Even in Dictation mode, you can use certain voice commands, such as "force num," "new paragraph," and "spell it." Each of these commands and the others available to you will help you rely almost solely on speech recognition.

You can also switch between modes easily so that you can accomplish almost anything just by using your voice. For example, you can begin dictating into Microsoft Word, then switch to Voice Command mode to use the menus to take actions on the text you just spoke. This enables you to have a virtually hands-off experience with your application—at least in theory.

In practice, however, the Input Panel speech recognition is still a bit behind the times in speech-recognition usability. Applications such as Dragon Naturally Speaking and IBM Via Voice are ahead of the included speech recognition, especially when it comes to usability. With that said, every word that you see in this chapter was spoken using the speech-recognition capabilities included in Windows XP Tablet PC Edition. For technology that is built into the operating system, the speech-recognition capabilities for the Tablet PC are amazing.

One more thing that you can do is enable voice commands to work during dictation. Be warned, though, that this may lower the accuracy of speech recognition. To enable voice commands in Dictation mode, perform the following steps:

1. Tap the **down arrow** at the right side of the Speech bar in the Input Panel, and choose **Voice Command Configuration**.
2. Tap on **Working with text** in the category column.
3. Tap the **Details** button at the bottom right of the dialog box.
4. Check the **Enable during dictation** check box.
5. Tap **OK** twice.

Although this enables voice commands and Dictation mode, it also reduces the ability for the speech engine to recognize your commands, and may also impair speech recognition in Dictation mode. Play with the setting to determine if it is worthwhile for you.

Common Commands

Understanding the commands that you can use in each mode is important so that you can be as effective as possible using speech recognition. Table 9.1 shows some of the most common commands available in Dictation mode, and Table 9.2 covers handling common symbols and punctuation in Dictation mode.

TABLE 9.1   Common Voice Commands in Dictation Mode

Voice Command	Action	Example
Dictate into foreground application		
"Force num <number>"	Speak numbers instead of words.	Force num 2
"New line"	Insert a single carriage return.	New line
"New paragraph"	Insert two carriage returns.	New paragraph
"Spell it <spelling>"	Spell a word exactly.	Spell it <humperdink>
"Spell that"	Spell a word in all caps.	Spell that <HUMPERDINK>
Controlling Speech		
"Microphone"	Turns microphone off.	Microphone
"Voice command"	Switches to Command mode.	Voice command

TABLE 9.2   Common Symbols and Punctuation in Dictation Mode

Symbol	Voice Command	Symbol	Voice Command
&	"Ampersand"	+	"Plus sign"
*	"Asterisk"	#	"Pound sign"
@	"At sign"	?	"Question mark"
\	"Backslash"	;	"Semicolon"
^	"Carat"	/	"Slash"
:	"Colon"	~	"Tilde"
,	"Comma"	_	"Underscore"
--	"Dash"	"	"Quote"
$	"Dollar sign"	"	"End quote"
°	"Dot"	(	"Open paren"
=	"Equals"	)	"Close paren"/"end paren"
!	"Exclamation"	<	"Less than"
-	"Hyphen"	>	"Greater than"
¼	"One quarter"	[	"Bracket"
½	"One half"	]	"Close bracket"/"end bracket"
%	"Percent sign"	''	"Single quote"
.	"Period"		

Whereas Tables 9.1 and 9.2 deal with voice commands in Dictation mode, Table 9.3 deals with voice commands in Command mode. The fun part here is that you don't just see words appear, you actually make things happen on your computer. If the computer recognizes your voice, and your application supports it, you can do just about anything using voice commands. Table 9.3 shows many of the common commands that you'll use when commanding your computer. This is not all of the commands, but the ones that I have found work most of the time and provide most of the benefit.

TABLE 9.3 Commonly Used Voice Commands in Command Mode

Voice Command	Action	Example
Starting and Switching to Applications		
"Launch <application name>"	Starts the application you specify. You can also use "Open" and "Start" to do the same thing.	"Launch Microsoft Word"
"Switch to <application name>"	Switches to the open application you specify.	"Switch to Microsoft Excel"
Selection and Correction		
"Correct <phrase>"	Selects the phrase and gives you choices for correction.	"Correct <your application>"
"Correct that"	Provides correction options for the selected text.	"Correct that"
"Delete <phrase>"	Deletes the specified phrase.	"Delete <your application>"
"Delete <phrase> through <phrase>"	Deletes a large section of text.	"Delete <your application> through <voice commands>"
"Scratch that"	Undoes the last word or phrase dictated.	"Scratch that"
"Select line"	Selects the entire current line, from left margin to right margin.	"Select line"
"Select <phrase>"	Selects the specified phrase.	"Select <your application>"
"Select <phrase> through <phrase>"	Selects a large section of text.	"Select <your application> through <voice commands>"
"Select next phrase"	Selects the next phrase.	"Select next phrase"
"Select paragraph"	Selects the entire current paragraph.	"Select paragraph"

Voice Command	Action	Example
Selection and Correction		
"Select sentence"	Selects the current sentence.	"Select sentence"
"Select word"	Selects the word that the cursor is currently on.	"Select word"
"Unselect that"	Unselects the selection.	"Unselect that"
Navigation		
"Go to beginning of line"	Moves the cursor to the beginning of the current line.	"Go to beginning of line"
"Go to bottom"	Moves the cursor to the bottom of the current page.	"Go to bottom"
"Go to end of line"	Moves the cursor to the end of the current line.	"Go to end of line"
"Go to top"	Moves the cursor to the top of the page.	"Go to top"
Uppercase and Lowercase		
"All caps that"	Capitalizes all letters of the selection.	"All caps that"
"Cap that"	Capitalizes the word or phrase selected.	"Cap that"
"Capitalize"	Capitalizes the word or phrase selected.	"Capitalize"
"No caps that"	Uncapitalizes the word or phrase selected.	"No caps that"
"Uncapitalize"	Uncapitalizes the word or phrase selected.	"Uncapitalize"
Editing Operations		
"Copy that"	Copies the selection to the clipboard.	"Copy that"
"Cut that"	Cuts the selection from the document and adds it to the clipboard.	"Cut that"
"Paste that"	Pastes the contents of the clipboard into the document.	"Paste that"
"Undo that"	Undoes the last action.	"Undo that"
Keyboard Simulation		
"Backspace"	Deletes the character to the left of the cursor.	"Backspace"

TABLE 9.3 (continued)

Voice Command	Action	Example
Keyboard Simulation		
"Delete"	Deletes the selection or character to the right of the cursor.	"Delete"
"Enter"	Inserts a carriage return.	"Enter"
"Move down"	Moves the cursor down one line or cell in the document.	"Move down"
"Move left"	Moves the cursor one character or cell to the left.	"Move left"
"Move right"	Moves the cursor one character or cell to the right.	"Move right"
"Move up"	Moves the cursor one character or cell up.	"Move up"
"Next cell"	Moves the cursor to the next cell in the selection, or the next cell to the right.	"Next cell"
"Page down"	Moves the document down one page.	"Page down"
"Page up"	Moves the document up one page.	"Page up"
"Space"	Inserts a character space.	"Space"
"Tab"	Inserts or executes a tab.	"Tab"
Controlling Speech		
"Dictation"	Switches to Dictation mode.	"Dictation"
"Microphone"	Turns the microphone off.	"Microphone"

Menus and Buttons

Varies by application. Several common commands will be covered in the chapters dealing with Microsoft Office 2003.

Application-Related Commands

Many Tablet PC applications feature application-sensitive commands. You can find these commands in the Menus and Buttons section of the What Can I Say dialog box. Items such as being able to select the File or Edit menu or perform actions like bolding or italicizing text are included in this section.

Whenever you start a new application with which you want to use speech tools, be sure to look at the Menus and Buttons section of the What Can I Say dialog box to determine what additional commands can be used within the application.

> ## tip
>
> Always consult the What Can I Say dialog box when you want to use voice recognition with a new application. This will help you understand what you can use in the way of voice commands with that application.

Using Speech Recognition

Now that you've learned the basics of voice dictation and voice command, you're ready to start using them in a real way. The application I use voice recognition with most is Microsoft Word, so the examples that follow will come from Microsoft Word 2003.

In this section, I'll show you how I've used voice dictation and voice command to write this chapter.

Dictating to Word 2003

Dictating is easy, but at least initially the edits that you'll have to make may be significant and frustrating. Once you get into the flow of things, however, you'll be able to dictate long pieces of text with only minor edits.

When you're in Dictation mode, you will use very few commands. You will mostly be speaking text that you want to show up in your document. The main things that you need to consider when dictating are to speak clearly and at a speed that the computer can recognize, and to say the names of the various punctuation marks you need to use. (You'll learn how to use speech recognition to edit your text in the next section.)

To dictate, switch to Dictation mode and just start talking. As you begin to speak to your computer, you'll learn what the computer will recognize and what it won't. If you work in a specialized field, such as medicine or law, that uses a lot of nonstandard words, you might need to look at another package such as Dragon Naturally Speaking to handle a large specialized vocabulary.

Editing Text with Voice Commands

Editing text in speech recognition takes some getting used to. I usually keep at least one hand near the keyboard so that I can hit backspace, delete, or capitalize a letter quickly. But all of this can be done using your voice.

I've had much less success controlling applications than I have had editing text with voice commands. In fact, sometimes I cannot get voice recognition to recognize even simple voice commands such as "format," "file," "edit," and so on. I've also had some problems using simple editing commands that the What Can I Say dialog box says are available to me. For these reasons, I'm going to use this section to share with you a few of the tools that I use most when editing using Voice Command mode. In fact, these are some of the commands that I used when dictating this chapter.

Select Commands

The "select word," "select line," "select sentence," and "select paragraph" commands enable you to select the word, line, sentence, or paragraph on which your cursor currently rests. You can use these commands to move quickly through your text, as well as to apply formatting or changes to an entire selection.

Go To Commands

The four big navigation commands, "go to beginning of line," "go to end of line," "go to top," and "go to bottom," are useful for navigating through a page of text. Just say the command and the cursor will move to that location.

Move Commands

The move commands ("up," "down," "left," "right," and "next cell") move the cursor one character or cell at a time. You can also use the familiar keyboard-equivalent commands, such as "page up," "page down," "home," and "end" to move the cursor around.

Deletion Commands

The "delete" and "backspace" commands are just like their keyboard equivalents: "delete" deletes the character or selection to the right of the cursor, while "backspace" deletes the character or selection to the left of the cursor. These are commonly used commands.

Undo Commands

Just after you've done something that you didn't want to do, you can use the "undo that" or "scratch that" commands. If one of these commands is issued immediately after dictation, the entire dictation will be undone. If one of the commands is used after an action has taken place, the action will be undone.

Caps Commands

This is one of my favorite sets of commands. Especially when writing this book, in which I frequently needed to capitalize words in the middle of a sentence, I used the "cap that" command often. When you want to uncapitalize a selection, use the "uncapitalize" command. If you want the entire selection to be capitalized, use the "all caps" command.

Copy, Cut, and Paste Commands

The "copy that," "cut that," and "paste that" commands are exactly like the menu commands you use on a regular basis. Each works with the clipboard to enable you to copy, cut, and paste a selection. To use these commands, simply select the text you want to act on, and say either "copy that" or "cut that." You can then switch applications or move your cursor and use the "paste that" command to paste the selection into the current document in the spot where your cursor is located.

The "Correct <Phrase>" Command

"Correct <phrase>" is a great command to use when voice recognition is not 100%. Figure 9.12 shows what it looks like when the "correct <phrase>" command is issued within Microsoft Word. In this instance, I had said "correct your application."

If there could be multiple interpretations of your dictation for that phrase, you will see multiple items that you can choose from when you issued the "correct < phrase>" command. To select one of the items using speech recognition, just say the number next to the desired selection.

note

This command does not always work. If not, just get your pen out to select the text, and then click on the green icon in the upper-left part of your selection to access the correction tool.

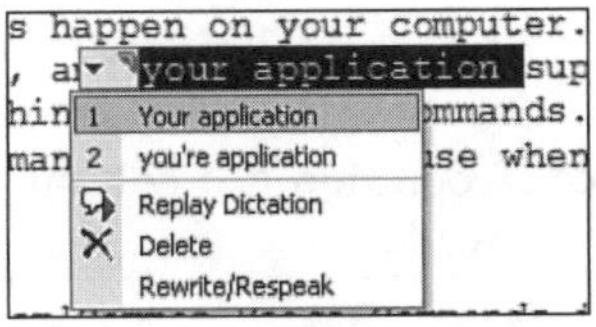

FIGURE 9.12

The "correct <phrase>" command helps you correct a phrase using speech recognition.

Real Voice Input Samples

Table 9.4 shows a list of samples of things I said versus what the computer thought I said. Notice that unexpected words and phrases often cause inaccurate interpretation.

TABLE 9.4   Dictation Samples and Their Results

What I Said	The Computer's Interpretation
"Now is the time for all good men to come to the aid of their country"	Now's the time for all good men to come to the aid of their country
"Four score and seven years ago our fathers brought forth on this continent a new nation comma conceived in liberty and dedicated to the proposition that all men are created equal period now we are engaged in a great civil war comma testing whether that nation or any nation so conceived and so dedicated can long endure period"	Four score and seven years ago our fathers b rought forth on this continent a new nation, conceived in liberty and dedicated to the proposition that all men are created equal. Now we're engaged in a great civil war, testing whether that nation or any nation so conceived and so dedicated to catalog and you are.
"We the people of the United States comma in order to form a more perfect union comma establish justice comma ensure domestic tranquility comma provide for the common defense comma promote the general welfare comma and secure the blessings of liberty to ourselves and our posterity comma do ordain and establish this constitution for the united states of america period"	We the people of the united states, in order to form a more perfect union, establish justice, ensure domestic tranquility, provide for the common defense, promote t he general welfare, and secure the blessings of liberty to ourselves and our posterity, do more dame and establish this constitution of the united states of America.
"We hold these truths to be self-evident comma that all men are created equal comma that they are endowed by their creator with certain unalienable rights comma that among these are Life comma Liberty comma and the pursuit of Happiness period"	We hold these truths to be self-evident, but all men are created equal, that they are and down by their creator with certain unalienable rights, that among these are life, liberty, and the pursuit of happiness.
"Voice recognition is great, but it doesn't always work. "	Voice recognition is great, but it doesn't always work.

As you can see above, voice dictation is not perfect, but it is really good. By speaking clearly and steadily, you can increase recognition capability. You don't have to speak slowly. Just avoid erratic speech.

Now go use speech recognition to write your next document. Happy speaking!

tip

If you find that your computer is responding incredibly slowly after you finish using speech recognition, you may need to manually shut down the tabtip.exe process. To do this, right click on the taskbar and choose **Task Manager**. Then click on the **Processes** tab and look for the process that is taking up the most resources. If tabtip.exe is taking up more than a few CPU percentage points, then tap on **tabtip.exe** and then tap **End Process**. This will shut down that process, and free up your processor. I have to do this frequently after using speech recognition on my Tablet PC, but it may not be an issue for you.

THE ABSOLUTE MINIMUM

Here are the key points to take away from this chapter:

- You must enable and train the speech tools before you can use speech recognition. Do this by turning on speech recognition in the Tablet PC Input Panel.

- Voice recognition will improve as you use speech recognition and as you complete additional training sessions.

- Use the What Can I Say dialog box to discover the commands that you can use in Dictation and Voice Command modes.

- Get to know the voice commands that work best for you. You will probably use only a subset of the total available commands during your speech-recognition sessions.

- The included voice tools are very good at what they do, but they're not perfect. Expect some time in editing, as well as some frustration at the start. Your accuracy and your skill with the tools will improve over time.

- For even better speech recognition and control capabilities, consider purchasing either the Dragon Naturally Speaking or the IBM Via Voice package.

PART **IV**

DATA COMMUNICATION AND PROTECTION

10

WIRELESS NETWORKING

As wireless networking (Wi-Fi) becomes more prevalent in public places, you will probably see more options for connecting and for security. Wi-Fi provides the capability to access Internet and corporate resources without wires. Right now, however, most Wi-Fi connections are unsecure, so be sure to take precautions when using Wi-Fi.

Setting up Wi-Fi at home is easy as well. Many consumer-oriented technology stores (Best Buy, Circuit City, CompUSA, and the like) have several offerings for wireless gateways that let you share your cable or DSL Internet connection with several computers in your home. Be sure to follow safe computing practices so that you don't open up your computers to prying Wi-Fi hackers, however. It is important to use some form of firewall, such as Internet Connection Firewall, which is included with Windows XP, and which I discuss in Chapter 11, "Keeping Your Data Safe and Synchronized."

Finally, connect to the Internet wirelessly when you're away from your desk by going to a hot spot. Hot spots are public wireless access points that let you connect to the Internet, such as those found at some coffee shops, airports, and book stores.

What Is Wi-Fi?

Wi-Fi stands for Wireless Fidelity, and is a wireless network protocol. Wi-Fi is becoming a prevalent way to connect to networks and the Internet. Wi-Fi usually refers to an 11 Mbps protocol (a *protocol* is a defined way to communicate electronically) called 802.11b. 11 Mbps is about as fast as 10 Mbps Ethernet, and about one-tenth as fast as 100 Mbps Fast Ethernet. Wireless often seems slower than Ethernet. 802.11b operates at the 2.4 GHz frequency range, which can conflict with other devices such as walkie-talkies and microwave ovens.

Other options for wireless networking include 802.11a and 802.11g. See Table 10.1 for the differences between each protocol.

TABLE 10.1   Wireless Standards

Characteristic	802.11b	802.11a	802.11g
Maximum speed	11 Mbps	54 Mbps	54Mbps
Frequency range	2.4 GHz	5 GHz	2.4 GHz
Install base	Large	Small/medium	Small, but growing
Strengths	Most common deployment, so you're most likely to find access points in other locations.	High speed. Less-used frequency, thus less possible contention.	High speed. Compatible with 802.11b.
Limitations	2.4 GHz band can interfere with cordless phones, Bluetooth, walkie-talkies, and other items. Slowest option.	Incompatible with 802.11b, which has the largest install base.	2.4 GHz band can interfere with cordless phones, Bluetooth, walkie-talkies, and other items.

One big problem with 802.11g implementations is that typically they do not in practice reach the same speed as 802.11a due to interference and other issues. Also, 802.11g has been shown to be much slower than 802.11a if you have a mix of 802.11b and 802.11g devices on the same network all accessing a 802.11g access point. However, because of its compatibility with 802.11b, I still expect the 802.11g protocol to win the battle in the near term, or at least until there is an even faster, more secure wireless protocol.

Components of a Basic Wi-Fi Network

Wi-Fi is composed of a router or access point and wireless network adapters for the Tablet PC, other computers, and peripherals that will access the Wi-Fi network. Figure 10.1 shows a diagram of a simple wireless network in a home.

A company has different needs for protection than home users. The entire office network must be protected from intrusion. For this reason, the router and firewall are usually separate devices in an office deployment because most offices have a different type of connection to the Internet than a cable or DSL link. Notice in Figure 10.2 that the Wi-Fi access point is inside the firewall, and that it is connected directly to the network switch/hub.

In this scenario, you will want to make sure that you are protected on the wireless side as well as at the Internet connection point. Wi-Fi can inadvertently allow people from outside the company to access resources if proper security precautions are not taken. The last section in this chapter, "Securing Your Wireless Network," will detail ways to tighten security on your wireless connections. For a more in-depth coverage of wireless networking, see Appendix A, "Additional Resources," for books about the subject.

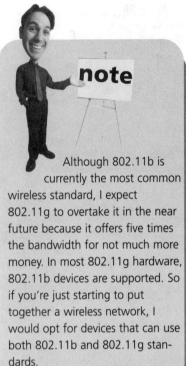

note

Although 802.11b is currently the most common wireless standard, I expect 802.11g to overtake it in the near future because it offers five times the bandwidth for not much more money. In most 802.11g hardware, 802.11b devices are supported. So if you're just starting to put together a wireless network, I would opt for devices that can use both 802.11b and 802.11g standards.

note

If you're just setting up a home network, wireless may be less expensive and easier to install—although it will be slower than Fast Ethernet and less secure because others can connect if you don't establish good security practices.

FIGURE 10.1

A simple home wireless net-work.

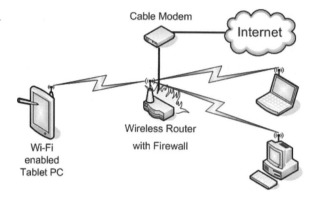

FIGURE 10.2

A simple office wireless net-work.

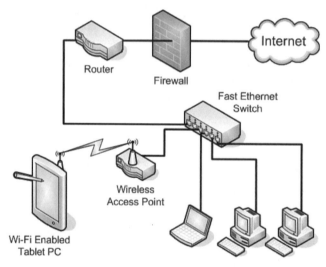

Finding and Connecting to Public Access Points

Wireless hot spots are places you can go to get connected to the Internet via Wi-Fi. There are thousands throughout the United States and the world. Major U.S. cities have many spots available already, and more will be added over the next few years.

Starbucks is one company that has made a concerted effort to make all its cafés Wi-Fi friendly (and free). Next time you want a cup of joe and a romp on the Net, go to Starbucks or your favorite wireless java house, or even one of your favorite book stores.

To find hot spots near you, visit one of the following sites:

- www.80211hotspots.com
- www.nodedb.com
- www.t-mobile.com/hotspot/default.asp?nav=hm
- www.ezgoal.com/hotspots/wireless

> **caution**
>
> When connecting to public hot spots, make sure all file sharing is turned off. You may also want to have Internet Connection Sharing enabled on your wireless connection (discussed more in Chapter 11).

Each of these sites list hot spots around the United States, and the first two list sites around the world. If you want to connect to a hot spot in your area, look it up.

T-Mobile currently has the greatest number of hot spots in the world. T-Mobile offers several plans for regular hot-spot users, including annual, monthly, prepaid, and pay-per-use plans. Plus, T-Mobile has set up the hot spots in Starbucks and Borders book stores, so you will have lots of choices.

How to Connect to an Access Point

Now that you know what a wireless network is, and how to find where public hot spots are, let's get you connected. First thing, of course, is to make sure your machine is ready for wireless.

If your Tablet PC has built-in Wi-Fi capability, all you need is an access point to connect to. If your Tablet PC is not Wi-Fi ready, purchase a Wi-Fi adapter that will work with your Tablet PC and follow the instructions to install it in your machine.

Once you have the required equipment on the Tablet PC side, you will want to find a wireless network to connect to. If your office has a wireless access point, ask your IT staff how to connect. If you've set up a wireless network at home or are ready to get connected at your favorite coffee house, try to connect there.

Once you have the information about where you're going to connect, if it's not already on, turn on your wireless networking. Some Tablet PCs don't have a switch, but others do. (If you're not immediately connected, read on.)

Making Sure Your Wireless Connection Is Enabled

If you know you are in range of an access point but you aren't connecting, make sure your Tablet PC's wireless networking features are enabled. To do this, you can go to Start, right-tap on **My Network Places**, and then tap on **Properties**. The Network Connections window, shown in Figure 10.3, opens.

FIGURE 10.3

The Network Connections window.

In the Network Connections window, right-tap **Wireless Network Connection**. If you have the option to enable, you need to do so. If, however, Disable is an option, do nothing here.

Setting Wireless Connection Properties

Once you are sure that your wireless network connection is enabled, you will want to check the properties of the connection. With the Network Connections window open, right-click **Wireless Network Connection** and choose **Properties** to open the Wireless Network Connection Properties dialog box, similar to the one shown in Figure 10.4.

In this dialog box, tap the **Show icon in notification area when connected** check box to select it. Doing so configures Windows XP to display a network connection icon in your system tray whenever you are connected to a wireless network. It also configures your Tablet PC to notify you when you're in range of a wireless network.

FIGURE 10.4

The Network Connection Properties dialog box for wireless networks.

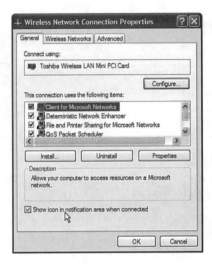

Now that you've checked the box, click on the **Wireless Networks** tab in the Wireless Network Connection Properties dialog box (see Figure 10.5). In this tab, you can configure secure wireless networks by specifying security parameters such as WEP keys and SSID.

Notice that I have multiple Wi-Fi networks defined. The circle around the antenna on the 1604 network in the top box indicates that I am currently attached to that network. If you don't see an antenna with a circle, be patient. You still may have some minor configuring to do before you can get connected.

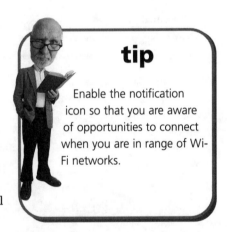

tip

Enable the notification icon so that you are aware of opportunities to connect when you are in range of Wi-Fi networks.

If you have configured your access point for a secure connection (see the section later in this chapter called "Securing Your Wireless Network"), you will need to specifically identify the network that you have made secure. To do so, click the **Add** button in the Wireless Networks tab to add a network definition to the list of preferred networks. Doing so opens the Wireless Network Properties dialog box; if it's not already displayed, click the **Association** tab, shown in Figure 10.6.

FIGURE 10.5

The Wireless Networks tab lets you define networks and their specific settings.

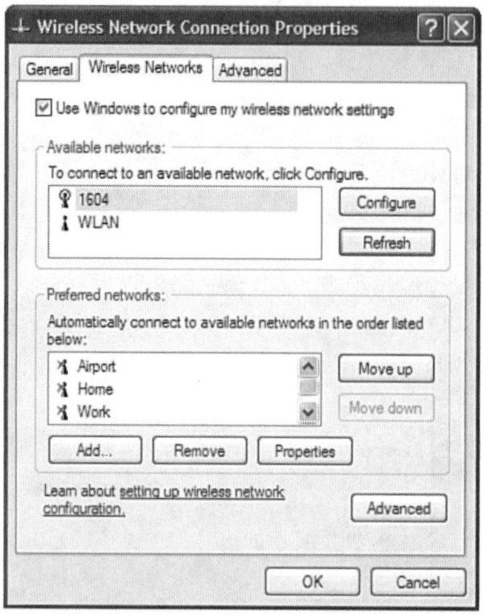

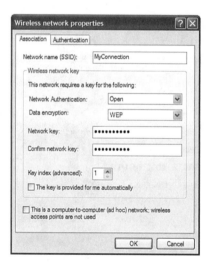

FIGURE 10.6

The Wireless Network dialog box's Association tab, where you define the security characteristics of your Wi-Fi network.

The Association tab is where you enter the SSID and other characteristics of your Wi-Fi connection. Follow these steps to configure your network connection:

1. Enter the SSID of the access point you want to connect to.

2. Choose the network authentication type. This is usually Open.

3. Choose whether you have WEP enabled or disabled.

4. If WEP is enabled, enter the network key twice. This will be a series of alphanumeric characters.

5. If you use a key other than the key index of 1, change it.

6. Check the **The key is provided for me automatically** check box if the key is provided automatically, in which case you will not need to enter the keys above.

7. Finally, check the **This is a computer-to-computer (ad hoc) network...** check box if the connection is to other computers or devices, instead of to a wireless access point.

After you have entered the requested information in the Association tab, click on the Wireless Network Properties dialog box's **Authentication** tab, shown in Figure 10.7.

FIGURE 10.7

The Authentication tab lets you configure advanced security settings for your Wi-Fi connection.

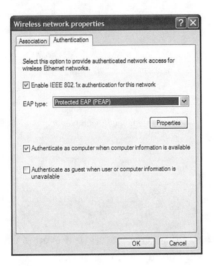

If your access point supports and uses IEEE 802.1x authentication, enable it here by checking the top check box. For most networks, this will be disabled.

Getting In Range of an Access Point

Now that you have configured your wireless network connection, you can try to get connected. When your Tablet PC picks up a signal and you get connected, you will see a status balloon like the one shown in Figure 10.8.

Notice that when your Tablet PC first connects, it says there is no signal. But if it's connected, there must be one, so be patient. After a few moments, hover your cursor over the wireless network icon in the system tray and you will see a message similar to the one shown in Figure 10.9.

FIGURE 10.8

You see this status balloon when you are connected to a wireless access point. "1604" is the SSID of my access point   it will be different for you.

FIGURE 10.9

When you're connected, you can hover your cursor over the wireless network connection icon to see the status of your connection.

Your signal strength will vary based on several factors, but even a Very Low strength indication can work well. If you ever get out of range or there is a disruption in your connection, you will see a status balloon like the one shown in Figure 10.10.

FIGURE 10.10

When you have a disruption in your connection, you will be notified by a status balloon.

If you have access to multiple Wi-Fi networks, you may see a dialog box similar to the one in Figure 10.11.

FIGURE 10.11
When you have multiple connection options for Wi-Fi networks, you may be prompted to choose one.

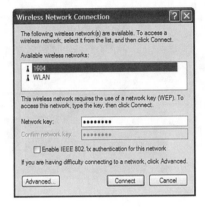

Once you connect to a wireless network, you should automatically be able to gain access to the Internet. If you are accessing a pay-for-use access point (such as one in a public place), the first time you connect to the Internet you may be asked to pay for your connection. After disconnection, you may be required to pay another fee, depending on the service provider.

Checking Wireless Network Status

If you want to check the status of your wireless network, you can double-click the **Wireless Network** icon in your system tray, or right-click it and choose **Status**. When you do this, you will see the dialog box shown in Figure 10.12.

This dialog box shows whether you are connected, how long you have been connected, the speed of your connection, signal strength, and the amount of data that has been sent and received by your Tablet PC.

> **note**
>
> Wireless access speeds can be affected by many factors, including signal strength, walls and objects between your Tablet PC and the access point, and more. If you have a hard time connecting, you may need a signal booster to enhance your wireless signal.

If you want to see additional information about your link, click on the **Support** tab. You will then see a dialog box similar to the one shown in Figure 10.13.

FIGURE 10.12

The Status dialog box shows what's going on with your connection. You can access additional information by clicking the Support tab and the Properties button.

FIGURE 10.13

The Support dialog box shows the TCP/IP characteristics of your connection.

If you click the **Details** button, you will see even more detailed information, such as a DNS server list, gateway, and other information you probably won't need unless you're troubleshooting your connection.

Back on the General tab, you can click the **Properties** button to open the Wireless Network Connections dialog box shown in Figure 10.11. There, you can click the **Advanced** button to open the Advanced dialog box, shown in Figure 10.14. This dialog box enables you to specify whether your Tablet PC can connect to ad-hoc networks, and whether it will automatically connect to non-preferred networks (that is, networks that you have not specifically defined).

FIGURE 10.14

The Advanced button lets you enable access to unsecure and ad-hoc wireless devices.

If you are still not able to connect to a wireless network that you know exists and is working correctly, you will probably need to contact your IT staff, or the technical support of the company providing the access point. Going any further here is beyond the scope of this book.

Securing Your Wireless Network

Although it is easy to connect to wireless networks, that ease is also its greatest downfall. Security is a concern that all wireless users should think about. In addition to setting up file security on your Tablet PC (covered in Chapter 11, "Data Management and Synchronization"), you need to secure your wireless network access points.

One of the best ways to secure your wireless network is to perform the following (you'll learn more about each of these steps in the sections that follow):

1. Physically protect your Tablet PC.
2. Disable SSID broadcast and create a nonsensical SSID.
3. Enable WEP.
4. Change your default password.

Step 1: Protect Your Tablet PC

The first way to secure your data is to limit physical access to your Tablet PC. Carry it with you, lock it up, use mobile security alarms and locks, and the like. This is crucial if you have critical data on your machine.

In addition to limiting physical access to your Tablet PC, you should protect the files on your Tablet PC using file system security, as described in Chapter 11. Good security practices and data management will always be the first layer of protection. That way, even if people get onto your network, you can prevent infiltration by blocking them from your files.

Step 2: Disable SSID Broadcast

If your wireless access point or router broadcasts its System Security Identifier (SSID), anyone in the vicinity with a wireless network adapter will be able to detect it. Once that is done, the person can connect to your network just by clicking a button.

> **tip**
>
> To totally protect yourself when you're not using the Internet, disconnect your Tablet PC from the network and turn off your Wi-Fi connection. If you're not using it, why not have 100% protection?

WHAT'S IN AN SSID?

An SSID is just the name of your access point. On Linksys access points, for example, the SSID is "Linksys". Since that's a known SSID, it is inherently unsecure. You can usually change the SSID to whatever you like, but you're limited to basic characters and no spaces.

Disabling the broadcast of your SSID will prevent the casual hacker—one who is simply looking for open wireless networks to infiltrate—from exploiting yours. More sophisticated intruders could be persistent enough to get your SSID, however, and thus access your network. If your access point does not broadcast the SSID, an intruder will have to guess (or use an application like Network Stumbler) in order to gain access to your network. Make sure your SSID is not composed of words or numbers that relate to you or your organization, such as the company name, an address, a person's or pet's name, and so on.

For a person to connect to your network, that person must have the correct SSID assigned in his or her wireless network settings. If you have created a nonsensical SSID and stopped broadcasting it, you will prevent the majority of casual intruders.

Step 3: Enable WEP

Once you have disabled SSID broadcast on your access point, the next thing to do to increase protection is to enable Wired Equivalent Privacy (WEP). WEP, though basic, is the most common form of security in wireless networks. Although WEP is not perfect, it is a second measure that can enhance security. Some people use WEP instead of disabling the SSID broadcast, but used in combination, they provide a formidable defense against intrusion for the novice wireless hacker.

WEP is a security method used by most Wi-Fi access points. Enabling WEP can enhance security significantly, but it is not bullet-proof. When you enable WEP, you should create a WEP pass phrase that is nonsensical (for example, h7kqY73). This pass phrase will be used on both the access point and the wireless network adapter to create a "handshake." This handshake ensures that both sides of the connection know about the other side. By using the same pass phrase, the access point identifies your Tablet PC as friendly.

Not all access points use pass phrases, however. If yours doesn't, you will be asked to enter a WEP key. A key is 10 or 26 hexadecimal characters (0–9 plus A–G). You can use 40- or 128-bit encryption (protection scheme). A 40-bit key will use 10 characters, whereas 128-bit encryption requires a 26-character key. 128-bit encryption is stronger.

If you enable WEP on either the access point or your Tablet PC and not the other, you will be unable to connect. Make sure all your WEP settings are identical on your access point and your Tablet PC.

Step 4: Change Your Default Password

Once you have your access point/router configured, change the default password. Most hackers can guess the device's default password if they can determine the manufacturer of your network device. Changing the password to a "strong" password will prevent a hacker from changing your access point's configuration. A strong password consists of upper and lowercase letters, numbers, and special characters such as punctuation marks.

One last note on Wi-Fi security: As of September 1, 2003, the Wi-Fi Alliance requires all wireless products to have Wi-Fi Protected Access (WPA) security in order to carry the Wi-Fi compliant seal of approval. WPA is a subset of the 802.11i standard that is mentioned in the following sidebar.

DEVELOPING WI-FI STANDARDS

A few new standards are just over the horizon that promise to improve Wi-Fi: 802.11e and 802.11i. 802.11e adds Quality of Service (QoS) functionality that lets it stream video and audio more capably than any of the other Wi-Fi standards. By giving priority to audio and video streaming, 802.11e can improve streaming quality, making Wi-Fi more capable in home theater and broadcast situations. 802.11i promises significant security enhancements by improving the way wireless devices connect and transmit data. This is a much-needed upgrade to Wi-Fi, as Wi-Fi is mostly unsecure.

THE ABSOLUTE MINIMUM

Here are the key points to take away from this chapter:

- Use wireless networking to be more mobile and to escape the tyranny of the wire.

- Be diligent in security, because others can access your machine when you are connected over wireless.

- Enable the wireless network icon in your system tray so that you will be notified of available connections.

- Define the characteristics of your preferred networks. If you don't, you may not be able to connect.

- Turn off wireless networking when you don't plan to use it in order to further protect your Tablet PC and your files from others.

- Connect to wireless hot spots when you want to get on the Internet and are away from home.

- Enable security on your wireless connections so that you will be less exposed.

11

KEEPING YOUR DATA SAFE AND SYNCHRONIZED

Why use a computer unless it's for dealing with important information, data, files, and the like? If your data is important, it's important enough to take care of. Securing your machine and files against unknown prowlers is just as important as making good backups. In addition, keeping your data synchronized with other file-storage areas will help others keep up with the changes you make to documents, or allow you to use multiple computers (though I don't know why you'd want to use anything other than your trusty Tablet PC).

Establishing Good Security Practices

Security is important for your Tablet PC—especially because it's possible for intruders to tap into your Tablet PC wirelessly. If you turn off wireless networking and don't have your network cable connected, you're safe from data thieves as long as your machine is in your possession.

If you let the machine out of your sight, however, others could access your files. That's when you want other levels of security. This section will help you establish safe computing practices and help you lock down your computer as much as practical. You can certainly take serious measures to protect your machine, but for most users, these protection schemes can get in the way of getting work done. The protection scheme you choose depends on your ability to accept risk, and the sensitivity of your data.

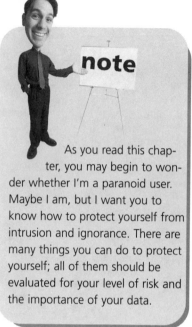

As you read this chapter, you may begin to wonder whether I'm a paranoid user. Maybe I am, but I want you to know how to protect yourself from intrusion and ignorance. There are many things you can do to protect yourself; all of them should be evaluated for your level of risk and the importance of your data.

User Accounts and Passwords

The first thing you need to do to protect your Tablet PC is to establish user accounts for those who will use the machine. (Note that it's possible that user accounts were set up before you received your machine.)

To get to the user account setup, go to the Control Panel, then choose **User Accounts**. In the User Accounts dialog box that appears, you will see a list of current users, as shown in Figure 11.1.

In the list, you see Administrator, which is a system account that cannot be changed. You also see my login, CMATHEWS. Notice also that there are two different domains. The CMATHEWS domain is just the local computer; the MCKIMCREED domain is the domain I log on to at work. A *domain* is a trusted security grouping that recognizes users by username and password. If your computer is not part of a work domain, you will probably want to

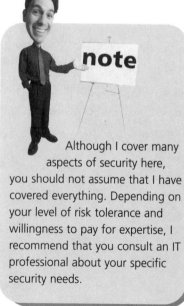

Although I cover many aspects of security here, you should not assume that I have covered everything. Depending on your level of risk tolerance and willingness to pay for expertise, I recommend that you consult an IT professional about your specific security needs.

have just two users, Administrator and your username. The domain will just be the name of your computer.

FIGURE 11.1

The list of user accounts on my machine.

To add a user, simply click the **Add** button and follow the prompts. If you intend to add multiple users, you may want to establish groups. To do this, tap on the **Advanced** tab and then tap the **Advanced** button to open the Local Users and Groups window, as shown in Figure 11.2. This window displays a list of all your named users. Guest is disabled, as denoted by the circled X.

FIGURE 11.2

A more in-depth look at the user accounts on my machine.

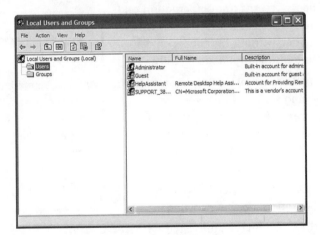

To boost security, make sure that the Guest user is disabled and that the Administrator user has a unique password (unless your IT department set it up for you, in which case you will want to ask them how your security is configured). To disable the Guest account, double-click the **Guest** username and check the **Disable account** check box. Leaving the guest account enabled is a potential security hazard.

Requiring Ctrl+Alt+Delete for Secure Logins

To configure your Tablet PC to require users to log in securely, again open the **User Accounts** dialog box (choose User Accounts from the Control Panel), but this time tap the **Advanced** tab. There, tap the **Require users to press Ctrl+Alt+Delete** check box; this will require a secure login, which users perform by pressing—you guessed it—Ctrl+Alt+Delete. Any time people log into your Tablet PC, they will then need to press Ctrl+Alt+Delete to log in.

Require Login When Returning from a Power-Saving Mode

In addition to configuring your Tablet PC to require users to log in securely, it's a good idea set up your machine to require a login every time it boots, returns from hibernation and standby, and resumes from a screensaver. This will prevent anyone without the proper credentials from getting into your machine easily.

Establishing good usernames and passwords is important. Making sure that passwords are required is the next step. If you allow your Tablet PC to return from standby or hibernate mode without asking for a password, it can be easy for someone to access your machine.

To require a password when returning from standby or hibernation, do the following:

1. Open the Control Panel and choose **Power Options**.
2. Click the **Advanced** tab.
3. Check the **Prompt for password when computer returns from standby** check box.

caution

Always disable the Guest user account. In fact, any accounts that you are not sure of are suspect. If yours is a company-owned machine, check with your IT department about how to secure your machine within the company's parameters. If not, limit the number of accounts you have set up on your machine and make sure each has a secure password.

caution

If you don't set up password recovery from standby or hibernation mode, all your other security measures can be compromised from a person sitting down in front of your machine while you're away.

Require Login When Returning from Screensaver

You also have potential security risks when you walk away from your machine for a while. You can make your screensaver require a login when resuming from the screen saver. If you're away long enough for your screensaver to kick in, it's long enough for someone else to gain access to your machine.

To establish this policy, open the Control Panel and choose **Display Properties**. Click on the **Screensaver** tab, and check the **On resume, password protect** check box.

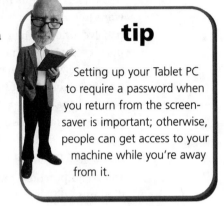

tip

Setting up your Tablet PC to require a password when you return from the screensaver is important; otherwise, people can get access to your machine while you're away from it.

Install and Configure Virus Protection

Virus protection is an important safety precaution if you think you'll ever connect to the Internet or a network (which is a big reason for getting the Tablet PC in the first place). Basically, you need it.

There are numerous virus-protection packages available, including Symantec's Norton Antivirus, McAfee's VirusScan, and packages by Computer Associates and Trend Micro. McAfee and Symantec have the largest installed bases and are always excellent choices.

Install the software according to the instructions provided with your package. Usually, accepting the defaults will yield a reasonable protection level. When you first install the application, you will probably be required to scan your hard drive before doing anything else. After that, you can configure your anti-virus product to scan on a regular basis, such as once a week, and also to protect in real-time, checking all files coming into your computer.

If your Tablet PC is company-owned, your IT staff may have already set up virus protection for you. Ask them how often the virus definitions get updated. If it's any less than a month or week, ask if they can make it more frequent. I have my company's virus files updated daily.

caution

In today's world, if you're not protected from viruses and you share information with anyone else, you are opening yourself up for a world of hurt. Install virus protection software as soon as possible.

Use a Firewall to Protect Against Internet Attacks

If you're using your Internet connection for multiple users, you will want to purchase a firewall device. These are inexpensive, and can be purchased in a multipurpose device, such as a wireless broadband router/firewall/switch combination. If you're setting up a network at home to include wireless access to the Internet, I'd encourage you to purchase and configure one of these devices. If you don't have a firewall at work, put this book down and go get one right now. Seriously.

You could purchase any one of probably a hundred or so different firewall products. I have used both the Linksys and D-Link broadband router/firewall/switch combos, and have been pleased with each. The amount of security you need will determine your device requirements.

> **caution**
>
> Firewalls are important for anyone using the Internet. If you leave yourself open, there are just too many ways malevolent people can get control of your machine.

If you plan to create a wireless network, refer to Chapter 10, "Wireless Networking," for more information on what to buy and how it should be configured.

Enabling Internet Connection Firewall

If you're only going to have your Tablet PC connected to the Internet (and not multiple machines), you don't have to have the hardware-based firewall, even though I recommend it. Windows XP includes the Internet Connection Firewall (ICF) as an option. Using this, you can protect your machine at a basic level against data thieves and other miscreants. Internet Connection Firewall prevents others from coming through the Internet and getting on your computer.

> **tip**
>
> Use Internet Connection Firewall only if you don't have a hardware-based firewall. ICF takes up computing resources and can interfere with other applications.

The Internet Connection Firewall can slow down your system and interfere with other services on your Tablet PC, but it is an option for those who don't want to buy a firewall device.

To enable the ICF, do the following:

1. Choose **Network Connections** from the Control Panel, or double-click the **Network Places** icon on your desktop and then choose **View network connections**.

2. Choose the connection that you want to protect (dial-up, wireless, or LAN are the most common choices). The shortcuts window on the left will then show several options, as shown in Figure 11.3.

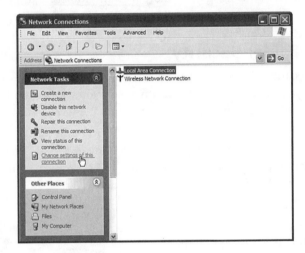

3. Tap **Change settings of this connection**.

4. Tap the **Advanced** tab.

5. As shown in Figure 11.4, check the check box at the top to enable **Internet Connection Firewall**.

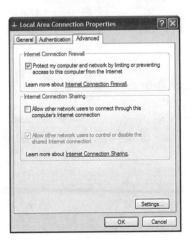

If you find that enabling ICF interferes with anything you need to do, you can follow the same procedure, but uncheck the check box to disable ICF.

For more information on ICF, enter the phrase "Internet Connection Firewall" into Help and Support (**Start**, **Help and Support**). The Internet Connection Firewall overview explains what ICF is, and how it works. It also details issues that you may need to be aware of when enabling ICF on your system, such as possible contention with Internet Connection Sharing (ICS) and not enabling it if not connected directly to the Internet. Because this book deals more with the Tablet PC than Windows XP, you may want to find a good Windows XP book for information on items like this.

Setting Up File and Folder Security

File and folder security allows you to establish even greater control over what files are protected. If you have particularly sensitive files, you will want a firewall, anti-virus program, sign-on accounts and passwords, and file-level security.

Folder- and file-level security is only available on NTFS-partitioned drives. Many Tablet PCs have FAT32 partitions, while others will have NTFS. NTFS is a more secure and higher-performing partitioning method than FAT32. You can convert from FAT32 to NTFS easily, but you cannot readily go back to FAT32.

To convert your C: drive to NTFS, you can do the following:

1. Make sure you want to convert. You cannot go back to FAT32 without significant effort.

2. Back up your system in case there is a problem.

3. Tap **Start**, then **Run**.

4. In the dialog box that opens, type `convert c: /fs:ntfs` and tap **OK**.

The process may take quite a bit of time, depending on the size of your hard drive and the amount of data you have.

To establish file- or folder-level security, drill down in My Computer or Windows Explorer to the folder or file on which you want to establish higher security. Then right-click the folder or file and choose **Sharing and Security**, as shown in Figure 11.5.

> **caution**
>
> For most people, setting up file- and folder-level security is not necessary. Use this only if you need to protect particular data from others, as it could make it more difficult for you to gain access to files at some point.

FIGURE 11.5

To enable folder-level security, right-click the folder you want to add security to and choose Sharing and Security.

After you do that, you will see the *Folder* Properties dialog box (where *Folder* is the name of the folder). Click on the **Security** tab, and you will see something similar to what is shown in Figure 11.6.

FIGURE 11.6

Reduce the groups and users to the fewest who need access to your files. This is only available on NTFS-partitioned drives.

Notice that only a few of my users and groups can access this folder. I could further reduce the number of potential users by eliminating all but my account. This could be problematic, though, if my account was re-created or destroyed for some reason.

The main thing to keep in mind here is that if you want your files secure, you need to limit access to only those who need access, and no more. Likely, this will be just you. You (or your network administrator, if you are using your firm's Tablet PC) will need to determine whether you want the administrator to access your folder(s). You probably will, but if you do, make sure that the administrator password is secure.

File and folder security can be implemented on everything you have on your machine, but I would recommend you take other precautions before going to this extreme. I basically allow myself and the administrator to have rights to my system, and I have control over both accounts. Of course, I'm also in charge of IT in my company.

If you get a message that you cannot remove a user or group because "this object is inheriting permissions from its parent," you can get around this by clicking on the **Advanced** button on *Folder* Properties dialog box's Security tab, and then deselecting the first check box.

You may want to refer to a more in-depth Windows XP book for more information on file and folder security. Alternatively, you might want to speak with someone in the IT field who can help you with your specific data-protection needs.

Disable Folder Sharing

When your computer comes to you, it will probably have drive and folder sharing enabled. If it does, all it takes is one person knowing that he or she can access your hard drive by using the \\computername\c$ access method to thwart your other security measures.

The easiest way to remove folder sharing is to do the following:

1. Open My Computer.
2. Right-click the **C: drive** and choose **Sharing and Security**.
3. Click on the **Do not share this folder** option button to select it.

Before you performed step 3, did you notice that your C: drive was shared as C$? This is an administrative share that most people don't know about, but that is easily compromised.

You can certainly choose to share any folder that you want on your machine, but I'd recommend making it a folder that you're sharing, and not the entire drive.

caution

If you don't remove the administrative share on your hard drive, you will automatically allow anyone with a proper username and password to access your entire hard drive. Protect yourself and remove this share.

Data Management

Keeping your system "clean" is also a good practice. To do so, you should regularly remove unneeded files and defragment your hard drive; this will keep space available for new files and applications, and will help your system to run at optimal speed.

Using Disk Cleanup

Disk Cleanup is a tool that can help you remove unwanted and unused files from your Tablet PC. This helps you maintain free disk space, which provides room for other applications and data files.

To start the Disk Cleanup tool, tap **Start**, then **All Programs**, **Accessories**, choose **System Tools**, then **Disk Cleanup**. Windows checks the contents of your hard drive, noting its progress in the dialog box shown in Figure 11.7.

FIGURE 11.7

The Disk Cleanup tool helps you keep your hard drive clean.

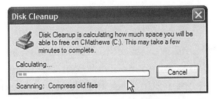

After Windows scans your hard drive, it suggests files that you can delete to free disk space, as shown in Figure 11.8. This is when you select categories of files to remove. The dialog box will tell you how much disk space can be freed in each area. Few of the categories contain files you need to hold on to; if you want, you can choose to view the files before you delete them, but in most cases, I'd just send them to oblivion.

FIGURE 11.8

The Disk Cleanup dialog box lets you choose categories of files to delete in order to free space.

In addition to the categories on the Disk Cleanup dialog box's Disk Cleanup tab, there is also a More Options tab, which gives you—you guessed it—more options. Figure 11.9 shows the More Options tab and the associated choices.

FIGURE 11.9

The More Options tab lets you choose even more ways to increase free disk space.

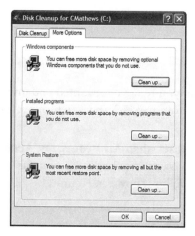

To remove items like Fax Services and Windows Messenger from your system, click the **Clean up** button in the Windows components area of the More Options tab. The dialog box shown in Figure 11.10 opens; Uncheck the check box next to the item(s) you want to remove (you can reinstall them at any time if you change your mind) and then tap **Next**.

FIGURE 11.10

Removing Windows components can help free disk space and, because those components will no longer load when your Tablet PC starts, could improve your system performance.

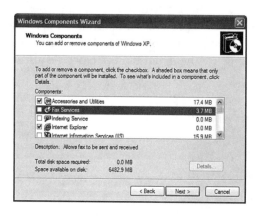

Clicking the Clean up button in the More Options tab's Installed programs section takes you to the Add/Remove Programs dialog box, which you can also access from the Control Panel. In the Add/Remove Programs dialog box, you can select applications to remove from your system, which will free disk space and possibly reduce boot-up time.

Clicking the Clean up button in the More Options tab's System Restore section removes all but the most recent restore point. A restore point is usually created just before you install applications and drivers so that you can rollback to the point before the installation if there is a problem. Unless you're running low on disk space, you may not want to choose this option, because you may need to roll back your system to a prior point in time (such as before loading a program that causes problems).

Using Disk Defragmenter

Disk Defragmenter should be your friend. If you haven't met, get to know it. It can significantly improve system performance by optimizing the disk space usage on your system. After a while, files stored on your hard drive get fragmented. That is, a single file may be stored in several pieces (fragments) across the hard drive, requiring more time to read the file. Disk defragmenter puts all the pieces that make up a file in one place so that the hard drive doesn't have to move as much to retrieve a file.

To start Disk Defragmenter, right-tap **My Computer** and choose **Manage**, then tap **Disk Defragmenter**. You can also tap **Start**, then **All Programs, Accessories**, choose **System Tools**, then **Disk Defragmenter**. When you do, you will see a window that looks like the one shown in Figure 11.11. (The window shown here is displayed on Tablet PCs with the DisKeeper plug-in, which adds some additional options; if you don't have this plug-in, your window will differ slightly.)

To begin the defragment process, click the **Defragment** button; blocks of color will begin to appear on the display in the right side of the window. Red is bad (fragmented files), and all other colors are fine. The more red you have, the longer it will take to defragment your drive. Defragmenting your hard drive often will prevent the process from taking forever each time you run it.

Run Disk Defragmenter once a week, and you'll be kept in good shape. This will improve the speed at which the computer can access information from the hard drive because it only has to go to a single spot on the hard drive for a single file, instead of pulling fragments of a file from multiple places on the hard drive.

FIGURE 11.11

Disk Defrag-
menter helps
you keep your
hard drive(s)
optimized. This
screenshot is
from DisKeeper,
which has
even more func-
tionality.

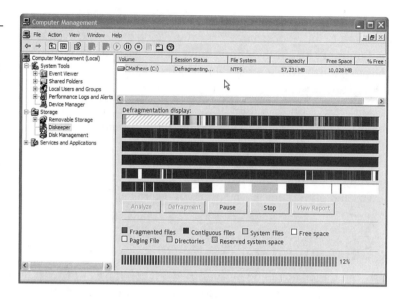

If you want to upgrade to scheduled defragmentation, you can buy DisKeeper by Executive
Software. It adds a few more tools, and actually
shows the multiple bars like you see in Figure
11.11. There are several other features that
make DisKeeper a good option to buy, such as
automatic scheduling and the ability to defragment the boot sector.

Protecting Yourself with Backups

Backups are critical for ANY machine that holds one-of-a-kind data, but are especially so for a Tablet PC because it is more mobile and thus more prone to theft or
damage. Your failure to back up your files could mean the loss of days or even years
of work in the time it takes your hard drive to crash.

There are several ways to back up your system, a few of which I will show you here.
If your Tablet PC was distributed to you by your firm, please check with your IT
department or network administrator about their recommendations for backing up
your data.

tip

DisKeeper is a great tool to
have on your Tablet PC. It
provides a deeper level of
defragmentation and hard-
drive optimization. It also
allows you to set up scheduled defragmentation.

There are numerous options for backup software and hardware. Windows XP includes a backup application called Backup. You can start it by going to **Start**, **All Programs**, **Accessories**, and then **System Tools**. It starts in wizard mode the first time you run it, which will guide you through backing up your files.

Backing Up to a Network Share

If your Tablet PC contains information related to your firm, you will probably want to back it up on your network. If your IT department has not told you where your data files should reside, please check with it first.

If you have a network file server, you can often back up your files to a network share. A network share could be a drive letter on the network, or it could just be an address that you go to to get files (such as \\Server\Folder). If your network administrator allows data backups to the network share, then you should establish procedures for doing so.

Before backing up to the network share, you will need to ensure that there is enough disk space on the server to comfortably hold your files. If not, your backup could prevent others from working. Always work with your IT group if there's any question about what you should be doing.

There are a few ways to back up your files to the network share. The first and easiest is to simply copy the files you want to back up from your computer to the server. Do this once a week, over-writing earlier versions of the files on the server. This can be time-consuming on the first backup.

The second way is to create a batch file that backs up just those files that have changed since the last backup. Use a script such as the following to copy everything in the C:\Files folder to the N:\Backup folder:

```
xcopy c:\files n:\backup /m /e /f /h /r /y
```

caution

Anyone who doesn't backup his or her system and who keeps unique data on it is asking for trouble. Everyone should regularly back up data that does not exist elsewhere. A good backup plan is important for your mental health!

caution

If your firm owns your Tablet PC, please check with your IT staff before dropping several giga-bytes of data onto the network server. They will appreciate it, and so will the other people who you may have prevented from work-ing by filling up the server.

The switches in this script instruct Windows to copy only those files that have changed since the last backup, in all subfolders, without asking you for approval. To actually create the script, open a new file with Notepad, insert the script, and then save the file with a .bat extension; you can run it whenever you want to back up your files. If you have multiple folders to back up, include multiple lines similar to the one above in your batch file.

The third method is to get a utility like Second Copy 2000, which is a simple but powerful tool to help keep your files backed up and synchronized with another file storage location. Follow the directions that come with your program to ensure that your computer is backed up.

Backing Up to an External Hard Drive

The same three methods you learned about for backing up to a network share can also be used to back up to an external hard drive. If you have an external hard drive, such as a USB hard drive or a FireWire drive, you can copy your files directly, with a batch file, or with a utility like Second Copy 2000. If you use a batch file, make sure the destination drive and folder are correctly identified in the script.

My preferred method for backup is my external USB 2.0 hard drive. You can get an external drive pretty cheaply. Because desktop hard-drive sizes are significantly greater than those in laptops and Tablet PCs (200 GB max versus 80 GB), external hard drives give you the ability to store your Tablet PC's backup data and much more. The external drives usually use a desktop drive (3.5-inch) as the storage medium, making them much less expensive than smaller drives based on portable, 2.5-inch drive technology.

Backing Up to a Tape Drive or CD-ROM Burner

Using tape drives can get hairy. I have had more problems with tape drives than any other type of hardware. They do, however, have several advantages over other storage media, such as cost per megabyte for backup, and their ability to be easily used in other computers.

On the other hand, although CD-ROM burners and CD-RW drives are inexpensive, they are limited to 700 MB of data, which could be much less than you need. I am a collector of information (data hog), and I have two external 200 GB drives filled with data, audio files, video, and backups. There is no way I'm going to use CDs to back up my data. Until some of the compatibility issues are resolved with DVD burners, DVD burning may not be the best option, even though they can back up much more than CDs.

General Backup Recommendations

To tell you how to back up your computer with your backup device and software is beyond the scope of this book, but I will make a few suggestions.

1. Make a full backup of your unique files at least once a month. I suggest once a week.

2. Back up files that change on a more regular basis, such as every day.

3. Store backup media somewhere other than where your Tablet PC is usually located. This ensures that if something happens to the building in which your Tablet PC lives, you will still be able to recover it if needed (even though you may need to buy a new Tablet PC).

Using the System Restore Feature of Windows XP

System Restore protects your computer from changes that you make or that other people or programs make to your system. If you start having lots of problems after installing a particular application or driver, you can use System Restore to roll back your system to the state it was in before you installed the suspect item.

This restore process restores the operating system settings only; that is, it does not affect any data files. Even so, if you religiously make backups before implementing any system changes, you can use the backup to restore your files, and use System Restore to restore your system in the event of a problem.

To access System Restore, tap **Start**, then **All Programs**, **Accessories**, choose **System Tools**, then **System Restore**. You will then see the window shown in Figure 11.12.

From here, you can tap the **System Restore Settings** link on the left side of the window if you want to change the amount of disk space that System Restore uses. Clicking this will also enable you to turn off System Restore.

caution

System Restore rolls back your system to a prior state, so you should make sure that you want to do this before continuing. Any system changes that you've made since the restore point (such as installing applications or drivers and changing operating system settings) will be lost if you continue. Restore points are usually created automatically when you install applications and drivers.

FIGURE 11.12

The System
Restore window
lets you recover
from installing a
problematic
product.

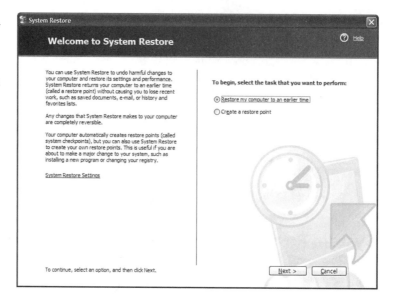

If you don't wish to make changes to System Restore's settings, you have two basic
options:

- If you are planning to install a potentially contentious program or driver, tap
  the **Create a restore point** radio button. That way, if there's a problem
  with the installation, you can restore your system to its state at the time the
  restore point was created. After you tap Create a restore point and then tap
  Next, you must type a name for the restore point, then tap **Next** again. The
  restore point will be created, and then you will tap **Close** to finish.

- If you've installed a program or made some other change to your system, but
  discover that the change has negatively affected your system, tap the
  Restore my computer to an earlier time radio button.

After you've made your selection, tap **Next**. If you have chosen to restore your computer to an earlier time, you'll see a calendar of dates with restore points, as shown
in Figure 11.13. (Bold dates are the ones with restore points.) Choose the date from
which you want to restore, and then click **Next**.

After you've chosen the restore point you want to use, you'll see a window similar to
the one shown in Figure 11.14. If you really want to restore to this point in time, go
ahead and click **Next**; Windows will shut down and then restart after the changes
have been rolled back.

FIGURE 11.13

Choose the date
of the restore
point from
which you want
to restore.

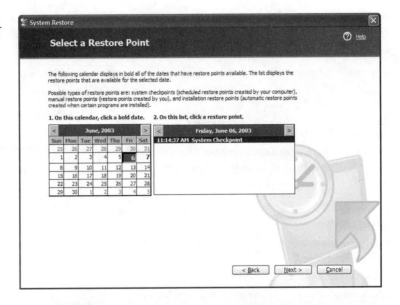

FIGURE 11.14

Warnings try to
keep you from
making a mis-
take.

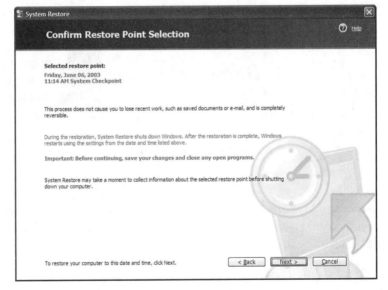

Data Synchronization

Synchronizing your data is similar to backing up your data, but instead of just putting what you have on your Tablet PC onto another storage device, synchronization
involves keeping your Tablet PC in synch with files in another location. So if files

change on a network share, for example, you will have the most recent files on your Tablet PC when you synchronize, and the files you've changed on your Tablet PC will also be changed on the network share.

This is useful when you are using multiple computers, or when you are sharing files with others and need to have the most recent versions on hand.

Synchronizing with a Network Share

Data synchronization can be handled with a third-party program, such as Second Copy 2000, and it can also be controlled by Briefcase and offline file management. Windows XP Backup is another option, but it has fewer features.

Briefcase

Briefcase is included with Windows XP Tablet PC Edition and allows you to configure file synchronization with a server or other computer. Briefcase allows you to create a storage folder (briefcase) for storing files that you want to keep synchronized. You create the briefcase and then drag your source files onto the briefcase. Although many people think this is a great way to manage files, it is best for only a few files and not several major folders full of files.

After you have created the briefcase, you can work with the files in it. If you change files, you will be able to synchronize with the source files later on.

> **tip**
>
> Briefcase is not as helpful for large amounts of files or multiple folders. Use another means of synchronization if you find yourself with either of these scenarios.

Example

You create a briefcase called Files where you store all your important documents. The briefcase is stored on your Tablet PC's C: drive, and the source files reside on your server. The files that you add to your briefcase from the server are now the same as those on the server. You pack up your Tablet PC, go home, and then do some work with a few of the files after the kids go to bed.

When you return to the office the next day, you again synchronize your Files briefcase, and the files that you changed on your Tablet PC are then updated on the server.

To create a briefcase, just go to the folder where you want it to reside, right-tap in the folder, and choose **New**, then **Briefcase**. Name your briefcase, and then double-tap it to open it; when you do, You'll see the dialog box shown in Figure 11.15.

FIGURE 11.15

Briefcase lets you keep your files synchronized between two locations.

After you've read the information in the dialog box, tap **Finish**. You can then add files to the briefcase. When the briefcase is open, you'll see a window similar to the one shown in Figure 11.16. When you add files to the briefcase, they will show up here just like in a folder. Notice the Update all items link to the left of the file area in Figure 11.16; you can click it to synchronize your files at any point.

FIGURE 11.16

Click the Update all items link to synchronize files.

If any files have changed, you will see a dialog box like the one in Figure 11.17. This dialog box asks you what you want to do with the changed files. If you want all the changed files to be updated, choose **Update**. You may be given additional options if both files have changed. Be sure to look at Help on Briefcase if you want more information about how to use it.

FIGURE 11.17

If files have
changed, you
will see this dia-
log box, which
asks you what
to do with
changed files.

Offline File Management

Offline file management allows you to work with files on another computer whether
you have a connection to it or not. If you lose your connection, or go mobile with
your Tablet PC, you will still have access to the files you set up for offline access.

To make sure the Offline Files feature is enabled, do the following:

1. Open My Computer or Windows Explorer.
2. Choose **Tools**, then **Folder Options**.
3. Tap the **Offline Files** tab.
4. Make sure the **Enable Offline Files** check box is checked.

To specify which files and folders you want to have access to offline, just right-click
the folder or file, and choose **Make Available Offline**. The first time you use this
feature, you'll need to step through a series of dialog boxes; you can accept the
defaults or change whatever items you want. After you have completed the setup
process, you'll see the Synchronizing dialog box, shown in Figure 11.18.

FIGURE 11.18

The Synchroniz-
ing dialog box
provides status
information
about the offline
files being
copied from the
source folder.

If you disconnect from the file source (file server or other computer), you will see a message similar to the one shown in Figure 11.19.

This just means that you are working on files that used to be online, but now reside on your Tablet PC. When you reconnect to the file source, the Offline Files tool will automatically begin synchronizing changed files.

Synchronizing Using a Third-Party Application

You will need to use a third-party utility primarily when you don't have a Windows-based network server or are synchronizing with files on another computer or external storage device.

If you choose multiple source folders for offline files, all the files will appear in the same folder on your computer. This can be confusing, and is one reason I prefer not to use this feature.

I prefer Second Copy 2000 for synchronizing and backing up files, although there are numerous utilities that may work for you. With Second Copy 2000, you have the option to copy files, create exact copies of folders (including file deletions), and synchronize files, which ensures that the most recent files in either location are synchronized so that both file-storage locations have the most recent versions of files. Configure your utility according to the instructions, and be sure to specify the way you want files handled—copy or synchronize. Figure 11.20 shows the options available in Second Copy 2000 for file copying.

FIGURE 11.19

When you disconnect from the file source or network, you will see a message similar to this.

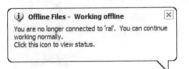

ⓘ Offline Files – Working offline   ☒

You are no longer connected to 'ral'. You can continue working normally.
Click this icon to view status.

FIGURE 11.20

Second Copy 2000 offers several ways to copy files—on a schedule or not.

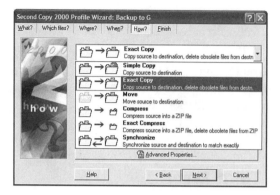

Accessing Data While Offline

When you're traveling, it's always great to be able to have access to your important information. More than likely, you have multiple places that you store data. Email, local hard drive, network share, external hard drive, CDs, and more are available to make file storage virtually limitless. Of course, all these options also make keeping track of files difficult.

When you're planning to be away from the office, you'll probably want to take your data with you. This section will help you work offline almost as effectively as online.

Files

Keeping your files synchronized with other data sources has already been covered. To find out how to use the Offline Files feature or third-party programs for synchronization, look at the preceding section, "Data Synchronization."

Email

More and more, people are storing important information in email. When you do that, you just need to make sure you have access to email when you need it. By enabling offline email, you'll be able to have access to email even when you're not connected to the network or Internet. In this section, I'll detail how to set up offline email in Microsoft Outlook because it is the most-used program in the corporate world. If you use a

The following instructions are for Outlook 2003 only. If you use another email application, you will need to find out how to make it work with offline data.

different email application, check with the program's documentation or with your IT staff to find out how to enable this feature.

In Outlook (and I'm not talking about Outlook Express), you can set up email to be stored offline automatically. It will take up space on your local hard drive to do this, but it is worth it.

To enable offline email in Outlook 2003, do the following:

1. In Outlook 2003, click **Tools**, then **E-Mail Accounts**.

2. In the dialog box that appears, choose **View or change existing e-mail accounts** and click **Next**.

3. Choose the account that you want to modify, and click the **Change** button.

4. In the dialog box that appears, click the **More Settings** button.

5. Click the **Advanced** tab.

6. Make sure that the **Use local copy of Mailbox** check box is checked.

7. If you want to confirm the location of your data file, click the **Offline Folder File Settings** button. You should see a file path with an .ost extension. If this is correct, you are set up for offline email.

Now that you have offline email enabled, you can view your email, calendar, contacts, tasks, and more—even when not connected to the network.

Web Sites

Sometimes when you travel, it's beneficial to have access to Web site information. Often, data changes frequently enough that you don't want to just make a local copy that will be out of date in a few days.

To have access to Web sites offline, the sites need to be in your Favorites list. Once the site is a favorite, you can right-click the **Favorites** link to the site and choose **Make available offline**. The Offline Favorite wizard starts. Click **Next** on the first screen that appears; you'll see the screen shown in Figure 11.21. There, choose whether you want pages that are linked to the favorite site to be downloaded as well, and the depth of links that you want to download, and click **Next**.

note

Not all Web sites are good for viewing offline. Sites that use a database or dynamic data to present information (such as a Web-based catalog site) may not provide good offline data. Always try a site out before you need it to make sure you get what you expect from it.

FIGURE 11.21

Choose whether you want additional linked pages to be downloaded, and to what depth.

Next, you'll be asked whether you want the synchronization to occur manually or automatically on a regular schedule. Then you'll be asked whether the site requires a password. When you finish with that dialog box, the site will be downloaded, and the synchronization will follow the schedule you set, if any.

To remove a favorite site from offline synchronization, just right-click the **Favorite** link and choose **Make Available Offline** to remove the check mark. You will then be asked if you're sure you no longer want the data available offline. Once you click **Yes**, the offline site content will be deleted and you will no longer have offline access to that site.

THE ABSOLUTE MINIMUM

Here are the key points to take away from this chapter:

- Protect your data.
- Buy a firewall and set it up to protect your machine(s).
- Establish login requirements for returning from standby, hibernate, and screensaver.
- Set up folder- and file-level security only if you are really serious about data protection and want the highest level of operating-system protection.
- Use Disk Cleanup and Disk Defragmenter (or DisKeeper) to keep your hard drive clean and running at optimum speed.
- Make good backups on a regular basis and store them offsite regularly.
- Establish file synchronization routines if you regularly share data with others.
- Set up offline email and Web site synchronization if you want access to these resources when not connected to the network or Internet.

PART V

Using Other Included and Free Applications

12

STICKY NOTES

Almost everyone is used to the little yellow squares of paper that are stuck all over people's desks to remind them of impending doom. Now you have the same ability with your Tablet PC. Sticky Notes is a great tool to use for all those small notes you need to keep on various subjects, but that defy organization or long-term need.

Sticky Notes is easy to use, and with it, you can even add voice annotations to a note. You can use sticky notes by themselves to leave notes on your desktop, and you can also use sticky notes inside some other applications.

Why Use Sticky Notes?

Sticky notes are often used to keep notes handy, when notes are not part of a longer document, and when they are of short-term use. You will usually not use your Tablet PC's Sticky Notes feature to store information that you want to have access to long term. Using sticky notes for items such as contact information, addresses, telephone numbers, and other data that you may want to have access to later is not a good idea.

Although it's nice to be able to take some quick notes and have ready access to them, Sticky Notes does not allow you the flexibility of multiple notes displayed at one time on the desktop, like some other "sticky note" applications (just search for "sticky" at www.download.com). You can, however, use the Sticky Notes feature to place a stack of sticky notes on your desktop.

> **tip**
>
> Sticky Notes is fine for quick notes that you will move to other applications or discard later, but you may want to limit your use of them because they are not easily managed.

In addition, you can copy notes to other applications, like Word, as well as import notes from other locations. If saving notes like this seems to you to be a great way to lose your mind, or if you want to store something for longer than a week or so, use a planner like TabletPlanner or Outlook so that you can easily find what you're looking for.

Did I discourage you from using Sticky Notes? No? Then read on.

Sticky Notes Basics

Creating sticky notes is easy. This section shows you how to create written and audio sticky notes. You can take a single note, or you can create a stack of notes. You cannot have several unattached notes at once with Sticky Notes. The stack metaphor lets you move among several notes to find the one you want.

Creating a Sticky Note

To create a sticky note, tap on **Start**, **All Programs**, and then **Sticky Notes**. A sticky note will appear; Figure 12.1 shows a sticky note that has already been written on.

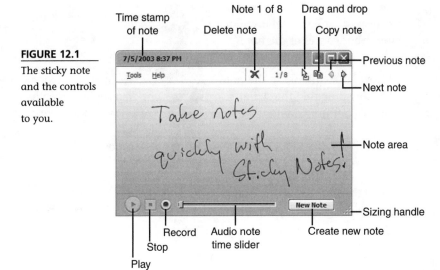

FIGURE 12.1

The sticky note and the controls available to you.

Time stamp of note

Note 1 of 8

Delete note

Drag and drop

Copy note

Previous note

Next note

Note area

Sizing handle

Record

Audio note time slider

Create new note

Stop

Play

As the callouts show, you can do several things with your note. You can click the **Drag and Drop** button at the top right of your note to drag-and-drop the note into another application, such as Word. The **Copy Note** button allows you to copy the contents of the note into another application. The **Next** and **Previous Note** buttons let you navigate among a stack of notes. Finally, the **Delete** button enables you to delete the note, and you can click the **New Note** button to create a new note. (Most of these options are available only after you have made your first mark on the sticky note.)

Once the sticky note appears, you can write your note, as shown in Figure 12.2.

FIGURE 12.2

Writing on the sticky note in Sticky Notes is as easy as writing on the real thing.

One nice feature of sticky notes is that you can resize them. If you have a larger or smaller note, just drag the bottom-right corner of the note window to resize it, as shown in Figure 12.3.

Figure 12.4 shows how I added more to the note shown in Figure 12.2. By dragging the sizing handle, you can make your note area larger.

tip

Make more room for notes by dragging the sizing handle at the bottom right of the Sticky Notes window to create more writing area.

FIGURE 12.3

Resize the note by dragging the bottom-right corner of the note.

FIGURE 12.4

Once you've made the note bigger, you can add to it.

Recording a Voice Note

Ever feel like it's easier just to say something than to have to type it or write it? Well, now you can dictate quick notes. Sticky Notes allows you to add voice notes as well as handwritten notes. Up to 30 seconds of audio can be added to each note.

Recording a voice note is as easy as clicking a button and speaking into the microphone. Just click the red circular **Record** button next to the slider at the bottom of the note, and your Tablet PC will start recording from your microphone. You have up to 30 seconds of audio per note; as you record, the slider bar will inch across to the right, telling you how much time you have left (see Figure 12.5).

To stop recording, just tap the square **Stop** button. To play back the recording, tap the larger circle with the triangle, which is the **Play** button, just like on a VCR or CD player. If you don't like the note you recorded, simply tap the **Delete** button to delete it.

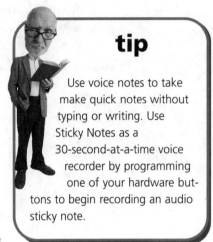

tip

Use voice notes to take make quick notes without typing or writing. Use Sticky Notes as a 30-second-at-a-time voice recorder by programming one of your hardware buttons to begin recording an audio sticky note.

FIGURE 12.5

As you record an audio note, the slider inches to the right, showing how much of your 30 seconds has been used up.

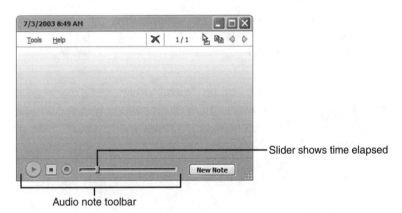

Slider shows time elapsed

Audio note toolbar

Advanced Stickies

In addition to creating basic sticky notes, you can also organize your notes and search on them for content. You can import and export notes as well, allowing you to share notes with other people and machines.

Organizing Sticky Notes

Sticky notes are organized into a stack. A stack can be managed as a group, but cannot be split up. Stacks can be combined with other stacks, but stacks are only managed as a single group of notes. For that reason, you can't have multiple stacks open at the same time. This is a sore spot for those who want a screen filled with yellow notes.

Organizing sticky notes is really a misstatement. You really have no choice but to keep your notes in a stack, and only one stack may be open.

To see how many notes you have at any given time, look at the numbers to the right of the Delete button on the Sticky Notes window's toolbar. The first number represents the number of the currently displayed note, while the second number indicates the total number of notes in the stack.

You can easily move between notes by tapping the right and left arrows for forward/back, respectively. Sticky notes will always be arranged from oldest to newest in the stack.

note

Sticky Notes keeps notes in a stack. You cannot separate notes from the stack, so get used to a single window for all your notes.

Exporting Sticky Notes

You can export your stack of sticky notes to a file for backup or sharing purposes. When you export, the entire stack is exported, not just the current note.

To export a stack of notes, tap on **Tools**, and then **Export**. Enter the name of the sticky notes file and the location where you to store it and tap **Save**. When you export, your notes still remain in the stack; to remove them, you will need to delete them one at a time.

tip

You can export sticky notes to create a backup of your notes stack. It's better, however to use another application for long-term storage of notes.

Importing Sticky Notes

After you or another Sticky Notes user has exported a sticky notes stack, you can import the stack. When you import, you have the option to merge with the existing stack, or to replace it.

If you save a stack for backup purposes, and then import the stack using the merge option, you will duplicate all the existing notes. If you import using the replace option, you can move stacks of sticky notes between active and archive states. Best bet, as stated earlier, is to use Sticky Notes for less important, more time-sensitive notes.

When you import a stack of notes, the combined stack (existing and newly imported) will be rearranged so that the oldest note is first, and the newest is last in the stack.

Copying Sticky Notes to Other Applications

Sticky notes can be copied to other applications by two methods: drag-and-drop, and copy/paste. To use drag-and-drop, select the note you want to copy, tap the drag-and-drop icon, and then drag the note to the selected application. You cannot drag-and-drop voice notes. You can, however, copy and paste them by tapping the **Copy** button, and then pasting into the destination application.

tip

Copying sticky notes to other applications can be done through drag-and-drop and copy/paste. Each application is different in how it handles notes, so try both methods to determine which works best for your application.

It's often easier to drag-and-drop notes when Sticky Notes is on top, or when the other application is not maximized. You can temporarily set the Always on Top setting so that Sticky Notes is on top when you want to drag-and-drop. To do this, tap **Tools**, **Options**, and then **Always on Top**. You can do this again to make Sticky Notes go behind other applications again.

Figure 12.6 shows a sticky note that contains directions, which I want to drag into an appointment.

FIGURE 12.6

Here is the diagram I want to include in an appointment.

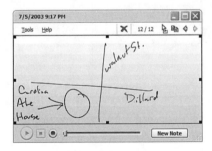

Notice in Figure 12.7 that I have dragged the note into my appointment, and that the note shows up as an attachment, which you can double-click to open. The same things would happen if I tried to copy and paste the note to an appointment.

FIGURE 12.7

Here is the
appointment
after I drop the
note into it. I
can double-click
the note to
open it.

There are some differences between drag-and-drop and copy/paste. Notice in Figure 12.8 the difference between the two notes inside Word 2003. The drag-and-drop operation created a note look-alike, whereas the copy/paste operation just copied the contents of the note—not the note's Ink.

FIGURE 12.8

Differences
between
drag-and-drop
and copy/paste
operations into
Word 2003.

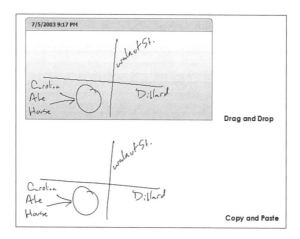

Now look at the note pasted into Word in Figure 12.9. This time, there is only an audio note, and no Ink. The only way to get audio notes copied into Word (and some other applications) is to make sure there is no Ink in the note. If there is Ink, the copy operation will copy the Ink only. Drag-and-drop will not copy audio into other applications.

FIGURE 12.9

FIGURE 12.9
This note is an
audio-only
copy/paste
into Word.
Drag-and-drop
will not copy the
audio into
Word.

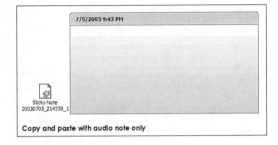

Applications operate differently with respect to how notes appear with the two copying methods. Test both methods when you want to copy a note to see which works best for your needs.

Enabling the Scratch-Out Gesture

To enable Sticky Notes to allow you the ability to scratch out parts of your note, you must enable the scratch-out gesture, which is just like the scratch-out gesture in Input Panel. To do so, tap **Tools**, **Options**, and then tap the **Enable Scratch-out Gesture** check box to check it. When this check box is checked, you can use the scratch-out gesture, as shown in Figure 12.10. You can also use the eraser on your pen, if you have one.

FIGURE 12.10
Use the scratch-out gesture to remove parts of a note you don't want.

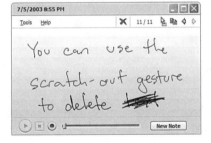

Make Stickies Open at Startup

Another way to improve your note-taking prowess is to have Sticky Notes start when your computer does. This will enable you to jot quick notes whenever you need to capture some information quickly.

To enable this setting, tap **Tools**, **Options**, and then tap the **Open at Startup** check box to

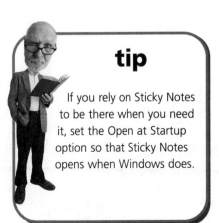

tip

If you rely on Sticky Notes to be there when you need it, set the Open at Startup option so that Sticky Notes opens when Windows does.

check it. As long as that check box contains a check mark, Sticky Notes will open when Windows does, and you will always have it available for you.

THE ABSOLUTE MINIMUM

Here are the key points to take away from this chapter:

- Sticky notes are useful for jotting down or recording quick notes for reference later, or for reminders.

- Use sticky notes only if the information is not valuable over a long period of time.

- Sticky notes are stuck in a stack of notes, which cannot be broken into individual notes.

- You can use both drag-and-drop and copy/paste operations to copy notes into other applications. The look of the resulting note in the application will depend on the method used and the application itself.

- Enable the Scratch-out Gesture setting to be able to use the scratch-out gesture to remove unwanted Ink.

- Enable the Open at Startup setting to always have Sticky Notes available.

13

PowerToys for Tablet PC

PowerToys are small applications that increase functionality and enjoyment of the Tablet PC. Some PowerToys are distinctly businesslike in their functionality; those are the applications I discuss in this chapter. Specifically, you will see a calculator and some display-management tools. (The Snipping tool is probably the most useful of the bunch, because it enables you to grab a portion of the screen and copy it into another application, such as an email program.) Other PowerToys are designed with fun in mind, and you'll read about some of them in the next chapter. That's not to say that you'll learn about every PowerToy in this book, however. There are a few that I've chosen not to cover because I found them to be problematic or of little use.

In any case, to download PowerToys, go to www.microsoft.com/windowsxp/tabletpc/downloads/powertoys.asp. Because the PowerToys are so easy to install (just follow the instructions provided by the installation wizards), I don't cover the details of installing each application. Accepting the defaults for each will be sufficient.

Calculator for Tablet PC

Calculator for the Tablet PC is a calculator that lets you use the pen for numeric input. Instead of using the keyboard, you use the pen to tap on buttons and *write* numbers. Other than the ability to accept pen input, there is nothing new with this calculator. Instead of using the Calculator for Tablet PC, you could easily just tap buttons on the calculator that comes with Windows XP.

Calculator Modes

The Calculator for Tablet PC comes with two modes: Standard and Scientific. The Standard mode looks like Figure 13.1.

FIGURE 13.1

This is the Standard mode of the Calculator for Tablet PC.

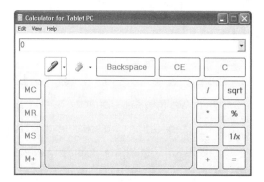

The other mode, Scientific, is shown in Figure 13.2.

FIGURE 13.2

This is the Scientific mode of the Calculator for Tablet PC.

After installing Calculator for Tablet PC, open the application by tapping **Start**, **All Programs**, **PowerToys for Tablet PC**, and then **Calculator for Tablet PC**. To use the Calculator, just write a number in the box in the center, and then tap one of the operator buttons, such as plus, minus, or times. When you tap the operator button, the number is recognized and the appropriate action (addition, subtraction, multiplication, or what have you) is performed. Keep writing numbers and tapping operator buttons until you are ready to view the final result, and then tap the equals button.

Figure 13.3 shows what it looks like when you write numbers in the Calculator for Tablet PC window's text area. In this case, I wrote the number in the top text box (here, 5.76), tapped the plus button, and then wrote the number that's currently in the text area; the calculator is waiting for me to tap another operator button or the equals button.

> **caution**
>
> Unless you like the novelty of writing numbers instead of tapping number buttons, this tool may not be that useful to you. In fact, because there's the distinct possibility of inaccurate recognition (and no view of the recognized numbers before entry), you may have inaccurate results and not know it.

FIGURE 13.3
To enter numbers into this calculator, write the number, and then tap an operator button.

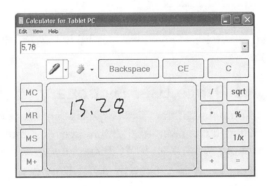

One drawback with this calculator is that, except for the first entry, you never see what it recognized from your handwriting. So if it misrecognizes a number, you'll never know if your answer is accurate. As a proof-of-concept for how handwriting recognition can be used, however, the PowerToy makes its point.

Dictionary Tool for Tablet PC

The Dictionary tool for Tablet PC enables you to manage your Tablet PC Dictionary for handwriting recognition. If you're having a problem getting your Tablet PC to recognize certain words that are not in most dictionaries, you can add the entries into your Tablet PC Dictionary by using the Dictionary tool for Tablet PC.

Adding and Removing Dictionary Entries

To add an entry in the Tablet PC Dictionary, type the word in the **Enter Dictionary entry here** text box at the top of the Dictionary Tool for Tablet PC dialog box, as shown in Figure 13.4, and then tap the **Add** button.

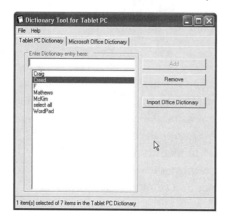

FIGURE 13.4

Use this tool to add or remove entries from your Tablet PC Dictionary.

To remove an entry, simply tap the entry that you want to remove, and tap the **Remove** button.

Importing Entries from the Office User Dictionary

If you have invested a fair amount of time building a custom dictionary in Word or another Office application, you can leverage that time spent by importing the contents of your Office Dictionary into the Tablet PC Dictionary.

Before you do, however, it's a good idea to tap the **Microsoft Office Dictionary** tab in the Dictionary Tool for Tablet PC dialog box to see a list of the words you've added to the Office Dictionary, as shown in Figure 13.5. If you want to add or delete entries in your Office Dictionary, tap the **Open Office Dictionary** button and edit the list as needed.

When you're satisfied with your Office Dictionary, import the contents of that dictionary into your Tablet PC Dictionary by tapping the **Tablet PC Dictionary** tab in the Dictionary Tool for Tablet PC dialog box, and then tapping the **Import Office Dictionary** button. Notice in Figure 13.6 that entries were added to the Tablet PC Dictionary from my Office Dictionary.

FIGURE 13.5

The Dictionary Tool for Tablet PC lets you manage your Office User Dictionary.

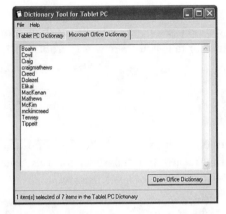

FIGURE 13.6

After I tapped the Import Office Dictionary button, entries from my Office Dictionary were imported.

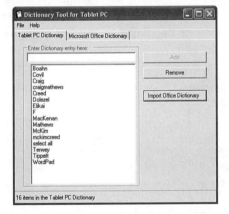

Importing Entries from a Text File

If you have another source that contains a list of words that you frequently use, you can put them into a text file and import the list that way. To do so

1. Tap **Start**, **All Programs**, **PowerToys for Tablet PC**, and then **Dictionary Tool for Tablet PC**.

2. Tap **File**, **Import text file**.

3. When asked, supply the name of the text file you want to import. (Make sure the file you select is a plain text file; otherwise, you may receive an error.)

caution

When you tap the Import Office Dictionary button, you are not asked to confirm the import. Be sure that you want to import your custom dictionary before tapping the button.

4. Tap **Open** to begin the import process.

5. The Import Complete dialog box opens and tells you how many entries were added to your dictionary (or tells you there was a problem). Tap **OK** after reading the dialog box.

Hold Tool for Tablet PC

The Hold tool for Tablet PC enables you to turn off the press-and-hold feature of the pen for controls such as scroll bars, push buttons, slider controls, and more. This can make your tablet usage a bit easier and a lot less frustrating.

To enable the tool, just run it. (If you want it to start when you start your Tablet PC, you can put it in your Startup folder under the Start, Programs menu.) When the program is running, you'll see an icon in your System Tray that looks like a fat scroll bar. Click it and choose **About** to see the dialog box shown in Figure 13.7, which describes exactly what the tool does.

FIGURE 13.7

When you tap the Hold Tool icon in the System Tray and then tap About, you will see this dialog box.

To turn off the Hold tool, again tap the tool's **System Tray** icon, but this time choose the **Active** option to remove the check mark there, as shown in Figure 13.8.

FIGURE 13.8

Turn off the Hold tool by tapping its System Tray icon and then tapping the Active option to remove the check mark.

Snipping Tool for Tablet PC

The Snipping tool enables you to capture portions of a screen to include in other applications. Note that the Snipping tool does not capture the data itself, but rather creates a picture of the portion of the screen that was snipped. You could, for example, use this tool to capture a picture of part of a Web page, which you could then include in an email message.

To Start the Snipping Tool, tap **Start**, **All Programs**, **PowerToys for Tablet PC**, **Microsoft Snipping Tool for Tablet PC Preview Release**, and then **Microsoft Snipping Tool**. When you first start Snipping tool, you'll see a welcome screen like the one shown in Figure 13.9.

FIGURE 13.9

The Snipping tool welcome screen.

Snipping Contents from the Screen

After you have started the Snipping tool, you can tap on the **Snipping Tool** icon in the System Tray (shown in Figure 13.10) to activate the tool. When you tap the icon, it turns green, and the Snipping Tool toolbar appears. In the toolbar, the Lasso tool becomes active, enabling you to select the portion of the screen you want to "snip," as shown in Figure 13.11.

FIGURE 13.10

The Snipping Tool icon resides in the System Tray for quick access.

FIGURE 13.11

When you activate the Snipping tool, you will be in Lasso mode, which you can use to encircle the section of the screen you want to snip. You can then add ink.

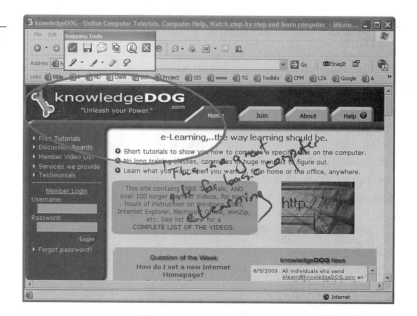

As soon as you snip the section of the screen you want, you can add ink anywhere on the screen. When you're finished, tap either the **Save As**, **Email**, or **Copy Image to Clipboard** button to save, send, or copy the contents of the snip and the ink you added. Any ink you add after selecting the portion to snip will be saved as well, regardless of where you added the ink. For example, Figure 13.12 shows what happened after I snipped a section of a Web page, made an ink comment (outside the snipped section), and then tapped the Email button on the Snipping Tool toolbar.

If you choose to copy to the Clipboard, you can then paste the image into any number of applications, including Word, Excel, and PowerPoint. If you tap the **Save As** button, be sure to save the image in a common graphic format, such as JPG, so that other applications can use the file easily.

Note that the Snipping tool does not support multi-monitor systems. If you attempt to use it on a multi-monitor system (like the system I typically use), you will see the dialog box shown in Figure 13.13.

FIGURE 13.12
The email created when I tapped the Email button after snipping and inking.

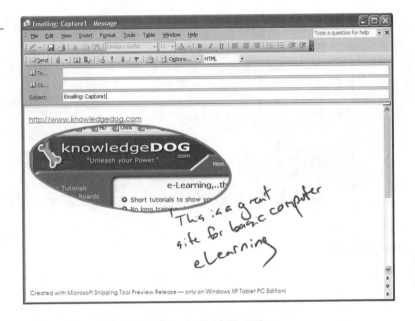

FIGURE 13.13
The Snipping tool does not support multi-monitor configurations.

Using Other Capture Modes

You can also use the Snipping tool to capture entire screens by right-tapping the **Snipping Tool** icon and choosing **Capture Screen**. Likewise, you can capture windows, dialog boxes, and the like within screens just as easily. The window-capture tool enables you to specify the window you want to snip—eliminating the extraneous detail around a dialog box or application window, for example.

The Snipping Tool Editor

The Snipping Tool Editor, shown in Figure 13.14, enables you to add ink to a snip and modify it using pen tools, such as pens, highlighters, and the eraser; these tools work just like all the other ink tools you're used to using. You don't need to use the Snipping Tool Editor. All the tools are available when you activate Snipping Tool. The Editor just enables you to edit the snip after you have saved it or copied it to the clipboard.

In the Snipping Tool Editor, you can set options, such as how the snip will be presented in an email , by opening the Tools menu and choosing **Options**. Doing so opens the Microsoft Snipping Tool Options dialog box shown in Figure 13.15.

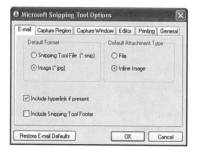

The Snipping tool is probably the most useful of all the PowerToys. It leverages the pen capability of the Tablet PC, and proves that the Tablet PC platform is superior to other computers—at least for some applications. Play around with it to learn how to make it work for you.

Thumbnail View Tool

The Thumbnail View tool lets you see small pictures of your Journal notes in the file system, just like you can see thumbnails of image files in Windows XP. The

Thumbnail View tool becomes a part of the Windows XP interface so that you can view Journal notes as thumbnails anywhere notes files exist.

After you install the Thumbnail View tool, whenever you navigate to a folder that includes Windows Journal files and choose to view the contents of the folder in Thumbnail mode, you will see Journal files in a way similar to what's shown in Figure 13.16. To view folder contents in Thumbnail View mode, tap **View**, and then **Thumbnails in My Computer or Windows Explorer**.

FIGURE 13.16

Windows Journal files can be viewed as thumbnails with the Thumbnail View tool.

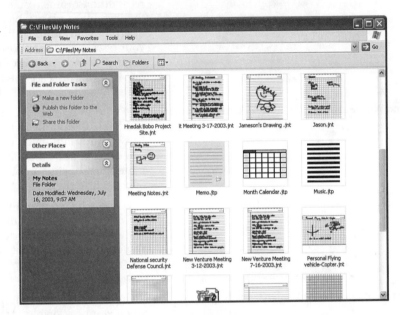

Complete List of PowerToys as of Late 2003

Table 13.1 contains a complete list of PowerToys and their descriptions as of August 2003. (Note that the descriptions are taken from Microsoft's PowerToys Web site.) It also indicates the chapter in this book (if any) that discusses each PowerToy.

TABLE 13.1 A Complete List of PowerToys

PowerToy (Chapter)	Description
Art tool for Tablet PC (not covered)	Use this coloring book and your imagination to create awesome pictures. A variety of templates are included, and you can also load your own pictures to color.

TABLE 13.1 (continued)

PowerToy (Chapter)	Description
Calculator for Tablet PC (Chapter 13)	Use the Calculator for Tablet PC in place of your handheld calculator. Simply use your pen to write the numbers for calculations.
Dictionary tool for Tablet PC (Chapter 13)	To improve your handwriting-recognition results, you can customize the dictionary your Tablet PC uses to interpret your handwriting. You can add your own words or import them from a text file or the Microsoft Office dictionary. You can also use the Dictionary tool to remove words from the dictionary.
Drawing Animator Toy for Tablet PC (not covered)	Free your imagination and enjoy creating colorful animated images. The Drawing Animator Toy for Tablet PC lets you draw your own doodles and animate them, including picture rotation, bounce, and more.
Extended Desktop for Tablet PC (not covered)	This PowerToy creates a window on your Tablet PC that shows a duplicate image of the desktop on the external monitor. You can then manipulate the objects on the extended desktop within this window.
Hoop Strategy Game for Tablet PC (Chapter 14)	If you enjoy unconventional games, you'll want to download the Hoop Strategy Game for Tablet PC. In this game, you build your own strategy to get the ball in the hoop. Draw a path and be creative—but keep in mind that gravity, velocity, and trajectory play a big part in your success.
Hold tool for Tablet PC (Chapter 13)	Annoyed by the press-and-hold functionality of your tablet pen? Download the Hold tool for Tablet PC and disable this functionality for certain controls. Scroll bars, push buttons, check boxes, option buttons, spinner controls, slider controls, and tab controls will respond immediately when the pen tip touches them.

PowerToy (Chapter)	Description
Maze Game for Tablet PC (Chapter 14)	Try a classic maze game—Tablet PC style. Try to escape this maze as fast as you can by using your pen to draw a line from start to finish.
New York Times Crossword Puzzle for the Tablet PC on MSNBC.com (Chapter 14)	A must for fans of crossword puzzles and the Tablet PC, this challenging game lets you use the tablet pen instead of a keyboard to solve puzzles. Get the latest crossword puzzle from MSNBC.com and take it with you on the go. Save puzzles in progress, and then continue them at your leisure. This PowerToy features two levels of difficulty; get clues and reaffirmation at the regular level, or play the old-fashioned way.
Pool for Tablet PC (Chapter 14)	Download the pool game that is optimized for Tablet PCs. Using your tablet pen, compete against the computer or another person. You can even play another Tablet PC user in real-time across a wired or wireless network.
Puzzle Game (Chapter 14)	Like jigsaw puzzles? Puzzle Game lets you drag and click pieces together using the tablet pen. You can choose from the default pictures, or use your own pictures to create a customized puzzle. Different levels of difficulty make this game as challenging as you want it to be.
Snipping tool for Tablet PC (Chapter 13)	Snipping tool for Tablet PC enables you to easily "snip" anything onscreen and share it with other people. The whole screen becomes an inkable surface to which you can add comments, and which you can mark up however you like. You can then save the annotated image to use later, or send it to someone else in an email message.
Tablet PC Music Composition tool (not covered)	With this music-composing tool, you can create and play your own music files. Use your pen to write notes on the staff and then play your tune.

TABLE 13.1   (continued)

PowerToy (Chapter)	Description
Thumbnail view (Chapter 13)	View your Journal files in a new light. Use the Windows Explorer Thumbnail view to preview your Journal files. Navigate to your notes with quick visual recognition for JNT and JTP files.
Tic Tac Toe (Chapter 14)	How about a game of tic tac toe? Put a twist on this classic game as you play against the computer. Just use your tablet pen to write your selection instead of typing it.
Writing Recognition Game (Chapter 14)	Have fun practicing and improving your writing recognition. To score points, write the letters before they hit the ground. The higher your score goes, the faster the letters drop, making this game even more challenging and fun.

The Absolute Minimum

Here are the key points to take away from this chapter:

- Go to the PowerToys site to download various helper applications called PowerToys.

- The Dictionary tool helps you manage your Tablet PC Dictionary for better handwriting recognition. You can also use it to manage your Office Dictionary.

- To make pen usage easier with scrollbars, sliders, and other controls, use the Hold tool for Tablet PC. After running it, the delay usually seen when using these controls is eliminated, allowing for a more natural experience.

- The Snipping tool is useful for capturing portions or all of a screen for inclusion in another application, such as capturing part of a Web page for inclusion in an email message. You can add ink to the captured region as well.

- The Thumbnail tool is helpful for viewing smaller (thumbnail) versions of your Windows Journal files. Put the tool in your Startup folder so that it starts automatically when you start Windows.

- There are numerous other PowerToys available from the PowerToys site. You may want to look at some of the applications that I have not covered in this chapter or the next chapter.

14

INKBALL AND OTHER FREE GAMES FOR THE TABLET PC

The pen interface of the Tablet PC provides an entirely new way to interact with games. In this chapter, you will look at a few free games that leverage the pen interface. As with the PowerToys covered in the last chapter, these games can be downloaded from www.microsoft.com/windowsxp/tabletpc/downloads/powertoys.asp. After you download the applications, run the installation programs and accept the defaults.

The games covered in this chapter are made to use the pen interface. Other games come with your Tablet PC, such as 3D Pinball, but they are not covered here. Because many Tablet PCs are relatively powerful, they can play most of the games on the market as well. Only the games requiring high-end graphics processors and speedy CPUs will drag on your Tablet PC.

Hoop Strategy Game

Hoop Strategy Game is basically a way to play basketball with a pen. To play the game, you draw a path for the ball to follow to get to the basket. The path can be any shape you want, but some shapes are more effective than others.

You do not have to draw a path from where the ball starts at the top left of the screen, but can draw a path anywhere within the drawing box. Figure 14.1 shows what a sample path looks like. This path seems to work almost regardless of where the basket is.

FIGURE 14.1

To play Hoop Strategy Game, just draw a path for the basketball to follow into the basket. This path seems to work quite well for almost every shot.

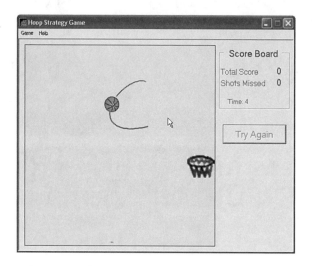

There are three levels of play in Hoop Strategy Game, including Beginner, Intermediate, and Expert. To change the level, tap the **Game** menu and then tap the desired level. The only thing that changes between the different levels is the size of the basket. In the Expert level, the basket is smallest.

To start a new game, press **F2** or tap **Game** and then **New Game**. To see a demo of how to play the game, tap **Help** and then **Show Demo**.

To play against other players, use the scoreboard to keep score. Challenge other Tablet PC users to a game, setting a time limit. This is not a multi-player game, so you will need to keep track of high scores.

InkBall

In InkBall, the objective of the game is to get the colored balls into the appropriate-colored holes (the orange ball goes in the orange hole, the blue ball goes in the blue hole, and so on). As you get farther into the game, you may also experience gray holes, which should be avoided, because they do not give you any points. In some levels, The balls can even change color, making it even more difficult. Figure 14.2 shows a beginner-level game with just two colors.

FIGURE 14.2

The object of InkBall is to get the balls into the same-colored holes.

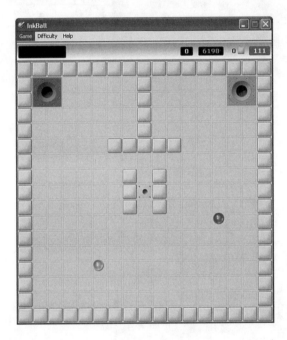

Figure 14.3 shows what happens when a ball goes into the wrong color hole.

To prevent the balls from going into the wrong holes, draw lines like the ones in Figure 14.4. You can make any number of strokes you want, as long or short as you desire. The balls will deflect off of the strokes you make according to the angle that the ball strikes the stroke. Because you can make as many strokes as you want without penalty, you can join a series of strokes together, thus protecting from multiple balls trying to get past your barrier.

FIGURE 14.3

This is what happens when you let a ball go into the wrong hole.

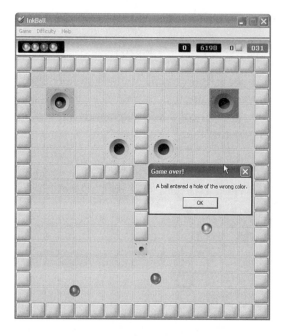

FIGURE 14.4

The lines I drew will prevent the balls from going into the wrong colored holes.

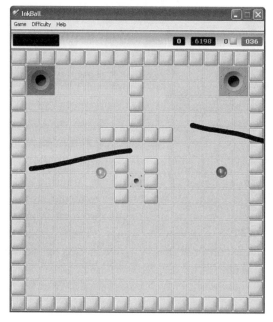

There are five levels of play: Beginner, Novice, Intermediate, Advanced, and Expert. As you increase the play level, the balls become more numerous and faster, and the boards become increasingly difficult.

As you advance in difficulty, you will also see different types of walls, as shown through the help screen in Figure 14.5.

FIGURE 14.5

There are numerous obstacles you will be presented with. It's your job to figure out how to get the balls into their matching holes.

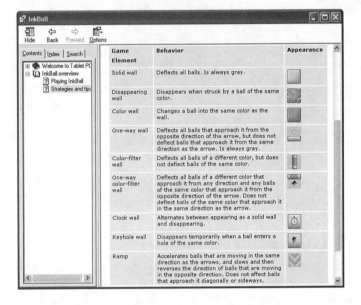

The play can get quite difficult when you advance levels. Figure 14.6 shows a particularly exciting Expert-level game board. Notice the multiple colors and varying obstacles.

InkBall can become addictive for some. It is a creative game for using the pen, and should provide lots of enjoyment for those who like Breakout-type games.

FIGURE 14.6

This is an Expert-level board with disappearing walls, color walls, clock walls, and keyhole walls of varying colors.

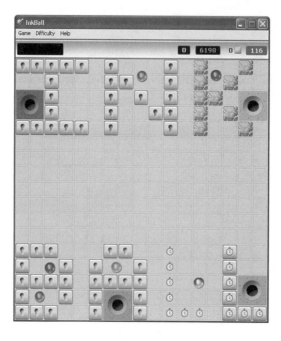

Maze Game for Tablet PC

Maze Game for Tablet PC is the same as a paper maze puzzle where you start in one location and work your way through the maze to the end. With the pen, you must draw your way through the maze without touching the walls of the maze.

Figure 14.7 shows what a simple maze looks like. There are four levels of mazes to choose from, depending on the challenge you desire.

FIGURE 14.7

Maze Game for Tablet PC is an ink training tool that challenges you to get from the green square to the red square without hitting any walls.

If you hit a wall on your way from the green square to the red square, you will need to tap the old line to turn it gray, and then begin drawing again from where you stopped. You cannot start from anywhere but where you hit the wall or lifted your pen.

There's no great strategy to the game, but if you like mazes, this is a good way to practice your inking and complete a few mazes in the process.

To change the maze's difficulty level, tap on **Game**, then the level at which you want to play: **Introductory**, **Beginner**, **Intermediate**, **Expert**, or **Master**. Figure 14.8 shows a Master-level maze.

FIGURE 14.8

This is what a Master-level maze looks like.

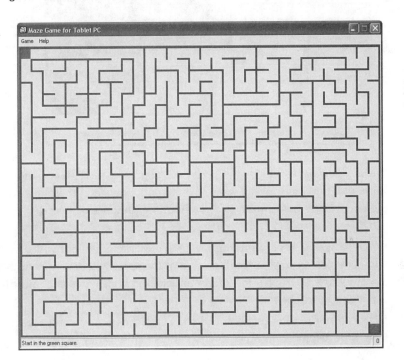

New York Times Crossword Puzzle for the Tablet PC

The New York Times crossword puzzle is widely regarded as the best crossword puzzle around, which is why MSNBC teamed up with the paper to create this little application. Simply download a new crossword puzzle from MSNBC every day to get your fix. Unfortunately, there is a little extraneous MSNBC content at the bottom (as shown in Figure 14.9), but you can just ignore it.

FIGURE 14.9

Here is a cross-
word puzzle I
downloaded.
Notice that you
use ink instead
of a keyboard to
enter the letters.

With Crossword Puzzle for the Tablet PC, you enter the letters using ink instead of a keyboard, making it much more like the paper version. There are even some cheating capabilities built in for those without the patience or knowledge to complete the puzzle on their own.

In the Standard level of puzzling, when you write a letter, it will show up green if you get it correct (and a small version of the letter will also appear in the box next to your written version). If it didn't understand your letter, the ink will turn blue. If it's wrong, it will be red.

In the Master level of game play, you get no cheats. You can't reveal letters, and all letters are displayed in blue, so you're never sure if they're right.

Downloading the Latest Crossword Puzzle

To download today's puzzle, tap on **Game**, and then on **Download Today's Crossword**. Alternatively, if you have a keyboard attached to your Tablet PC, you can press **F2**. When you do, you will see a dialog box similar to the one shown in Figure 14.10 asking what level of play you want.

FIGURE 14.10

When you download a puzzle, you will need to tell the application which mode to start the game in.

FIGURE 14.10

When you download a puzzle, you will need to tell the application which mode to start the game in.

To switch from Regular to Master mode or back, tap **Difficulty**, and then the difficulty mode you want.

Pausing, Exiting, and Continuing a Game

If you want to pause the game, tap **Game**, and then **Pause**. If you want to exit the game, tap **Game**, and then **Exit**. You will be asked if you want to leave, and if you want to save the game. After responding affirmatively, the program will close. The next time you start Crossword Puzzle, it will tell you that you previously saved a game, as shown in Figure 14.11.

To continue the saved game, tap **Game**, and then **Continue Game**.

note

You will need Internet access to download the puzzle for the day. Unless you save a game for later, you will need a new download every time you start the game.

Getting Help

When you're stumped by a puzzle, you can ask for some help if you're playing a Regular-level game. If you're in Master level, you're on your own.

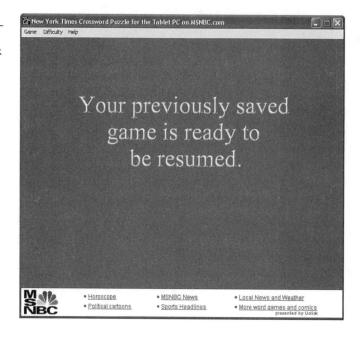

To get help, you can hover your pen over a square, then pull your pen back and tap on the **Reveal Letter** button in the lower-right corner of the screen. The correct letter will be displayed.

And as I mentioned earlier, when you're playing Regular level, the letters you write will be confirmed as being correct or incorrect as you go.

Puzzle Game for Tablet PC

Puzzle Game can be played with a mouse, but it is a great game for the Tablet PC because you can lay the Tablet PC flat and manipulate the game pieces with the pen. Figure 14.12 shows what Puzzle Game looks like when it starts.

The Easy mode (level 1) has only four pieces, whereas the Difficult mode (level 5) has 130 pieces. You can change the difficulty level of the game by tapping **Options**, and then **Difficulty**. When you do, you will see a dialog box like the one shown in Figure 14.13, where you will be asked to enter a number from 1 to 5 representing the difficulty level you desire.

FIGURE 14.12

Puzzle Game
starts in the
Easy mode,
where you have
just four pieces
to put together.

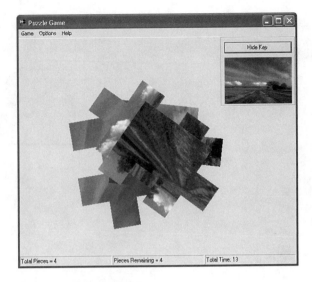

FIGURE 14.12

Puzzle Game
starts in the
Easy mode,
where you have
just four pieces
to put together.

FIGURE 14.13

To change the
difficulty level,
enter a different
number in the
text box.

In addition to changing the difficulty, you can also change the picture on which the puzzle is based. To do so, tap **Game**, and then **Select Picture**. You will then see a dialog box asking you to locate the picture you want to use. You can choose from several image types (JPG, BMP, and so on). Figure 14.14 shows a picture I took on a trip to New Mexico being used as the basis for the puzzle.

After you choose a picture and set the difficulty level, you can change a couple other settings. For example, if you tap **Options**, and then **Outline Pieces**, you will be able to see outlines on each of the puzzle pieces to help you align them better, as shown in Figure 14.15. You can also display or hide the key picture, which is the thumbnail view of the picture in the upper right corner of the game screen.

FIGURE 14.14

You can use your own photographs or other images as the basis for your puzzle to make it more interesting.

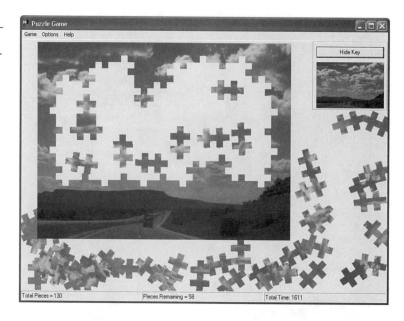

FIGURE 14.15

Choosing the Outline Pieces option lets you see the shape of the pieces more clearly.

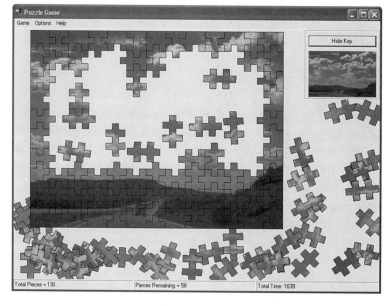

When you start the game, you will need to drag the puzzle pieces around the screen to match them up. If you drag the piece from the center, it will stay in the same orientation, whereas if you drag from an edge, you can turn the piece to rotate it the way you want. When you get the puzzle piece aligned with another one, and they match, push them together until they join. When they join, you will be able to move the pieces together. You cannot unjoin them.

As the game progresses, the Total Time counter will increase as, hopefully, the Pieces Remaining counter decreases. Challenge yourself and others to beat your previous low time scores for a more challenging Puzzle Game experience.

When you're ready for a new puzzle, or want to do the same one again, tap on **Game** and then choose **Reshuffle**. You will then start over.

Tablet Pool

Tablet Pool is one of the coolest games for the Tablet PC. It is a photo-realistic version of the classic table game, as shown in Figure 14.16. With Tablet Pool, you can practice your angles even in confined places.

FIGURE 14.16
Tablet Pool is a photo-realistic game where you can practice making your shots.

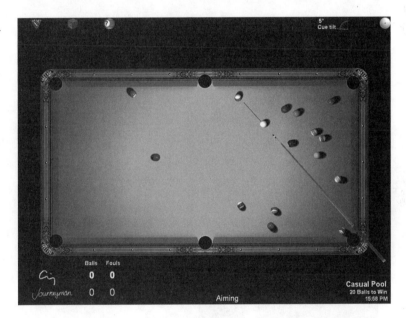

Placing the Cue Ball

To place the cue ball for the break, move the hand icon over the ball. The hand will then open up. Tap and hold over the cue ball and move it where you want, lifting the pen when the cue ball is in place.

Using the Cue to Strike the Ball

To aim the cue stick, move your pen around the cue ball until the cue stick is behind the ball. Tap and hold to ready the cue stick for the strike, and then move your pen across the cue ball at the speed you want to strike it. Make sure your hand moves as straight as possible to keep your aim true.

Tablet Pool Options

You can customize your game play by adding your own signature to the player list. To do so, tap on the rack icon in the upper-left corner of the screen and choose **New**. You'll see a screen like the one shown in Figure 14.17, which lets you choose the style of game (8-Ball, 9-Ball, or Casual Pool) and the players who will play. Click the **Create New player** button to add your signature in the Player 1 (local) list box.

FIGURE 14.17

This screen lets you change the game type and the players. You can also add your signature to the roster.

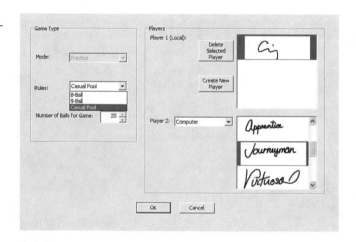

By tapping on the cue chalk icon at the top of the screen (see Figure 14.18), you can also set other options:

FIGURE 14.18

The options available in the Chalk menu.

■ **Aim Line**—When the Aim Line setting is enabled, the game displays the direction of the cue stick through the cue ball to the closest ball, as shown in Figure 14.19. You can use it to get a better aim since you can't sight down your cue stick.

FIGURE 14.19
Using the Aim Line option helps you fine-tune your aim.

■ **Kitchen**—When the Kitchen setting is enabled, the kitchen line—that is, the line across the table at the second marker, behind which you must put the cue ball after a scratch—is visible onscreen.

■ **Mute**—Click the **Mute** button to turn off all sound.

■ **Boss Button**—Enable the Boss Button setting to add a button to the right of the red-striped ball at the top of the screen (the one that has a question mark on it instead of a number). Click the **Boss** button at any time to shut off the game immediately.

Finally, you can adjust English and cue tilt for advanced shots. Do this by using the tools in the upper-right corner of the screen, as shown in Figure 14.20.

If you're a pool buff, this can make a long trip a bit shorter. Although it won't replace a real table, it can certainly make break time fun!

FIGURE 14.20
Use the Cue Tilt tool to adjust tilt. Adjust the placement of the blue dot on the cue ball to add spin, or English.

Tic-Tac-Toe

Tic-Tac-Toe is one of the simplest games of all time, but it wasn't until now that you could waste time playing it on your computer with a pen. Figure 14.21 shows what Tic-Tac-Toe looks like on a Tablet PC.

FIGURE 14.21
The Tic-Tac-Toe program lets you use ink to beat the computer (or not).

There really are no settings to adjust because Tic-Tac-Toe is such a simple game. Just tap the **New Game** button at the bottom of the screen to start a game. If you win, you'll see something similar to what's shown in Figure 14.22.

FIGURE 14.22

Just in case you don't see this yourself, I thought I'd share what it looks like when you win.

Writing Recognition Game

The purpose of Writing Recognition Game is to help you increase your writing-recognition accuracy. The object of the game is to write letters as quickly as possible to save Farmer Joe's crops. Figure 14.23 shows what the game looks like when you start it.

FIGURE 14.23

This is what Writing Recognition Game looks like when you start it.

To start the game, just tap the **New Game** button in the bottom-right corner of the screen. After you start the game, start writing letters in the green **Write Here** box and tapping the **Fire!** button in order to knock out the raindrops falling from the sky. The better your handwriting-recognition speed and accuracy, the higher your score. Figure 14.24 shows a game in progress.

FIGURE 14.24

Here is a game that is almost over.

Eventually, a raindrop will escape you, and the game will end. Your objective is to cause a drought.

Changing Difficulty Levels

You can change the difficulty level of the writing-recognition game by tapping **Game** and then selecting **Beginner**, **Intermediate**, or **Expert**.

Basic Strategy

The basic strategy of this game is to be accurate and fast with your handwriting. To get a higher score, you must be able to knock the most raindrops out of the sky. Therefore, you need to hit the raindrops before they hit the ground. The more raindrops you knock out before one hits the ground, the higher your score.

What works best for me is to first write the letters that I have the most problems with. For example, the letters I and K are problematic for me, so whenever I see them begin to fall from the sky, I try to knock them out first—even though other letters may be lower. It will take me more time to knock out those letters than the letters I don't have problems with. If I let one of my problem letters get farther down, it increases the chances that the raindrop will hit the field.

The other thing to keep in mind is to make sure that the letters you write are fully formed, and that you accurately tap the Fire! button.

How Well Does the Tablet PC Handle Other Computer Games?

All the preceding games are free. They either come with your Tablet PC, or you can download them at no charge. In addition to the free games mentioned here, your Tablet PC can also play most games on the market made for later generations of Windows. Because your Tablet PC is designed for lightness and battery conservation, however, it does not have the speed that many high-end desktop and laptop systems have. For this reason, it is important to read the system requirements of games before purchasing them—especially because opened software is not usually returnable.

The only games you should have problems with are ones that require significant graphics processing (first-person shooters and incredibly detailed strategy games) or extremely fast processors. Know what your processor speed is (in MHz or GHz) and compare that to the system requirements on software packages to be sure your system is compatible. Some games will also require significant RAM and hard drive capacity, so be sure you know what you have before buying and loading these games.

THE ABSOLUTE MINIMUM

Here are the key points to take away from this chapter:

- There are many games included with your Tablet PC, including InkBall, 3D Pinball, and many others.

- Downloading some PowerToys and other games will increase your Tablet PC enjoyment factor.

- Most games made for Windows can be played on your Tablet PC. The pen may even be beneficial in some. Some games requiring the fastest processors will be unacceptably slow on your Tablet PC, however.

PART VI

Using Microsoft Office 2003 with the Tablet PC

15

USING MICROSOFT OFFICE 2003 APPLICATIONS WITH YOUR TABLET PC

Office 2003 leverages digital ink (hereafter referred to as "ink") and voice input. Using ink, you can scribble notes in the margins of a document, and even include hand-drawn graphics. As you learn to utilize the pen and voice-input capabilities in Office 2003, you will find new ways to use the applications and new ways to impress others and gain efficiency.

In just the few months that I have been using the Tablet PC with Office 2003, I have had numerous people look at what I'm doing and say "Wow!" Inserting hand drawings in Word, annotating an Excel spreadsheet, writing down audience comments in PowerPoint during a presentation, and enabling pen input in Access is now possible.

This chapter assumes that you already know how to use each of the Office applications, or that you can find another book or resource to learn the applications. Because it is beyond the scope of this book to teach more, I will show you how to use each application's Tablet PC-specific tools only.

This chapter will show you the general tools available in many of the applications, and then will provide specific guidance for each application. You will soon discover that there is no reason to run any version of Office prior to Office 2003 when you have a Tablet PC.

How Office 2003 is Different from Office XP

One of the primary differences between Office XP and Office 2003 is that Office 2003 includes native ink support, whereas Office XP requires the Office XP Pack for Tablet PC. Even with the add-on, Office XP does not have the integrated feel of inking that Office 2003 offers.

For example, in Office XP, when you add an ink annotation, a box appears in which you must make the annotations, as shown in Figure 15.1.

FIGURE 15.1

In Office XP with the Office XP Pack for Tablet PC, you are able to add ink in boxes.

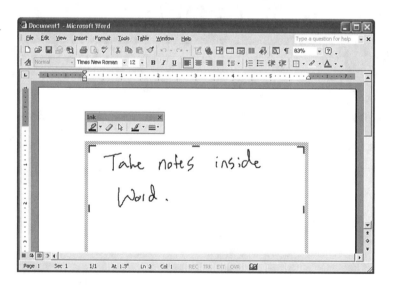

In Office 2003, however, ink can appear anywhere on the workspace in Word and PowerPoint. This means that unlike Office XP with the add-on, you can check off check boxes and annotate directly over text and other graphics, as shown in Figure 15.2.

FIGURE 15.2

In Office 2003, you can add ink anywhere you want in a document.

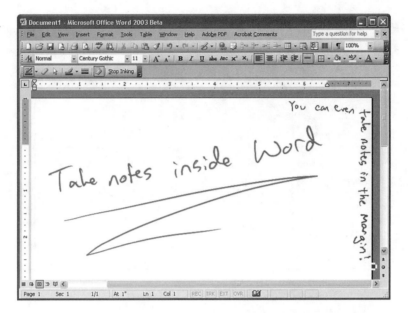

FIGURE 15.2

In Office 2003, you can add ink anywhere you want in a document.

Downloading Office XP Pack for Tablet PC

Downloading the Office XP Pack for Tablet PC will allow you to add functionality to Office XP and Windows Journal. You can download the add-on from http://www.microsoft.com/office/tabletpc/; once it's downloaded, simply install it on your machine.

The add-on to Office XP adds ink capabilities to Office XP applications that would otherwise not exist. In Word, for example, the add-on adds ink capabilities, as shown in Figure 15.3.

tip

Install the Office XP Pack for Tablet PC whether you have Office XP or Office 2003. The Pack adds functionality to Windows Journal as well as Office XP applications.

After you have finished installing Office XP Pack for Tablet PC, you will be asked if you want to run the tutorial. I recommend going through it (see Figure 15.4).

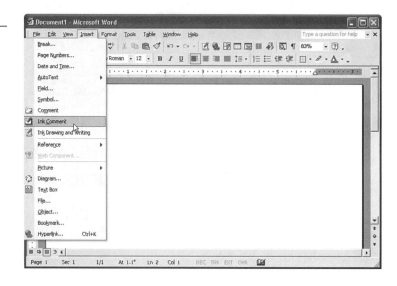

The Power of Ink in Office 2003

One of the main reasons we use paper instead of a computer is because we can doodle, sketch, and more fluidly communicate ideas on paper than through typing. Much of that has changed now with the Tablet PC. You can now type, doodle, annotate, and do about anything you can with paper—all by using your Tablet PC with simple applications that you're already familiar with.

Now your Microsoft Word experience can be as fruitful as a brainstorming session, with ideas generated on the keyboard, and sketches drawn beside the text. You can even include voice annotations and handwritten notes. The power of the pen has finally come to Microsoft Office!

Almost every member of the Office 2003 suite has the capability to add ink. And where you can add ink, you can erase it. In general, you can add ink to any part of a document, and in Word you can even add ink comments.

The main differences between the different inking styles are as follows:

- Ink annotations can be hidden, and do not require a special box. This is available in Word, Excel, and PowerPoint.

- Ink drawing and writing requires a special ink box, and is not hidden when the Hide annotations button is clicked. Word, PowerPoint, Excel, and Access can use ink drawing and writing.

- Ink comments are available only in Word 2003, and are just like comments used during collaborative writing, where the comments show in the margin and can be hidden.

The inking capabilities for each application will be covered in more detail in each application's section of this chapter.

The Power of Voice in Office 2003

As I explained in Chapter 9, "Speech Recognition and Voice Control," speech recognition and command allows you to dictate large amounts of text and control applications, all using just your voice. It is good enough that when writing Chapter 9, I did not type a single word.

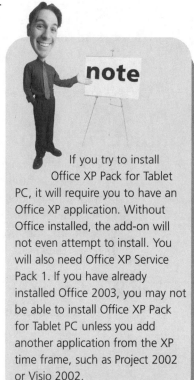

If you try to install Office XP Pack for Tablet PC, it will require you to have an Office XP application. Without Office installed, the add-on will not even attempt to install. You will also need Office XP Service Pack 1. If you have already installed Office 2003, you may not be able to install Office XP Pack for Tablet PC unless you add another application from the XP time frame, such as Project 2002 or Visio 2002.

Ink is powerful in Office, so spend some time getting used to it. Know what tools you have available in each application, and learn how to use them well so you can handle any inking situation with ease.

Word is the application in which most would use speech recognition, although it can be used anywhere in Office 2003. Ever wanted to just talk to someone instead of send email? You can. You can dictate to Outlook or include a voice recording with your message (which you could also do in Office 2000).

Each application has commands specific to it, so use the What Can I Say? command to determine the commands available to you.

Tablet PC Features in Office 2003

The addition/expansion of ink and voice-input capabilities in Office 2003 make the Tablet PC more powerful. Word, Outlook, Excel, Powerpoint, and Visio added powerful inking capabilities in 2003. Access has some capability, but because I'd have to get into programming to make the discussion useful, I am not including it in this book. InfoPath is a new application that facilitates data gathering through its forms-based software.

Ink in Word and Outlook 2003

Word has the richest set of inking tools, including ink Annotations, ink Drawing and Writing, and ink Comments tools. And because WordMail is basically Word, Outlook has the same set of features. However, WordMail allows ink comments and ink drawing and writing boxes, but not ink annotations without the ink box. Instead, you must use the ink drawing and writing box like that in Word XP, instead of the write-anywhere annotation inking in Word 2003. Figure 15.5 shows ink comments and annotations in WordMail.

Word will not convert handwriting to text, but it allows you to use as much ink as you want to get your point across. In fact, with Word 2003 and a Tablet PC, you can get your point across much faster because you can include ink comments and sketches, as shown in Figure 15.6.

To use ink in Word or WordMail, either access the pen directly from one of the ink toolbars, or choose **Insert**, then **Ink Comment** or **Ink Drawing and Writing**. You will then be able to add either a comment or an ink box. (In Word, you can also insert an ink annotation, which allows you to ink anywhere without a box.) You can change the color and style of the pen marks by using the Pen Style tool on one of the ink toolbars.

To display the ink toolbars if they aren't shown, go to **View**, **Toolbars**, then choose the ink toolbar(s) you wish to display. Figure 15.7 shows the three different toolbars available to you in Word.

FIGURE 15.5
WordMail offers most of the features of Word for inking, but requires an annotation box.

FIGURE 15.6
You can include handwritten notes and sketches directly in Word 2003.

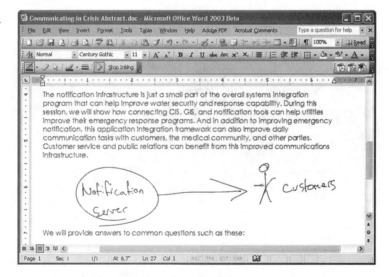

Ink Annotations toolbar

FIGURE 15.7

These are the three ink tool-bars available to you in Word.

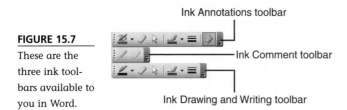

Ink Comment toolbar

Ink Drawing and Writing toolbar

I suggest using the ink Annotations toolbar if you intend to mark up the document directly. If you want space created for inking, then use the ink Drawing and Writing toolbar, which creates a graphics box that you can ink inside. Ink comments should be used only for callout-style comments in the document.

Enabling Word as Your Email Editor

If you need to enable WordMail in order to use ink in Outlook, click on **Tools**, and then **Options**. You will see the dialog box shown in Figure 15.8. Check the **Use Microsoft Office Word 2003 to edit e-mail messages** check box to enable Word as the email editor.

FIGURE 15.8

Check the Use Microsoft Office Word 2003 to edit e-mail mes-sages checkbox to turn on this feature.

Speech Recognition in Word and Outlook 2003

Word has an incredible list of commands that you can use to manipulate the pro-gram. Use the Input Panel's What Can I Say? feature to find the complete list of available commands; Figure 15.9 shows a small list. You can dictate directly into Word, as described in Chapter 9, and you can also command Word in Voice

Command mode by speaking the names of menus and commands. After writing Chapter 9, and proving the capabilities of speech recognition, I often choose to use speech recognition to dictate rather than type on a keyboard because it is sometimes faster and eliminates the artificial feel of keyboard input. Try it for at least ten hours to get the hang of it. It will open up a new world of input for you.

FIGURE 15.9

Here is a partial listing of voice commands within Word 2003.

Tablet PC Features in Excel 2003

Excel has fewer ink capabilities than Word. In Excel, you can only annotate a spreadsheet. There are no ink comments. The list of voice commands is also more limited. However, using ink in Excel can highlight key data points both through ink and through ink as a highlighter, as shown in Figure 15.10.

Notice in Figure 15.11 that when I tap the Hide Ink Annotations button, all annotations disappear, but ink drawing and writing objects stay.

FIGURE 15.10

Ink annotations
in Excel 2003.

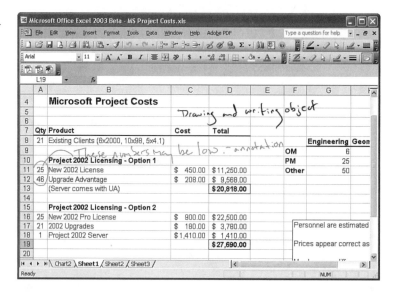

FIGURE 15.11

Ink annotations
are hidden, but
ink drawing and
writing objects
are not.

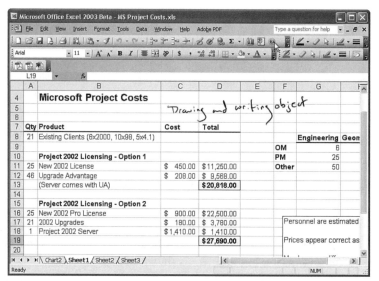

In addition to annotating spreadsheets, you can also annotate charts, as shown in
Figure 15.12.

FIGURE 15.12

Ink annotations
in an Excel 2003
chart.

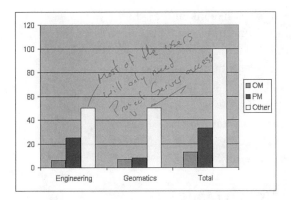

To add ink annotations to either a spreadsheet or a chart, just tap the **Insert Ink Annotations** button on the toolbar, as shown in Figure 15.13.

FIGURE 15.13

Use the Insert
Ink Annotations
button to insert
an annotation.

To insert ink that won't be hidden, choose the **Insert Ink Drawing and Writing** button instead, which is next to the Insert Annotations button, and has a blue whirl instead of a red one.

You can now use Excel 2003 to make more of an impact with handwritten notes, annotations, drawings, and highlights.

Tablet PC Features in PowerPoint 2003

The Tablet PC has some really cool benefits for PowerPoint. In addition to being able to draw when creating slides, you can also annotate slides *during* a presentation, enabling you to record feedback and get back to the same capabilities you had with overhead transparencies (but now with a single pen).

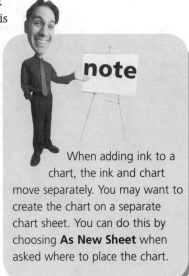

When adding ink to a chart, the ink and chart move separately. You may want to create the chart on a separate chart sheet. You can do this by choosing **As New Sheet** when asked where to place the chart.

Ink in PowerPoint works just like ink in the other Office applications. Ink annotations and ink drawing and writing are both available in PowerPoint. Figure 15.14 shows a presentation I gave and a slide where I presented some information graphically based on audience feedback.

Figure 15.15 shows how you can use blank lines in your slides to use as rules for text when you know that you want to get audience feedback.

Inserting Ink in Design Mode

To add ink to your slides before a presentation, just click on the **Insert Ink Annotations** button or the **Insert Ink Drawing and Writing** button, depending on your need for ink permanence. In Figure 15.16, I have added ink drawing and writing notes in white to show you the permanence of ink in this mode.

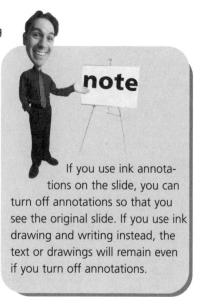

note

If you use ink annotations on the slide, you can turn off annotations so that you see the original slide. If you use ink drawing and writing instead, the text or drawings will remain even if you turn off annotations.

FIGURE 15.14

You can use the Tablet PC for PowerPoint presentations and mark on the slides as you're giving the presentation.

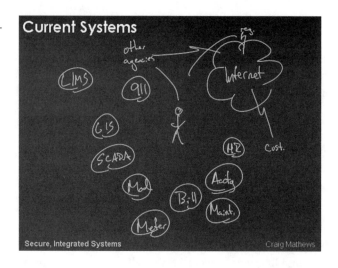

FIGURE 15.15
Use lines as
rules when you
want to record
feedback from
the audience in
your slides.

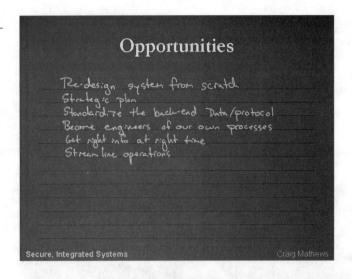

FIGURE 15.16
Ink drawing and
writing provides
a permanent
ink, whereas ink
annotations can
be turned on
and off.

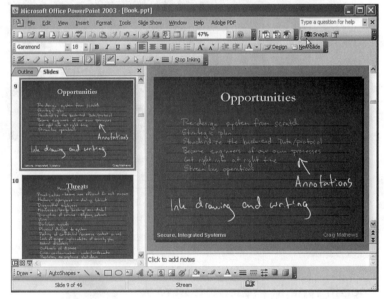

To hide ink annotations, just tap on the **Show/Hide Markup** button on the ink
Annotations toolbar, as shown in Figure 15.17.

FIGURE 15.17

Use the
Show/Hide
Markup button
to show or hide
ink annotations.

Once you hide the annotations, you will then see only the ink drawing and writing
marks you made, as shown in Figure 15.18.

FIGURE 15.18

Ink drawing and
writing objects
still show even
when ink
Annotations are
hidden.

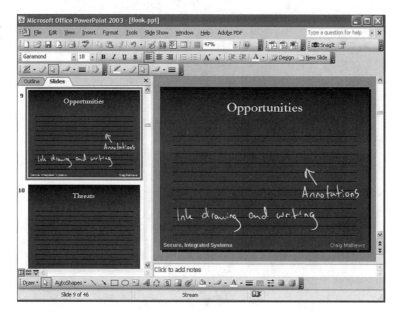

Note in Figure 15.19 that you can also add ink
to a slide master for ink that you want to show
on each slide.

Inserting Ink in Presentation Mode

Now that you know how to add ink during the
slide-creation phase, let's look at how to deal
with ink in the Presentation mode.

When you present on your Tablet PC, you'll
probably want to make sure your Tablet PC is in
landscape mode so that the projector can sit flat
on the table, or mounted on the ceiling, depending on your arrangement.

tip

Ink in PowerPoint is a
powerful presentation tool.
Understand how to use it
during a presentation to add
extra interaction with the
audience and to capture
the discussion in your presentation. (You do have two-way
communication in your presentations, don't you?)

FIGURE 15.19

Ink can also be
added to slide
masters.

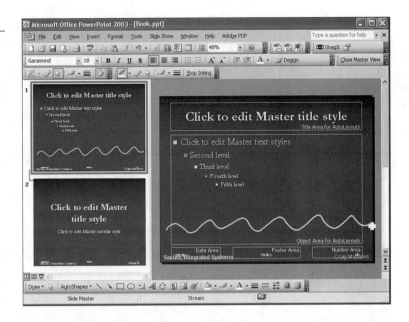

Once you have your Tablet PC in landscape mode, start your presentation by tapping the **Slide Show** button, or by pressing **F5** to start at the beginning of your
presentation, or **Shift+F5** to start at the current slide.

Now that you're in Presentation mode, you can add ink at any time by moving your
pen a little bit around the bottom left corner of the screen (move the pen too much,
and you'll open Input Panel). You will then see four buttons faintly displayed, as
shown in Figure 15.20.

FIGURE 15.20

The four buttons
available to you
in Presentation
mode are
Previous Slide,
Pen Tools,
Menu, and Next
Slide.

When you tap on the Pen Tool button, you will see a list of options like the one
shown in Figure 15.21. (Note that the Eraser and Erase All Ink on Slide items are not
available until there is ink on the current slide.)

The Pen Tools
menu. You can
choose pen
styles and colors
from this menu
for annotating
your slides in
Presentation
mode.

Figure 15.22 shows the use of all the tools on a single slide.

FIGURE 15.22

On this slide, I
used the ball-
point pen for
text, the felt-tip
pen for the
squiggle, the
highlighter, and
the eraser to cut
through ink.
The eraser is a
stroke eraser, so
it eliminates all
ink strokes it
touches.

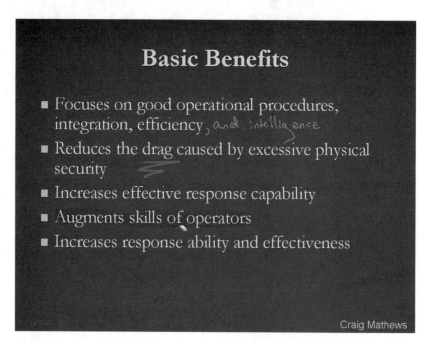

Tablet PC Features in InfoPath 2003

InfoPath, which is a new addition to Office in the 2003 version, is a forms tool that
helps capture data in a consistent way, just like using paper forms. The gathered
data can then be saved to a central data repository for analysis and action.

Suppose, for example, that you want to capture machine maintenance information
on a regular basis. InfoPath enables you to create a form that can be used for data
gathering, and then help you digitize the process.

InfoPath can utilize InkPicture fields in its forms to enable sketching, such as diagramming an accident scene in an insurance application. Figure 15.23 shows what a form could look like in InfoPath with ink included.

To insert an ink field in Design mode, click **Insert**, then **More Controls**. Then, drag the InkPicture control to the InfoPath form, as shown in Figure 15.24. If the Automatically create data source check box is checked, the data source will also be generated for you.

> ## tip
>
> To use ink effectively in your presentations, plan ahead, practice using ink in trial runs, and pick colors that show up well against your chosen slide background. Ink can add a lot to a presentation by providing more opportunities for recording feedback or highlighting points, but it can also backfire if you're fumbling to use the tools in your presentation.

FIGURE 15.23

An InkPicture field in InfoPath allows the user to diagram or notate something more fluidly than text alone.

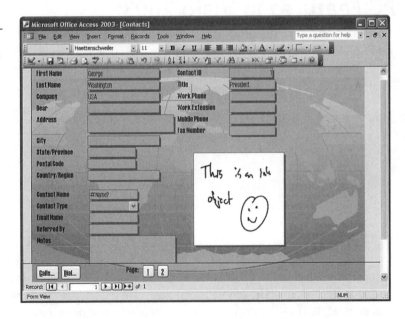

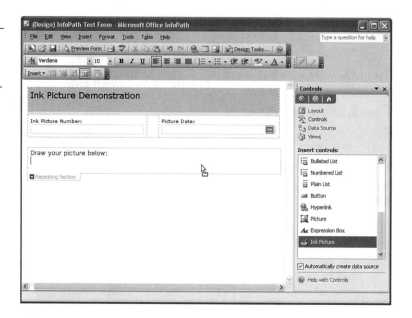

Tablet PC Features in Visio 2003

Visio 2003 allows you to draw as well as drag-and-drop objects. With ink, you can
add fine touches to your diagrams, and annotate them as you go. To add ink to a
Visio diagram, simply tap on the **Ink Tool** button on the button bar, as shown in
Figure 15.25.

You can also display the Ink toolbar by tapping on **View**, then **Toolbars**, and
checking the **Ink** toolbar. You will then have five pens to choose from; these pens
can be modified in the Customize Pens dialog, which is accessible from the Pen Tool
drop-down list on the main toolbar.

When you add ink to your drawing, you will see a selection box surrounding the ink after a brief moment, as shown in Figure 15.26.

FIGURE 15.26

Ink will automatically be clumped together as a single object until you choose another tool or tap the Close Ink Shape button on the Ink toolbar.

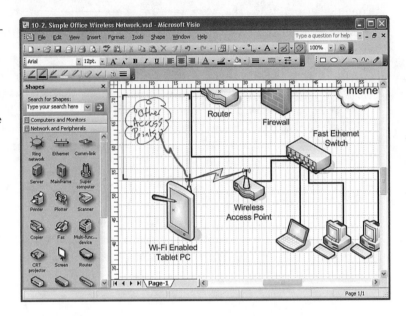

The ink you use is treated as an object. When you are finished drawing a shape, you can tap the **Close Ink Shape** button on the Ink toolbar to keep it as an object separate from other ink. Otherwise, all the ink you lay down while you have the ink tool open will be combined as a single object.

Because the ink is treated as an object, there is no annotation capability (where the annotations can be viewed/hidden).

THE ABSOLUTE MINIMUM

Here are the key points to take away from this chapter:

- Microsoft Office 2003 has the native ability to handle ink. Office 2003 is better for the Tablet PC than Office XP.

- Install the Office XP Pack for Tablet PC even if you have Office 2003.

- There are three modes of inking in Office: annotations (where ink can be placed anywhere on the document, and can also be hidden); drawing and writing (ink is inserted into the document, with or without a box, and cannot be hidden); and comments (where collaborative comments can be written instead of typed into Word).

- If you use Outlook for email, enable Word as the email editor so you can use ink in your email messages.

- Ink in PowerPoint can add new dimensions to your digital presentations, enabling on-the-fly annotations, drawings, and note-taking of audience comments. It turns PowerPoint into a full-fledged digital overhead projector.

16

MICROSOFT ONENOTE 2003

What is OneNote?

OneNote is the killer app for the Tablet PC. Not only does it allow you to take notes like Windows Journal does, it also lets you drop in Web pages and record audio from meetings. This is the application for anyone who attends meetings and seminars, and who does research on the Internet.

OneNote lets you store all the information you have on a subject in an ad-hoc manner, much like paper, yet with the ability to drop in Web pages and other content. It can be used for information storage, note-taking, meeting capture, and research. OneNote lets you capture all your information in one place, making it easy to use and find. the Tablet PC makes OneNote even more powerful because it lets you take notes and sketch in OneNote with the pen—making OneNote a true note-taking tool.

As you can see in Figure 16.1, OneNote accepts handwriting, text, graphics, and Web pages.

Because of its ability to incorporate lots of different media, OneNote is more powerful than any other single application for the Tablet PC. Notes and objects can be moved around in a document even more easily than in Word. OneNote can also recognize an entire handwritten document, allowing you to convert your handwritten notes into text more quickly than Journal or Input Panel.

For me, OneNote's most compelling feature is its audio-recording capabilities. Not only can OneNote record audio—say, at a meeting or lecture—but it also automatically ties together the audio recording with any notes you made during the recorded event. So notes and audio are now linked, even when you reorganize your thoughts.

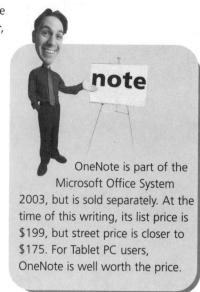

note

OneNote is part of the Microsoft Office System 2003, but is sold separately. At the time of this writing, its list price is $199, but street price is closer to $175. For Tablet PC users, OneNote is well worth the price.

tip

If you want to get the most out of your Tablet PC, get OneNote.

Benefits over Other Applications

OneNote is kind of like PageMaker, Publisher, and other desktop-publishing applications in that you can drag objects (text, graphics, Web pages, handwriting, and so on) to any place in the document.

FIGURE 16.1

OneNote can handle text, graphics, hand-writing, Web pages, and more—fluidly.

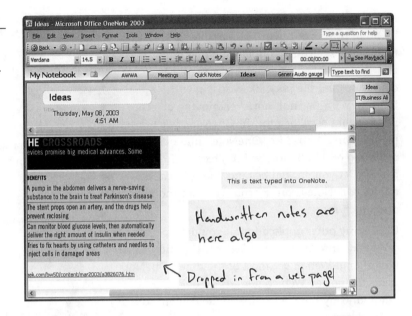

Unlike publishing applications, however, OneNote has no fixed size for a page, so you can extend to the right and down as far as you want. If you want to, however, you can define specific page sizes (for example, if you'll need to print the document you're using OneNote to create). In any case, the free-form ability OneNote gives you to move objects on the page means you can lay things out however makes sense to you, and then form logical connections between them. This can help in brainstorming and other activities that require linking ideas.

OneNote is fantastic for being able to put together free-form information, graphics, and ink.

Likewise, OneNote shares several characteristics with Microsoft Word. For example, like Word, OneNote has formatting and outlining tools, and lets you send notes as email messages. Unlike Word, however, OneNote lets you convert handwriting into text, and also lets you add audio to the notes you take. Although Word lets you add voice annotations and handwritten notes, it does not integrate them like OneNote does.

Finally, like Journal, OneNote lets you take notes by hand using your pen. This enables fluid note-taking and sketching, similar to paper note-taking. OneNote also enables you to move objects around the page like you can with Journal. With Journal, however, moving objects is somewhat cumbersome. In OneNote, you simply drag and drop. Also, OneNote's audio-recording and bulk handwriting recognition features let you go well beyond Journal's capabilities. OneNote is an alternative to Journal, but also much more.

Unlike any other application, if you drag portions of a Web site into OneNote, it keeps the formatting of the original Web page (most of the time). OneNote treats the pasted Web content as an object, and automatically provides a link to the content source Web address (URL).

Overall, OneNote is an application made for the Tablet PC. Through audio recording linked to notes and the ability to handle any type of media, OneNote is a must for the Tablet PC business user.

OneNote Basics

OneNote is simple to use, but you have to get used to its idiosyncrasies. Because of all OneNote does, it sometimes outthinks you, and assumes too much. For example, sometimes when you write, as you move your pen, it may decide you're starting a new thought and therefore start a new section, even if you're just continuing the sentence. Being consistent in where you begin sentences and your character spacing will help resolve most of this second-guessing.

In this section, I will introduce you to OneNote, and help you understand how to use the main features of the program. Before I begin, however, I recommend that you use the OneNote Tour. To

tip

Audio recording is one of the coolest features of OneNote. Any audio you record is linked to the notes you take in a time-based fashion.

note

OneNote is like Word, Journal, and a tape recorder all thrown together. You can work the way you want.

tip

If you do a lot of research, you'll find that OneNote offers a flexible tool for information gathering and deduction.

use it, tap **Help**, **Get Going with OneNote**, and then tap the
Start tour button to begin. When you do, you will
see the first screen of the Microsoft Office
OneNote 2003 Tour, as shown in Figure 16.2. Just
tap the arrow at the top of the dialog box to
move forward. Throughout the demo, you also
can see demos of the various actions that
OneNote can perform by tapping on the **Show
Me** button when it appears.

caution

OneNote takes a bit of
getting used to. Once
you're familiar with the
interface, though, you
can really be productive.

FIGURE 16.2

The OneNote
Tour helps you
gain a basic
understanding
of OneNote and
get started.

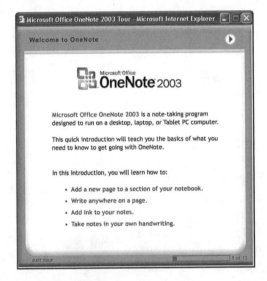

Introduction to the Interface

The OneNote interface looks similar to the interfaces found in other Office applications.
OneNote's interface does, however, have some
special features, which I cover here.

Figure 16.3 shows the main areas of the
OneNote interface.

tip

Use the OneNote Tour to
get up to speed quickly, and
then come back here for the
meat.

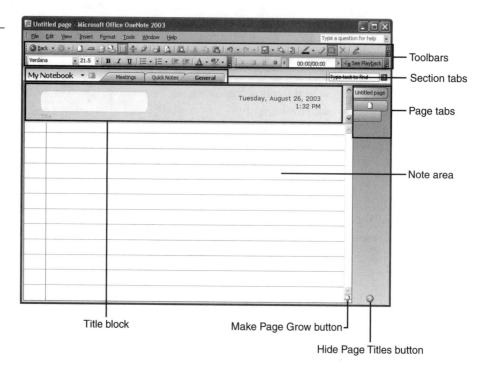

Toolbars

Section tabs

Page tabs

Note area

Title block

Make Page Grow button

Hide Page Titles button

These main areas are as follows:

- **Toolbars**—The toolbars are similar to those in other Office applications, although new tools are added to OneNote's. Especially notice the tools to the right, which deal with ink and audio recording. These toolbars are dockable. Standard, Formatting, and Audio Recording are the main toolbars I use.

- **Section tabs**—The section tabs are actually different .one files that have been loaded. Each .one file is a notebook by itself, but added together they make a multi-subject binder. Tap on a tab to switch sections.

- **Title block**—The title block has an area for the note title, and automatically inserts the date when you create a note. The date does not change when you edit the note.

> **tip**
>
> Use sections to organize your main types of note-taking.

- **Page tabs**—The page tabs help you keep track of different notes within each section. When you create a new note, a new tab is created. Sub-pages (covered later) show up as smaller tabs under the main page.
- **Note area**—The note area is where you write, type, draw, and manipulate objects. This is where the content goes.
- **Make Page Grow button**—The Make Page Grow button adds more space at the end of the page, letting you enlarge the document without adding additional pages.
- **Hide Page Titles button**—The Hide Page Titles button squashes the page titles to make more space for notes. When hidden, page titles become numbers.

note

The page tab on the right gets its name from the title block.

The Standard Toolbar

The Standard toolbar, shown in Figure 16.4, is where most of the tools in OneNote reside.

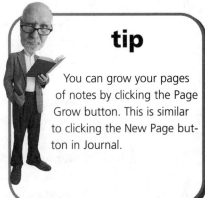

tip

You can grow your pages of notes by clicking the Page Grow button. This is similar to clicking the New Page button in Journal.

FIGURE 16.4

This is the Standard toolbar, the main toolbar in OneNote.

From left to right, here are the buttons found on OneNote's Standard toolbar:

- **Back and Forward**—These buttons enable you to go back and forth between pages and sections. They are similar to the back and forward buttons found in Internet browsers.

- **New Page**—Tapping this button creates a new page in the current section.
- **New Section**—Tapping this button creates a new section tab (and a corresponding .one file).
- **Email**—Tapping this button sends the current note as an email message.
- **Move Page To**—Tapping this button moves a page to another section.
- **Show/Hide Rule Lines**—Tapping this button either shows or hides the red and blue lines in the note area.
- **Insert Extra Writing Space**—This button functions just like the one in Journal, allowing you to insert space between objects.
- **Keep Window on Top**—Tapping this button keeps OneNote on top of other windows and applications.
- **Print and Print Preview**—These buttons act just like those found in other Office applications.
- **Research**—Tapping this button enables you to look up information in an electronic dictionary, thesaurus, and online tools.
- **Cut**, **Copy**, **Paste**, **Undo**, and **Redo**—These buttons are just like those found in other Office applications.

note

Many buttons on OneNote's Standard toolbar may look familiar to you. Pay attention to those that don't and learn what they do.

tip

Use note flags to mark important locations in your notes and to search for them later.

- **Note Flag**—Tapping this button enables you to add various types of flags to your notes. This is a drop-down button with five types of flags.
- **Note Flags Summary**—Tapping this button enables you to search for flags in your notes.
- **Create Outlook Task**—Tapping this button creates a task in Outlook, including the contents of your selection automatically.
- **Pen**, **Eraser**, **Selection**, and **Delete**—These buttons function just like those found in other Office applications.

- **Start/Stop Recording**—Tapping this button starts or stops OneNote's audio-recording function.

The Audio Recording Toolbar

The Audio Recording toolbar, pictured in Figure 16.5, is where you control OneNote's sound-recording and playback features.

FIGURE 16.5

The Audio Recording toolbar controls audio recording and playback.

Tap the red circle to begin recording. When you start recording, the slider in the middle of the toolbar moves to the right as time increases. (During playback, you can also use the slider in the center to move the time bar to the point you want it for a particular section of the audio.)

When you record audio, the audio files are stored in the My Documents\My Notebook folder by default. The files created will be Windows Media files and will have the .wma extension. As you enter other information, such as text, drawings, or handwriting, the audio will be linked to those objects based on time. As you insert other objects, the audio will link to the object that is active at the time of the recording.

> **tip**
>
> Try out OneNote's audio-recording feature while you take notes. Then play with the playback and see how it works. It's a powerful feature for people in meetings.

If you have highlighted an object that has audio attached, you can tap the **See Playback** button to begin audio playback. When you play back the audio, you will see the highlighted objects change over time, reflecting the links the audio recording made as you were making notes.

When you play back audio, you also can tap the triangular **Play** button, the square **Stop** button, and the double-lined **Pause** button. These work like normal tape or CD controls.

Section Tabs

To move between sections, you can use the Section tabs that appear across the top of OneNote, along with the My Notebook drop-down list, as shown in Figure 16.6.

You can you tap on the tabs to navigate between sections of your notebook, and you can also use the My Notebook drop-down list to find your notes, including deleted pages. The Deleted Pages folder stores the pages that have most recently been deleted.

Page Navigation and Control

To switch between pages within a section of your notebook, go to the right of the screen and use the page tabs you find there (see Figure 16.7). The top set of tabs will be your notes. The bottom two tabs are for creating new pages and sub-pages. Pages are basically new notes, whereas sub-pages are used to differentiate subordinate content levels within a page.

tip

Get a good quality external microphone that can pick up the type of audio environment you're usually in. This will help you get the most out of the audio recorder. With an external microphone, you can also reduce or eliminate pen tapping and typing sounds you might otherwise capture.

FIGURE 16.6

The Section Navigation area lets you quickly switch between sections of your notebook.

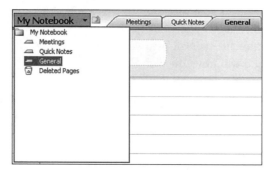

FIGURE 16.7

The page tabs in OneNote let you switch between notes easily instead of having to open files.

In Figure 16.7, notice the tab under Note 2, which denotes a sub-page. The tab names come from the title block of the note.

Taking Notes

To take notes, you need to decide how you want to capture your ideas. If you want to type or enter text through the Input Panel, you can tap where you want the text to appear in the body of the note, and a light gray box will appear, waiting for your input. You can then tap anywhere to enter text.

If you want to draw, just start drawing with your pen. You do need to make sure you are in Pen mode rather than Selection or some other mode. To get into Pen mode, tap the **Pen** button on the Standard toolbar.

If you want to write notes by hand, get in Pen mode and start writing. As you get toward the end of a line of text, the gray box surrounding your text will expand downward, allowing you to include more notes in the same object (see Figure 16.8).

You can define a new paragraph by leaving vertical space between your previous notes and your new handwriting. Figure 16.9 shows how I have created three paragraphs, each of which is considered a separate object.

The Importance of Object Segregation

It is important to know where your pen marks are getting grouped. You want all related ideas to be in a single group, rather than chunked into multiple groups. One way to do this is to write within

the gray boxes. In addition, using the Ruler Lines option is helpful for keeping your text together. Write on the lines, and OneNote will recognize your strokes as text.

If you notice that your ink strokes start appearing in different object blocks (gray boxes with control handles), you may want to change the way OneNote treats ink. If you are only going to be writing text, you can force OneNote to recognize ink as text by tapping **Tools**, **Pen Mode**, and then selecting **Create Handwriting Only**, as shown in Figure 16.10.

FIGURE 16.8

The gray box that appears when OneNote recognizes your ink strokes as handwriting helps you keep your text together instead of in multiple objects.

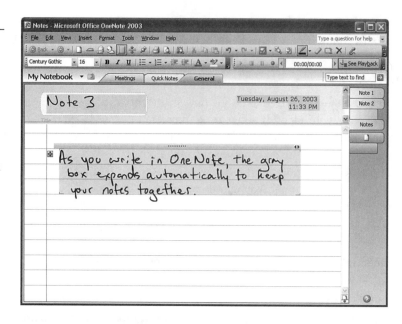

FIGURE 16.9

Separating paragraphs by a line helps OneNote tell them apart.

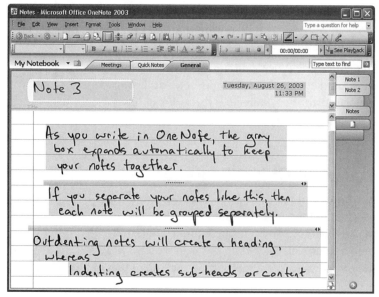

FIGURE 16.10
Select Create Handwriting Only to force OneNote to recognize your ink strokes as handwriting.

When you set OneNote to recognize only handwriting, the handwriting box appears, letting you expand the box and keep handwritten paragraphs together.

Rearranging Notes

Rearranging notes is easy in OneNote. Simply hover your pen or mouse over the text or object you want to move (see Figure 16.11), and then tap and hold the crossed arrow symbol that appears to the left of the object (this symbol is called the selection handle). As you hold your pen (or your mouse button) down, you can drag the object anywhere else in the note. When you lift your pen (or mouse), the object will stay where it was placed.

tip

To keep handwriting together in a single object, set the Pen mode to **Create Handwriting Only**.

FIGURE 16.11
OneNote lets you easily rearrange objects and notes by dragging the selection handle to the left of the object.

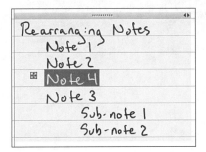

Another great feature of OneNote's drag-and-drop organization is that you can pull objects up and down in the outline hierarchy easily by dragging left or right. In Figure 16.12, notice that I have dragged the Note 4 section down between the two sub-notes, and then outdented (dragged to the left) the Sub-note 2 item. This easy rearranging makes OneNote a fantastic tool for outlining and brainstorming.

FIGURE 16.12

Ad-hoc note reorganization makes outlining easy in OneNote.

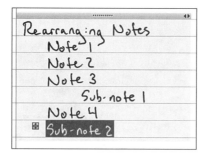

Grouping Notes

It's easy to group note objects in OneNote. Just select the object you want to combine by tapping on the control bar, as shown in Figure 16.13. Then drag up or down to combine the selected object with another object, as shown in Figure 16.14. The control bar also lets you resize the note by dragging the right-left arrow at the right.

FIGURE 16.13

Select the object you want to combine by tapping on the object's control bar.

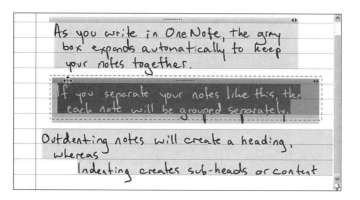

FIGURE 16.14

Drag objects together to combine them into a single object.

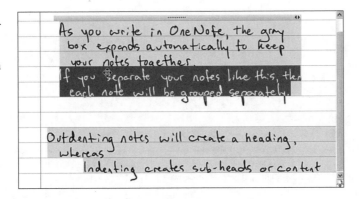

After you combine all the elements you want into a single group, it will look more like Figure 16.15.

FIGURE 16.15

Once combined, all the elements are treated as a single object in OneNote.

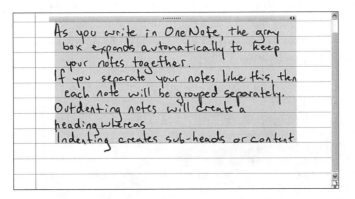

Creating Lists and Applying Bullets and Numbering to Your Notes

Notice that the last line of the handwriting is indented in Figure 16.14. This is the way OneNote differentiates between heading and bullet levels. If you want to create lists in OneNote like the one shown in Figure 16.16, just start writing, using the following suggestions:

- Keep items of the same level at the same indent.
- Indent significantly to change the level of the item.
- Leave a blank line between ideas.
- Going in and out creates a natural outline structure.

FIGURE 16.16
Creating a list
in OneNote.

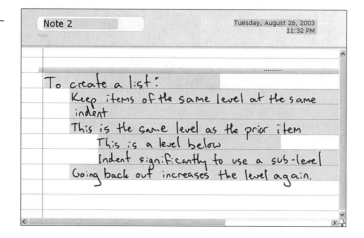

In the list in Figure 16.17, I selected the list and then tapped the Numbering button, which automatically added the outline numbering to my list. You can change the numbering format by tapping on the drop-down list to the right of the **Numbering** button, and then choosing a numbering style.

FIGURE 16.17
Tapping the
Numbering but-
ton after select-
ing the text
automatically
results in a
numbered list
based on the
indents that
OneNote recog-
nizes.

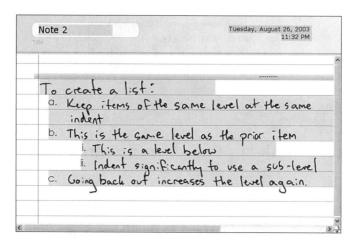

You can just as easily create a bulleted list by tapping the **Bullets** button on the toolbar, with the same drop-down selection capability.

Converting Handwritten Notes to Text

One great feature of OneNote is its capability to bulk-recognize handwriting so that an entire page or notes section can be converted easily to text. To convert a page of notes to text, simply right-tap the note page and select **Convert Handwriting to Text,** as shown in Figure 16.18.

FIGURE 16.18

You can easily convert a lot of handwritten notes to text.

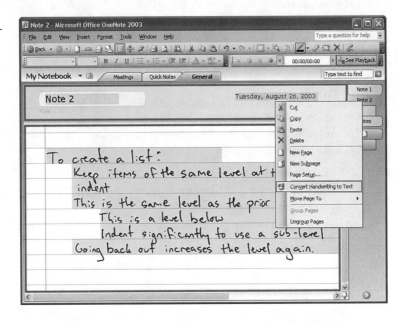

Once the text is converted (and cleaned up if the recognition wasn't perfect), it can be selected and copied into other applications, such as Word, where the formatting will appear just as you have it in OneNote. Figure 16.19 shows how the text looked after I converted this section of notes.

FIGURE 16.19

The text, once converted, lacked consistent formatting, and contained a couple of typos (due to my handwriting). This can be fixed easily.

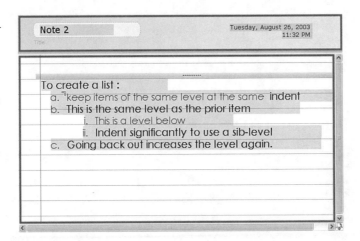

The formatting was a bit off in the text, so I selected all of it and made it uniform in font size to get the results shown in Figure 16.20. I also bolded the heading.

Organizing Your Notebook

It's easy to keep your notes organized in OneNote. The page tabs on the right keep your pages separated with easy access, while the section tabs at the top let you separate subjects just like you would in a multi-subject notebook.

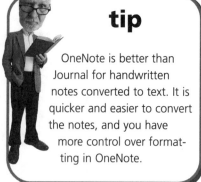

tip

OneNote is better than Journal for handwritten notes converted to text. It is quicker and easier to convert the notes, and you have more control over formatting in OneNote.

Slice and dice your notes any way that makes sense to you. If you want to move a page up or down along the right side, tap and hold on the tab you want to move, then drag to the right, to the edge of OneNote, and drag up or down. You should see a double arrow, as shown in Figure 16.21.

FIGURE 16.20
After only two formatting settings are adjusted, the text looks good.

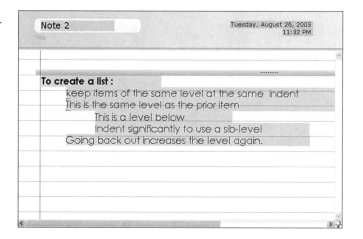

FIGURE 16.21
You can move pages up and down by tapping and dragging along the right side of the page tab area.

If you want to move a page to another section, right-tap the page, select **Move Page To**, and then tap **Another Section**. You will then see a dialog box similar to the one in Figure 16.22.

Choose the section you want to move the page to, and tap **Move** or **Copy**. Move moves the page from the source to the destination section and leaves nothing behind. Copy will duplicate the page in the destination section, leaving the page in the source section intact.

You can also choose **Create New Section** or **Create New Folder** for the page you want to move or copy by tapping the appropriate buttons. The Create New Folder button creates a new folder in the My Documents\My Notebook folder. This helps you organize your files. The Create New Section button creates a new .one file in your My Documents\My Notebook folder.

tip

Keep your notes organized so you can easily find what you're looking for later.

FIGURE 16.22

You can move a page into another section by right-tapping the page and then selecting Move Page To.

Using OneNote in Meetings

OneNote is made for meetings. It lets you take handwritten notes, doodle, type, insert images, charts, Web pages, and other documents to get your point across. And it lets you record the audio of the meeting, with the audio time-linked to the notes you take.

Voice Recording in OneNote

When you want to capture a meeting on your Tablet PC, OneNote can not only help you take notes, but also record the meeting itself. To turn on the audio-recording feature in OneNote, simply tap the **Record** button on the Audio Recording toolbar, as shown in Figure 16.23.

Double-Checking Ideas from a Meeting

If you have ever gotten back to your desk after a meeting, answered some phone calls and email, and then had a tough time understanding why you wrote the notes you wrote, OneNote can help!

In OneNote, you can listen to the audio that was recorded during a meeting. But wait, there's more: You can identify the notes about which you want to find more information, and OneNote will play back the audio from the point in the meeting at which those notes were taken.

tip

You can review a meeting as you drive by having your Tablet PC play back the audio from the meeting in the car. A simple cassette adapter or radio transmitter will let you listen over your car speakers.

Figure 16.24 shows an audio-playback icon next to a section of notes. If I double-tap the icon, the audio will begin playback at the point in the audio at which I took the notes. So if I was 15 minutes into the meeting when I jotted down a particular observation, I can begin the audio at the 15-minute marker just by double-tapping the audio icon next to the note to which it relates.

When playback begins, it will probably start well into the recording, as shown in Figure 16.25; this figure was shot after I double-tapped the speaker icon shown in Figure 16.24.

FIGURE 16.24

Double-tap the speaker icon next to a note to hear what was said when you were writing.

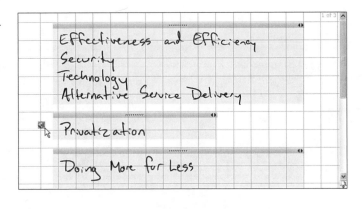

FIGURE 16.25

Audio begins playback from the time tied to the note you tapped on.

Using OneNote for Information Gathering

Not only is OneNote a great tool for meetings, it is also a great tool for doing research on the Web. It's easy to drag-and-drop Web content into OneNote. OneNote actually keeps the formatting of the source most of the time, making the research you do look good.

Drag-and-Drop Web Pages

Because you can move objects around easily in OneNote, you can make connections between items in your research results, drawing lines to connect related ideas and taking notes on things that stand out to you.

Figure 16.26 shows what a Web page about home MP3 players looks like when I dragged it into OneNote.

Although OneNote does its best, it is certainly not perfect when it comes to formatting Web pages. One of the main problems I've seen is with tables and frames. If you select just the text or graphics you want to include, however, you'll have better results.

tip

When dropping Web pages into OneNote, select the text or graphics you want to copy. Make it as simple as possible for the best results.

FIGURE 16.26

OneNote tries to keep source formatting for dropped-in Web pages.

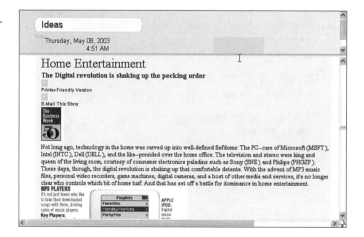

When you drop in a Web page, OneNote also inserts the URL of the source Web page so you can return there for more information. Of course, retaining the source page's formatting a bit better would be helpful, but it would be almost impossible to make every page look exactly the same in OneNote as it does in your browser. (Of course, you could always take a screen shot of the page and drop it into OneNote, but then you would lose the text-editing capability.)

THE ABSOLUTE MINIMUM

Here are the key points to take away from this chapter:

- OneNote is one of the best applications made for the Tablet PC. It can handle all sorts of content, such as handwriting, text, graphics, and audio.

- You can easily navigate your notes in OneNote by organizing them into sections and pages.

- Keeping objects separated is important if you want to treat ideas separately.

- Voluminous handwritten notes can be converted to text easily.

- Audio recording in OneNote links the audio to the notes taken over time, so that the conversation at the point in time that you take a set of notes is tied to those notes. You can access the audio recording directly from the notes.

- Web pages can be dropped into OneNote for help in research and information gathering.

EXTENDING YOUR TABLET PC

17

Hardware Options

From cameras and wireless communication to biometric security devices and barcode scanners, the Tablet PC is a platform that can be extended to meet the needs of many people.

Docking Stations

There are several options for docking stations. Some manufacturers, such as Compaq and Fujitsu, have docking stations specifically designed for their tablets. If your Tablet PC has that option, and if you're looking to buy a docking station, I recommended you try the docking station offered by your tablet's manufacturer first, because it will probably provide more functionality than a generic docking station.

What to Look For

Your connection options are USB and PC card interfaces. USB will not be able to offer the same capabilities as a PC card interface, but a USB docking station will be able to offer the main ports that you'll need.

MOBILITY ELECTRONICS EASIDOCK 1000EV

One docking-station option is the EasiDock 1000EV from Mobility Electronics. It is also sold as the docking solution for the Acer Tablet PC, and can be ordered from CDW and many other retailers.

The EasiDock connects to the Tablet PC or other laptop with a CardBus interface. It has ports for PS/2 mouse and keyboard, a serial port, a parallel port, and two USB ports. It also contains a video adapter that allows you to add an additional display, offering a third screen for most Tablet PCs.

The EasiDock 1000EV lets you add additional ports to your Tablet PC by simply inserting a CardBus card.

Special Features: CardBus adapter, includes extra video adapter and multiple ports

Where to Buy: PriceGrabber.com, CDW

Input Devices

The Tablet PC platform by nature begs for external input devices. If you don't want to attach a keyboard to your slate, you probably want a mouse or a headset for easier input. This section covers the main input devices for the Tablet PC, and provides suggestions for how to get the most out of each device.

Keyboards

Unless you have a docking station that supports a PS/2 keyboard, the USB keyboard is your only choice for a wired connection. Fortunately, there are myriad options for USB keyboards. If you have Bluetooth capability, you can use a Bluetooth-enabled keyboard, such as the Microsoft Bluetooth keyboard.

What to Look For

The main thing to look for is a keyboard that works with your Tablet PC. Chances are you'll be looking for a USB keyboard, so that will narrow your options considerably.

After you've hammered out the interface issue (that is, whether the keyboard should be USB, PS/2, or Bluetooth), you will want to look at the keyboard layout. Keyboards can be straight, curved, tilted, and flat. Most keyboards have standard-size keys, but some will be smaller to save space.

Once you've determined what style of keyboard feels best to you, narrow down the options by examining the various keyboards' extra features. If you don't need any, go for the basic model that feels good to you. Otherwise, identify which of the many keyboard add-ons you want: scroll wheels, surf buttons, application buttons, pointing devices, and programmable buttons.

MICROSOFT WIRELESS OPTICAL DESKTOP FOR BLUETOOTH

The Microsoft Wireless Optical Desktop for Bluetooth includes a keyboard and mouse that works with Bluetooth to provide wireless input on your Tablet PC. Whether or not your Tablet PC includes Bluetooth, you can use this dynamic duo. It includes a Bluetooth adapter. If you don't need it, great. Bluetooth will let you use your keyboard and mouse up to 30 feet away from your Tablet PC.

The Microsoft Wireless Optical Desktop for Bluetooth includes a keyboard and a mouse that use Bluetooth to communicate with the Tablet PC.

Special Features:	Bluetooth, programmable keys, ergonomic design
Where to Buy:	Office-supply and electronics stores

Mice

USB mice are your only options for wired connections unless you have a PS/2-capable port replicator. There are many types and brands. I recommend the Logitech Wheel Mouse, which isoptical and has a scroll wheel. The optical aspect of the mouse provides superior tracking on all but reflective surfaces (glass or high-gloss). Optical mice do not have the problems of dirty tracking balls and are better for travel because they work on most surfaces. I don't even use a mouse pad with my mouse in most places. If you happen to have a glossy surface and no mouse pad, just use a piece of paper or a low-gloss magazine.

Another option is the Bluetooth mouse. If your Tablet PC is set up to use Bluetooth, a mouse like Microsoft's Bluetooth mouse can be useful because it requires no wires.

What to Look For

Optical is the way to go for most users. Optical mice track well, and don't require cleaning. They can also operate on a sheet of paper or magazine. Wired mice are usually okay, but wireless mice have the benefits of reducing wire tangles.

KENSINGTON POCKETMOUSE PRO WIRELESS

Kensington makes a great little wireless mouse that's a fantastic companion for the mobile Tablet PC. The wireless adapter is small and connects to a USB port. When not in use, the wireless adapter can be stored in the mouse body, which then turns off the wireless equipment to save battery power. This is a small mouse, which is tough on large hands, but the portability and wireless feature makes it great for when you're traveling.

The Kensington PocketMouse Pro Wireless is small and a great addition to the Tablet PC.

Special Features: Wireless, small USB adapter

Where to Buy: Office-supply and electronics stores

Upgraded Pens

The pens that are available to you depend on the Tablet PC you use. If you use a Wacom-based Tablet PC, you will have more options than with other systems. Wacom and Cross, for example, are coming out with executive-style pens that look more like traditional high-end pens.

Because Tablet PCs like the Compaq use a battery-operated pen, the barrel cannot be much thinner than the one that comes with the tablet, which limits the ergonomics of potential pens.

Check with your Tablet PC manufacturer to find out what pens can be used with your Tablet PC. If you have a Wacom-based digitizer in your Tablet PC, you can go to Wacom's site (www.wacom.com) to find some additional pens.

What to Look For

Look for a pen that feels good in your hand and that also has the features you want. Some come with eraser tips on the back end (just like a pencil), and some come with switches on the barrel for right-tapping or assigning other functions. A good pen will let you work naturally.

Headsets

Headsets are kind of like headphones, except with a microphone. Headsets are usually the preferred way to speak to your computer, because they provide a close microphone and greater clarity of input.

When you look for a headset, you want to find one that is noise canceling, which means it disregards extraneous noise when you talk. This will give you the most accurate voice recognition.

There are many types of headsets, and unfortunately, many are incompatible with computers. Most are made for telephones, and are not readily compatible with the PC interface. You can get adapters for the ones that use the mini jack for cell phones, but the headsets made for stationary telephone sets are usually incompatible.

That said, you can find various types of headsets for use with your Tablet PC—ones that enclose your ears, that sit on your ears, that clip around one ear, and that wrap around your head.

I used the Logitech Internet Chat Headset and the Plantronics DSP-400 headset while I wrote this book and dictated chapters; I have included details about each in the following sidebars.

What to Look For

Find a headset that is noise-canceling. That's the most important aspect of the microphone. It will eliminate surrounding noise. Other than noise cancellation, the headphones should be comfortable, lightweight, and offer the audio performance you require. If you want a stereo headset, make sure you get one with two earcups or earpads that provide stereo sound. Otherwise, there are many headsets that provide monaural (mono) audio playback in a single ear, which may be sufficient for you.

Typically, the more padded the headset, the more comfortable it will be, but always try it on and think of how it will feel in a two-hour dictation session. If there's anything that bugs you about it when you first try it on, go to another headset. It's not worth being uncomfortable, because you won't use it as much if it is.

LOGITECH INTERNET CHAT HEADSET

The Logitech Internet Chat headset has excellent noise-canceling capability. As I am dictating this sentence, I'm flying in an airplane, and the recognition capability is still acceptable. For the price, this is a good headset. Sound quality from the headphones is not superb, but the microphone quality is excellent.

The Logitech Internet Chat Headset is a stylish, lightweight voice-recognition companion.

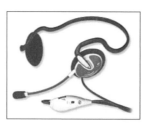

Special Features: Small, noise-canceling

Where to Buy: Office and electronics stores

PLANTRONICS DSP-400 FOLDABLE PC HEADSET

Another good choice is the Plantronics brand of headsets. Plantronics has been in the headset business for years, and offers a wide range of products. I have used the DSP-400, and found it to offer good sound quality and voice recognition. Although it is foldable, it is cumbersome with the audio adapter that plugs into your USB port. The headset adapter is an actual sound card, so it bumps up the quality of sound in low-end machines.

The Plantronics DSP-400 is another good voice-dictation headset that provides good audio sound as well.

Special Features: External sound adapter, foldable design
Where to Buy: Best Buy, PriceGrabber.com

Microphones

Microphones are similar to headsets in that they provide for voice input. However, they are usually stand-alone, and don't connect to your head. Most microphones for computers sit on a desk or attach to a monitor.

What to Look For

If you're looking for a microphone for speech recognition, it should be of the noise-canceling variety.

SONY ECM-ZS90 MICROPHONE

The best microphone I've looked at is the Sony ECM-ZS90 Switchable Stereo Microphone. This is a noise-canceling microphone that allows you to switch from super-directional (which enables you to pick out a sound source even from a great distance, such as a speaker in a lecture hall) to omni-directional (this mode functions much like a conference telephone, allowing you to pick up all the sounds within a more limited distance. I just wish I'd had one of these microphones and a Tablet PC when I was in my MBA program...).

The Sony ECM-ZS90 is a great microphone that has dual personalities: super-directional and omni-directional.

Special Features:	Switchable super- and omni-directional
Where to Buy:	PriceGrabber.com

Storage Devices

There are numerous types of storage devices, from drives to memory cards that are as small as the tip of your thumb. The type of storage device you use depends on your needs.

If you're looking for massive storage, you probably need an external hard drive. For more portable storage, however, you'll probably want to consider card-type storage media or USB key drives.

External USB 2.0 and FireWire Hard Drives

External USB and FireWire hard drives come in sizes ranging up to 250 GB, and will keep getting bigger. As digital media file collections grow, so too will the sizes of the storage equipment. Expect large external drives to remain the highest capacity options for storing and retrieving data well into the future.

note

This chapter covers only the peripherals that you can carry with you; it does not discuss drive arrays or other larger storage systems.

What to Look For

Look for USB 2.0 or FireWire, depending on which one your Tablet PC supports. Don't buy a USB 1.x drive even if your Tablet PC only handles USB 1.x. You might upgrade in the future, and your drive speed will remain slow. USB 2.0 is about 10 times faster than the previous version, and for data transfer, that's huge.

Other things to look for are the size and portability of the drives. Most will require access to AC power (or you can use an inverter for access in your car).

caution

Realize that by having data stored on portable media, it is also more susceptible to getting in the wrong hands. Protect your external media and use encryption tools if you have them.

WESTERN DIGITAL 250 GB FIREWIRE/USB 2.0 COMBO DRIVE

The WD 250 GB drive is a high-end drive that spins at 7200 RPM—faster than most hard drives. This enables it to have a higher data-transfer speed, retrieving your files faster. This is especially useful in digital media applications where video is stored on the drive. This drive also has a new look.

The Western Digital 250 GB USB/FireWire drive sports a new look and fast data transfer speeds.

Special Features:	Large capacity, fast drive, speedy interface, lots of cache
Where to Buy:	WDC.com

USB Flash Drives

USB flash drives are small, highlighter-size memory devices that plug into a USB port. As of this writing, these devices enable you to store up to 4 GB of data. I'm sure that as they pack more on a chip, the sizes will grow.

Some flash drives, such as the Gruvstick by CenDyne, or the MP3-BD256 by BUSlink, come with a built-in MP3 player and voice recorder, but most are just digital storage devices.

What to Look For

Although USB 2.0 devices should be faster than 1.1 devices, they rarely are, because the speed to read and write non-volatile memory is much slower than reading from a hard drive. All the same, USB 2.0 devices may offer a bit of an advantage.

Also look for any special features, such as MP3 playback, voice recording, and ActiveDisk support. ActiveDisk is something that the Iomega devices offer, which allows an application to run from the flash drive without being installed on the host machine. Not all applications support ActiveDisk, but many do.

IOMEGA 512 MB MINI USB DRIVE

The Iomega Mini USB drive is one of many out there. One of the few differentiators with this device is its support of ActiveDisk portable software. Otherwise, it is just like other USB memory sticks.

The Iomega
Mini USB drive
is a small,
keychain-size
device that can
store lots of
data, photos,
and ActiveDisk
applications.

Special Features:	ActiveDisk support, USB 2.0
Where to Buy:	iomega.com, CDW.com

Other Digital Media Options

SecureDigital, CompactFlash, XD, Memory Stick, and CardBus are all different storage formats for non-volatile memory products that can store gigabytes of data in the palm of your hand. Many Tablet PCs offer direct access to these media devices. For example, my Toshiba Portégé 3500 has an SD card slot and a CompactFlash card slot in addition to the standard CardBus slot. If that sounds confusing, it is. No single media has taken hold of the industry. As usual, Sony is trying to take the market with its Memory Stick media, while other manufacturers support various other media.

SD and XD cards are postage stamp–sized solid-state memory cards. This means they can be thrown around without jarring any mechanisms, unlike small hard drives.

What to Look For

If you need some portable storage, the main thing to look for is capacity, and the format that is easiest for your Tablet PC and the recipient's machine to accept. This could be any of the media formats. Just realize that none of the solid state memory products are going to be as fast as a hard drive. Sounds crazy, but the technology limits the speed of access and writing. Writing is slower than reading on any of the media formats.

HITACHI 1 GB MICRODRIVE

One exception is the Hitachi Microdrive (Hitachi bought IBM's disk drive business), which is a CompactFlash II device that can also be inserted into a PC card sleeve to be read from a PC card slot. I use a 1 GB MicroDrive in my camera, then take it out and insert it directly into my Tablet PC. It shows up as a hard drive (as all of these devices do), and I can then just move the images across. Hitachi is also coming out with a 4 GB version soon.

The Hitachi 1 GB Microdrive offers great speed, ruggedness, and lots of storage for digital media and files.

Special Features:	Small hard drive, high storage capacity, fast access, CF II format
Where to Buy:	Computer stores and online (CDW)

Bluetooth

Bluetooth is a wireless communication standard that allows devices in close proximity to communicate. Cell phones, headsets, PDAs, computers, cameras, mice, keyboards, printers, and many other devices are beginning to use Bluetooth to communicate. The service range is 10 meters, or 30 feet, so it is not good over long distances (Wi-Fi can connect over 100 meters).

Some Tablet PCs include Bluetooth, while others require a Bluetooth adapter. These adapters can be PC card, USB, CF card, and other form factors. If you have several of devices that you would like to connect easily, consider Bluetooth. If your current devices don't have Bluetooth, you can replace them over time when you consider upgrades.

Note that Bluetooth technology is based upon the 2.4 GHz unlicensed band, so it has the potential to conflict with other devices such as microwave ovens, baby monitors, cordless phones, and more. Bluetooth and Wi-Fi work together, but may experience some interference issues with each other.

One great use for Bluetooth is having a Bluetooth mouse and keyboard; You do not have to physically connect them, and they can be several feet away from your Tablet PC. Likewise, a Bluetooth phone can allow you to connect to the Internet or to your office from a remote location.

One limitation of Bluetooth is that each device has its own profile, or way of communicating with other devices. As of this writing, I have not been able to get a Bluetooth headset to connect to my Tablet PC, while it will easily connect to a Bluetooth-enabled cell phone. That's because the phones include the headset profile, while the Tablet PC does not.

There are numerous Bluetooth products on the market, and more are coming out each quarter. If you want to be as mobile as possible, use Bluetooth to gain freedom from wires. Now they just need to come up with wireless power…

3COM WIRELESS BLUETOOTH USB ADAPTER

The 3Com Bluetooth adapter lets you easily connect your Tablet PC to other Bluetooth devices. Work without wires and conserve your bag space with this small adapter.

The 3Com Bluetooth adapter enables your Tablet PC to connect to Bluetooth devices.

Special Features:	Small
Where to Buy:	CDW

HP BLUETOOTH WIRELESS PRINTER ADAPTER

The HP Bluetooth adapter lets you connect your old parallel printer without wires. Using Bluetooth, the adapter transfers data to the printer from across the room.

The HP
Bluetooth
printer adapter
enables your
Tablet PC to
connect to a
USB printer via
Bluetooth.

Special Features: Works with parallel printers
Where to Buy: CDW

Security Devices

Because your Tablet PC is so portable, it might just choose to get up and leave with a little help from someone else. There are numerous ways to protect your Tablet PC from thieves and intruders. Listed below are a few options.

Theft-Prevention Devices

There are several ways to protect your Tablet PC from theft. One of the most common is to use a cable lock that ties into your Tablet PC's security slot. It then connects to a heavy object, like a piece of furniture, to protect from theft. There are also alarms and security lockers available. One alarm I'd recommend is the Targus DEFCON 1.

TARGUS DEFCON 1 SECURITY ALARM

The Targus DEFCON 1 is a great way to protect your Tablet PC and other items from tampering or theft. With its motion sensor, unless you unlock it, the alarm will set off a 95 dB alarm to alert you of the intrusion.

The Targus DEF-
CON 1 can pro-
tect your Tablet
PC and belong-
ings from theft
and tampering.

Special Features:	Motion sensor, uses security slot on Tablet PC, alarm
Where to Buy:	Electronics and computer stores

Data Access Protection

Protecting from physical theft is one thing, but what about protecting your Tablet PC from someone who just wants your data? There are several ways to protect yourself from data theft, including security cards, password generators, and biometric (fingerprint and retinal scan) devices. Fortunately, the Windows XP operating system is built for data protection, unlike the Windows 9x and Me operating systems. This means that with the appropriate security access, your Tablet PC can be hardened against prying eyes.

> **caution**
>
> It is crucial that you at least consider access and data protection. Your files and the work they represent are at jeopardy. At the minimum, you should read Chapter 11, "Keeping Your Data Safe and Synchronized."

Access Control Devices

There are numerous hardware solutions for login and data-access security, including USB keys (about the size of USB flash drives), Smart Cards, and others. Each solution requires a hardware/software combination to protect your machine. Usually, a client application is loaded onto your machine; this application looks for the hardware piece when login occurs.

What to Look For

Look for devices that work the way you want to, without providing too much of a barrier to the way you use your machine. Some Tablet PCs (such as the Acer) include a Smart Card reader, so it makes sense to use what your platform supports. If your Tablet PC does not have built-in support for security cards, you can always get a USB or PC card–compatible device.

> **tip**
>
> If you're interested in more information about security products for your Tablet PC, look at www.scmagazine.com, which is the Web site for *Secure Computing Magazine*.

GRIFFIN TECHNOLOGIES SECURIKEY PERSONAL

The SecuriKey USB key protects your computer by requiring that the SecuriKey device be connected to your machine before you can access protected data. The software installs easily to let you define your levels of protection. Then it requires the same SecuriKey device to be attached when you access the secure data.

The SecuriKey USB access control device and software prevents people from accessing your data unless they havethe SecuriKey device used to encrypt your data.

Special Features: USB-based two-factor authentication

Where to Buy: TigerDirect.com

Biometric Devices

There are numerous biometric devices available for mobile computers, mostly based on fingerprint scanning. The intricacies involved in getting the software and hardware to work together preclude this from inclusion here, but if you want fingerprint-based security, you may want to look to manufacturers such as Precise Biometrics (www.precisebiometrics.com), or research this online. I just wanted point out that it is available if you have a need for this type of security measure.

Cell Phones

Phones like the Sony Ericsson T68i, Motorola V600, and Nokia 3650 can all use Bluetooth to communicate with the Tablet PC to share data and provide mobile Internet access. You can synchronize contact information not just through a cable interface, but through a wireless Bluetooth connection.

I used a T68i for a week, and it worked well with Bluetooth and my Tablet PC. While my wife was driving, I was able to connect to the Internet at 60 MPH. I also used a Bluetooth headset, which let me talk with the phone in my pocket and the headset around my ear. Not everyone has the need for wireless data, but it may come in handy with a computer as portable as the Tablet PC.

Other phones enable cable and infrared connectivity options, still enabling access to the Internet through a GPRS connection. You must find a cell phone service provider that handles phones with GPRS, and most major carriers do. When I was testing the T68i, it came with service from Cingular Wireless. AT&T Wireless also supports GPRS and Bluetooth-enabled phones. At the time of this writing, Verizon did not offer any Bluetooth phones.

What to Look For

Features to look for in addition to connectivity are things such as contact management, email synchronization, and Multimedia Messaging Service (MMS), which enables you to send pictures and, in some cases, have a mini video conference.

There is no doubt that a cell phone that holds your contacts and that can read email will benefit you through even greater portability than the Tablet PC. Used together, the cell phone and Tablet PC can be a powerful duo for highly mobile professionals.

Another feature to look for is GPS. GPS capability lets you locate your position in the world if you're lost, but in the case of phones, enables all sorts of new options, such as finding the nearest restaurant when you're walking or driving around. It can also be used for emergency location tracking so people can find you if you're hurt or lost. Privacy issues abound, but the technology is worth looking into.

Nextel is just starting to test its T1 speed data service. I haven't tried it yet, but it should be here by the time you're reading this. I don't know the price tag for such service, but usually, the GPRS service is expensive, so only those who really need it should consider the mobile Internet.

NOKIA 3650

This is the phone that has almost everything—voice command; Java capability; Real Media player; video recorder; camera; Bluetooth; calculator; and more. It can handle email and talk to your Tablet PC through Bluetooth, keeping you up to date when you're on the road.

The Nokia 3650 is a phone with tons of features.

Special Features:	Bluetooth, GPRS, voice dialing, camera
Where to Buy:	AT&T Wireless, T-Mobile

Headphones

Headphones are necessary to the extent that you use them to listen to digital music or digital audio books. If you intend to listen to either of these digital audio formats, good quality headphones are essential. Especially when you're traveling such as in an airplane or on a train, noise canceling and noise reduction technologies are important.

Headphones such as the Bose QuietComfort headphones envelop your ears in what are called "cans." The QuietComfort headphones have small microphones built into the outside of the headphone cover, enabling them to interpret the outside sounds and provide noise canceling waveforms that reduce or eliminate ambient noise. The Shure E5c headset, on the other hand, features and in-ear design that shuts out noise by blocking out ambient sound.

In addition to noise-reduction headphones, the standard types of headphones will also work, but they do not reduce noise.

Open-Air Stereophile Headphones

Some of the best headphones I've ever listened to do not provide noise reduction. In quieter environments, the Sennheiser headphones are among the best I've heard. They allow you to listen to environmental sounds (such as your spouse calling you for dinner) through an open air design, which keeps your ears from getting hot (which does occur when you use headphones with cans), yet provides highly accurate sound reproduction.

SENNHEISER HD 590-V1 HEADPHONES

If you're looking for excellent sound quality, comfort, and an open-air design for relatively quiet environments, Sennheiser open headphones are a great choice. The HD 590-V1are top-of-the-line headphones designed for serious audio enthusiasts. If you rip your CDs at less than 256Kb/s, you probably don't need headphones of this quality, however, because they will cause you to notice some flaws in your MP3s.

The Sennheiser HD 590-V1 headphones are for real audio enthusiasts.

Special Features:	Open-air design, audiophile sound reproduction
Where to Buy:	PriceTool.com, electronics stores

Active Noise Reduction (ANR) Headphones

Active noise reduction (ANR) cancels out noise with canceling waves—that is, sound waves that are produced to eliminate noise by emitting a wave of the opposite form as the noise. This reduces ambient noise significantly.

BOSE QUIETCOMFORT 2 HEADPHONES

Bose is well-known in consumer circles as a high-quality speaker manufacturer. Fortunately for us, the company has applied its expertise to a headset that you'll enjoy wearing on airplanes and in other noisy environments. The QuietComfort 2 headphones use active noise reduction (ANR) to sample the sounds in the environment, and then create canceling waveforms that eliminate the steady noises of airplane and car sounds and the like.

One of the great benefits of the QuietComfort headphones (versus sound isolation) is that you can still hear people around you. That may sound bad, but actually, it helps you hear the person next to you on an airplane better because the ambient noise is effectively eliminated or reduced. One other feature that the QuietComfort 2 headphones have that the first generation doesn't is the ability to disconnect the cable from the headphones when you just want noise reduction and don't want to listen to music. It allows you to get the benefits of noise reduction without the wire.

In fact, I'm using them right now as I watch the sun rise on my way to Florida on an airplane at 30,000 feet. I barely hear the sound of the airplane as I listen to some MP3 jazz playing from my Tablet PC. It's not because of the music that I can barely hear the plane; the headphone cans block some of the noise, but I can tell a definite difference when I turn off the noise-reduction switch. The rumble returns in force.

The Bose QuietComfort 2 headphones improve on the original design with folding ear cups for flatter storage.

| Special Features: | Active Noise Reduction, foldable, great sound quality |
| Where to Buy: | Bose.com |

Sound Isolating Earphones

Sound isolation is another way to approach noise reduction: it limits the noise that enters the ear instead of canceling it. Sound-isolating earphones are in-ear speakers similar to ear buds, but with sound-isolation qualities. They form a seal in your ear that reduces ambient noise.

SHURE E5C IN-EAR SOUND ISOLATING EARPHONES

These earphones reduce or eliminate noise by sealing the ear canal with a custom-fit ear adapter. When you place the earphones into your ears, most of the ambient noise disappears. When you turn on your music, you have incredible dynamic range and clear audio quality.

The E5c earphones are the top-of-the-line earphones, and will cost up to $500. However, they are a listening pleasure for the discriminating ear.

The Shure E5c earphones pack a lot of great sound into tiny in-ear packages.

Special Features:	Sound isolation, small, great sound quality
Where to Buy:	Shure.com

Standard Headphones

For most of us who want decent sound for not a lot of money, a pair of traditional headphones from your local electronics store should be sufficient. When I don't want the bulkier or more intrusive noise-canceling headphones, I usually use a pair of in-ear headphones that pack easily. About $20 or $30 will get you a good pair that you can beat up without worrying about them.

Most of all, look for comfort and sound quality. Most headphones claim a good dynamic range, which will reproduce most sounds well. If you're listening to audio books or low-quality MP3s, the quality won't matter quite as much.

Power Accessories

For now, no laptop can last all day. Even eight hours won't handle everything you may need, but most Tablet PCs offer only between two and four hours of battery life. This leaves a large need for lots of juice.

If you travel a lot, you will need alternate power. You'll probably want to have extra batteries (I carry two extra) on hand. More than one AC adapter is common (I leave one at the office, one at home, and one in my bag) and probably desired. A car adapter or AC/DC inverter can help if you're car-bound. And an airline adapter can help if you're often on an airplane.

Batteries

You have few options for batteries for your Tablet PC. Usually the manufacturer of your Tablet PC is the only one making batteries for it, although there may be others available.

AC Adapters

It's ideal to keep one adapter in the office, one at home, and one in your travel bag, though two will suffice if you don't travel often. There are few options other than the manufacturer's adapter, but the iGo Juice 70 is an interesting product, as described in the sidebar.

IGO JUICE 70 AC AND AUTO/AIR POWER ADAPTER

The Juice 70 is a 70-watt power adapter that plugs into AC outlets, car power outlets, and even airline armrests. This makes the Juice 70 the only power adapter you need.

The Juice 70 can make your traveling load lighter by combining AC, DC, and air power options into one unit.

Special Features:	Lightweight, triple-use adapter with tips for various notebooks and devices
Where to Buy:	iGo.com, CDW

Car Adapters and Inverters

Car adapters may be available for your Tablet PC from the manufacturer. If not, there are inverters that can do the trick, but they take up more space. An inverter changes the power coming from your car into power that can be handled by your Tablet PC or other AC-hungry devices (phones, cameras, personal audio players, and so on).

What to Look For

Look for an inverter that handles the power load and number of outlets you need. Some inverters have one outlet, others have two. I bought a one-outlet inverter and often want the second outlet (especially when in the car with the family). The maximum power load is important as well, because you'll want to provide enough power for your Tablet PC.

APC MOBILE POWER 140W INVERTER

APC is one of the best-known companies for PC-related power devices. The Mobile Power inverter provides power from your car to give juice to all your portable devices. If you need more power, look into APC's 340 W version, which has two outlets.

The APC inverter can keep your Tablet PC running when you're away from a power outlet.

Special Features:	Lightweight, low voltage disconnect
Where to Buy:	Electronics stores

Airline Adapters

Airline adapters connect your Tablet PC to the power outlet that may be available in a commercial airplane. These can be purchased from your travel and luggage store, or from a computer store such as CompUSA. There are a couple different airline power types, so be sure to get a package with both.

International Adapters

Your local travel store will have a slew of international adapters. You will need them when traveling to many other countries. These can be purchased from your travel and luggage store, or from a computer store such as CompUSA. As long as the adapter converts your plug to the destination locale's plug style, you'll be okay. Just make sure your travel destination uses the same input voltage as your home. For example, most countries use 110–120 volt AC power, which is compatible with most types of U.S. electronic equipment.

Other Complementary Devices

There are many more items that you could add on to your Tablet PC, but I'll cover the basic three here: scanning devices, photo-capturing devices, and printing devices. The Tablet PC is the perfect platform for storing digitized print, such as scanned documents, as well as digital photographs. Being able to print them for others who aren't fortunate enough to have a Tablet PC will probably be required at some point.

Scanners

Windows XP has excellent tools for getting the most out of scanners and cameras. Office XP and 2003 also offer the Office Document Scanning utility, which helps you scan and even use Optical Character Recognition (OCR) on your documents and images. This utility lets you scan text into your Word documents directly, without retyping. It is quite accurate, but stray marks and strange fonts can yield text that requires editing.

I recommend using a USB-based scanner. One that uses USB 2.0 will have a faster data throughput than one that uses USB 1.1. However, both your machine and the scanner need to support USB 2.0 for you to gain the speed benefit. Several Tablet PCs include USB 2.0, such as the Toshiba Portégé 3500.

Using scanners is a great way to avoid having to re-type a document, and they can also help you digitize photographs, articles, and more. Coupled with Adobe Acrobat, you can even convert articles to PDF format for later viewing on your Tablet PC so that you don't have to carry the paper version. This allows you to have a permanent copy of the article while being able to edit it in Acrobat (Acrobat Reader will not let you modify the document).

What to Look For

Look for the resolution you need with an interface that matches your Tablet PC (FireWire or USB). Also, look for at least 300 dpi (most scanners today are more than 1200 dpi) and 16-bit color. You will probably want it to include OCR software for converting pages to text.

Digital Cameras

This is an obvious extension for many who work out in the field. Insurance adjusters, construction supervisors, maintenance professionals, and many others can benefit from a built-in or linked camera.

There are several types of cameras that can be used with a Tablet PC, and some tablets may include cameras in the near future.

Overall, there are several ways to connect your Tablet PC to your digital camera. First is the traditional digital camera with a USB adapter; you simply plug in the USB cable when you are ready to transfer data. In many cases, you can control the camera from the computer when it is attached. You could, for example, set the camera on a tripod and zoom in/out and take pictures via your tablet. This could be an excellent tool for the digital photography studio.

Another type of digital camera has Bluetooth or infrared capabilities. This type of camera can connect and transfer data without any wires. With a camera like this, you could even have the camera mounted on a head strap like a miner's cap, or on a tripod, and control it from your Tablet PC—hands-free digital photography. Currently, however, there are few options for Bluetooth-enabled cameras.

A PC-card camera enables you to integrate the camera into the Tablet PC. No wires, no wireless. It is now a part of your computer. This can be handy for several applications, but probably will not yield the best results. As cameras get smaller, however, this may become more viable.

To find an updated list of cameras that I recommend, visit my Web site at www.TabletGuru.com and search for the term "digital camera." Because this field changes so quickly, I don't want to include a lot of details about the various models available here. I currently use the Canon G1, which is an excellent camera, but a few years old. It accepts the IBM Microdrive, which holds around 500 pictures. That may sound like a lot, but I'm a big believer in shooting first and cropping later. (I took 3,000 pictures on my last family vacation.)

Printers

If you're interested in wireless connectivity to your printer, you can use a Bluetooth-enabled printer, infrared-enabled printer, or add-on devices such as the 3Com or HP Bluetooth printer adapters. Most Tablet PCs will not have legacy devices such as parallel or serial connectors, so you will need either a wireless connection to the printer, a USB-based printer, or a printer connected to your home or office network.

Make sure that your printer supports Windows XP. Many older printers do not. If it supports Windows XP, then it will support Windows XP, Tablet PC Edition.

You will especially want to make sure the printer can handle photo-quality printing, enabling you to make physical copies of your digital photos.

THE ABSOLUTE MINIMUM

Here are the key points to take away from this chapter:

- Your Tablet PC is the base of your computing platform, on which you can add numerous devices to increase your enjoyment, security, and ease of use.

- Find a keyboard and/or mouse that helps you get your work done more efficiently—especially if your Tablet PC does not include a keyboard.

- With the voice capabilities of the Tablet PC, you will want to have a good headset for voice recognition. If you get a stereo headset, you will also be able to use it for listening to digital audio.

- If you have needs for portable storage (or backups), look into options for external or add-on storage, such as USB drives and USB flash drives.

- Bluetooth offers wireless communication with devices such as cell phones, mice and keyboards, and PDAs. If you want to connect your devices, consider using Bluetooth to untangle the wires.

- Consider options for protecting both your Tablet PC and the valuable data it contains. Often, the theft of a machine or loss of data is not as critical in business environments that have good backup practices. Where the problem arises is the data that the thief then has access to. At the very least, protect yourself with a data-protection tool such as a USB key.

- Consider all your power needs—extra batteries, AC adapters, and travel power sources such as inverters and airline adapters.

- Scanners, digital cameras, and photo-quality printers are excellent additions to the Tablet PC. With its ability to store digital paper and photographs, the Tablet PC is a perfect platform for reading and viewing. Because you'll store digital content on your Tablet PC, also think about the printer you'll need to maximize your experience.

18

Useful Software

There is no reason to buy a computing platform if there's no software to support it; being able to find software for your Tablet PC that helps you do your job more effectively is of critical importance. Because the Tablet PC is such a new platform, however, there is not yet available a plethora of Tablet PC–specific software. That said, there are numerous applications available for use on a Tablet PC, some of which are beginning to make the Tablet PC an indispensable tool for certain functions. Many of these applications can be also be used on a regular computer, without much sacrifice in capability.

I have included in this chapter a list of free and commercial general-purpose software that can help you perform various functions on your Tablet PC. (For information about niche applications, such as vertical industry applications, see the table at the end of the chapter.) I've included only those applications that I feel are the best in their class. For the sake of brevity, I have described each application in a minimal fashion, and have omitted details about how each one is used. Instead, I've explained their main features, and noted each application's intended audience. For more information about a particular application, visit its manufacturer's Web site.

Free Software

There's a lot of free software available, and several applications that are Tablet PC oriented. In this section you'll see readers, graphic tools, and productivity enhancers. Even though these applications are free, they still pack a lot of power.

Readers

Readers are applications that display digital content, such as eBooks and digital journals. For example, many magazines and journals are now published in electronic format, allowing you to use your Tablet PC as a reading platform.

tip

Just because these applications are free does not mean they aren't commercial quality. In fact, some of them have received awards as best products in particular categories. Try these first before forking out a ton of cash.

The Tablet PC is the perfect computer for enabling eBooks, because it's small and can be held in the hands like a book. You can download free and for-cost eBooks from numerous sites, listed here:

Amazon:	http://www.amazon.com/ebooks
eBooks.com:	http://www.ebooks.com
eBook-Hub:	http://www.ebook-hub.com
eBook Mall:	http://www.ebookmall.com
netLibrary:	http://www.netlibrary.com
PlanetPDF:	http://www.planetpdf.com
UVa eBook Library:	http://etext.lib.virginia.edu/ebooks/ebooklist.html

This is not a complete listing of sites that deal with eBooks, but it should meet most people's needs. The last link (University of Virginia) is a great source for classic works for free.

Adobe Acrobat Reader

Target users: Everyone

Web site: http://www.adobe.com

The most common of the readers is Adobe
Acrobat Reader. Most computer users have
encountered Acrobat PDF documents, like the
one shown in Figure 18.1.

Acrobat Reader is the viewing application, which
Adobe distributes free of charge. Acrobat
Professional, on the other hand, is the applica-
tion that lets you create and edit PDFs of your

tip

ScanSoft RealSpeak can
turn electronic books into
audio books through the
most human-like
text-to-speech engine
around.

own. Printing your files to PDF format (if you have the Professional version) lets you
store digital files that look exactly like the original. Anyone can then read the files
in Acrobat Reader.

FIGURE 18.1

Here's my
chocolate
chip–cookie
recipe in
Acrobat PDF
format.

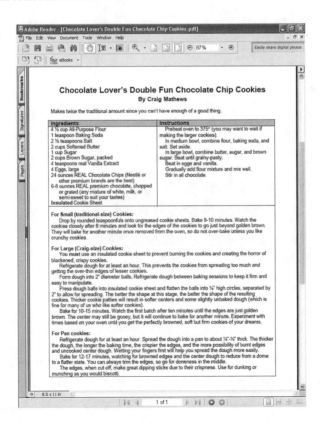

Microsoft Reader for Tablet PC

Target users: Everyone

Web site: http://www.microsoft.com/reader

The Microsoft Reader for Tablet PC is a great tool for reading digital content. You can even make your own eBooks with a free download you can get from the link shown here. Reader also allows you to annotate your eBooks with your pen, and understands Ink. Figure 18.2 shows a sample eBook in Reader.

FIGURE 18.2

Microsoft Reader lets you view a book just like you would in paper—except now you don't have to carry anything more than your Tablet PC.

To publish Word documents in eBook-reader format, you use the Read in Microsoft Reader (RMR) tool. Download the tool from www.microsoft.com/reader/info/rmr.asp. Once it is installed, you will have an additional icon in Word (Read) that builds the eBook for you. You can find more information about using RMR to create eBooks in the Tools section at http://www.microsoft.com/reader/downloads.

You can even have Reader read to you, as shown in Figure 18.3, by right-clicking the page number at the bottom of the page and then clicking the **Play** button.

FIGURE 18.3

Reader will even read to you if you want.

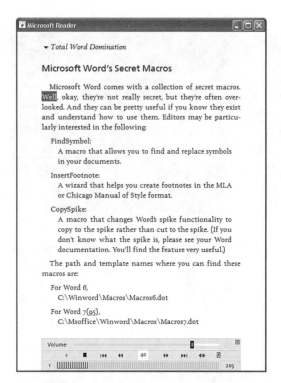

Zinio Magazine Reader

Target users: Everyone, magazine readers

Web site: http://www.zinio.com

The Zinio magazine reader is a tool for reading digital magazines. Many publications, such as *BusinessWeek*, *Harvard Business Review*, and *Motor Trend* are now available in Zinio digital format. Figure 18.4 shows a copy of *CIO Insight Magazine* in Zinio. Notice also that I have written and highlighted in Zinio, although Zinio does not recognize these strokes as Ink.

tip

If you like audio books, you can have Reader read to you. The voice takes some getting used to, but it opens up a lot of possibilities, especially for the visually impaired.

FIGURE 18.4

Zinio lets you highlight and mark up your magazines, just like you would do with paper.

With Zinio, you can turn pages just like you would a real magazine, as well as quickly flip through the magazine and tap on links to jump to other parts of the publication. The digital format also gives you the ability to print marked-up pages and store decades of magazines on your Tablet PC.

Graphics Tools

One of the great benefits of the Tablet PC is that it facilitates the use of the pen to sketch or generate ideas graphically. The following tools enable you to use your pen to communicate your ideas and create digital art.

Make sure that your pen settings are set for pressure sensitivity (if available). This will make whatever sketches or art you create more like real paper and pen, capturing the fluidity of your strokes and intention.

AutoDesk VoloView Express

Target users: People who need to view and mark up CAD drawings

Web site: http://www.autodesk.com

If you work with Computer Aided Drafting (CAD) files on a regular basis, VoloView Express and other CAD markup tools can enable you to provide red lines, mark ups, and comments on the CAD drawing in digital form. Although VoloView does not provide real Ink support, it is still as effective with the Tablet PC as a digital red-lining tool. Figure 18.5 shows a sample drawing with some hand-drawn notes. The notes were made using the Sketch tool, and can be viewed in AutoCAD, so a project manager or engineer can review and comment on drawings that a CAD operator drew. VoloView does not allow you to edit the drawing directly, so you can't move lines and such.

FIGURE 18.5

VoloView Express enables paper-reduced design firms, allowing project managers, engineers, and others to view and mark up drawings.

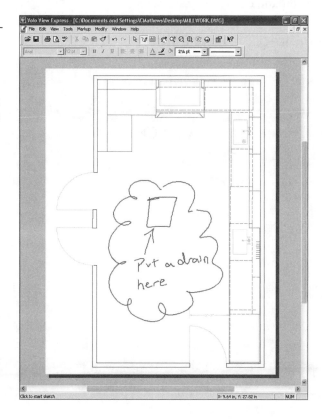

Denim

Target users: Web designers

Web site: http://guir.berkeley.edu/projects/denim/

Here's an idea: Why not create Web-site structures with a Tablet PC? The Group for User Interface Research at UC Berkeley has developed this application to quickly prototype Web sites—creating the structure and interconnections of the site without programming. Because most Web sites start out as sketches on paper anyway, this makes a lot of sense. Figure 18.6 shows simple site structure designed in Denim.

note

The version of Denim that I ran was good, but had a few interface issues. If you can get past those bugs, this is useful software.

Productivity Enhancers

This category includes a program that speeds up routine tasks by linking actions to gestures.

Leszynski inDirect Preview Edition

Target users: Everyone

Web site: http://www.leszynski.com

FIGURE 18.6

Denim allows you to sketch a Web site and create interconnections without programming.

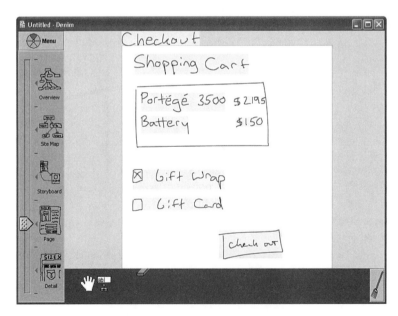

InDirect lets you activate shortcuts by using pen gestures. You can define what action you want a gesture to perform. This is similar in function to Sensiva Symbol Commander. Figure 18.7 shows how you can customize a gesture.

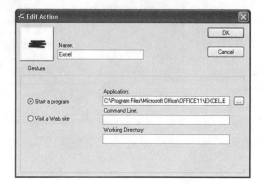

Video Tools

The Tablet PC is a great platform on which to create and view movies. Because you can carry the Tablet PC with you and hold it in any way, it gives you a portable movie studio and viewing room.

Microsoft Movie Maker

Target users: Those interested in editing digital video

Web site: http://www.microsoft. com/windowsXP/ moviemaker/ downloads/ moviemaker2.asp

tip

If you take digital video, or have a video camera and PC interface, Movie Maker is a terrific tool for making your videos more interesting.

Microsoft Movie Maker is an easy-to-use and powerful application for editing digital video. Movie Maker can create polished movies that are viewable on most computers. Figure 18.8 shows a video-editing session in which I took a video clip of my kids and added a title and transition effect. You will need a way to get the video clips onto your Tablet PC, but once they are there, Movie Maker can use most digital video formats as source material. It can also save videos in several formats.

FIGURE 18.8
Movie Maker
can help you
create great-
looking digital
videos.

Commercial Software

In addition to the companies that make free software, there are companies that actually want to get paid for their thousands of hours of work. This next list of software is what I've found to be helpful when using the Tablet PC.

Adobe Photoshop Elements

Target users: Those dealing with digital photographs

Web site: http://www.adobe.com

Price: $99.00

Photoshop Elements is the scaled-down version of the popular, but expensive, Adobe Photoshop. Photoshop Elements is a great tool for quickly editing the thousands of digital photos you've no doubt collected. Figure 18.9 shows just one tool that Elements offers: the Liquify tool.

Elements doesn't have all the features of Photoshop, such as scripting, but using it can save a lot of time through streamlined tools and quick fixes.

FIGURE 18.9

Photoshop Elements lets you do a lot of advanced photo manipulation, including stretching and morphing photos.

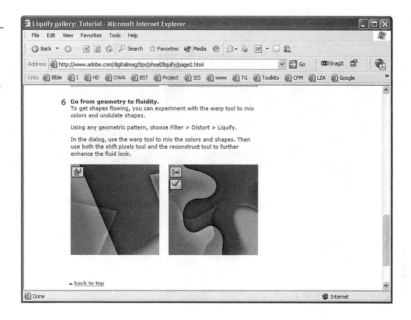

Alias SketchBook Pro

Target users:	Graphic artists and illustrators
Web site:	http://www.alias.com
Price:	$179.00

SketchBook Pro is an easy-to-use graphics tool that resounds with simplicity. Alias is the maker of Maya, the tool used to create the feature film *Monsters, Inc.* Clearly, Alias has some talent with making production-quality tools, and it shows in SketchBook Pro. Figure 18.10 shows a quick sketch I made in SketchBook Pro, which made it easy to create the image.

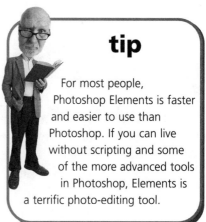

tip

For most people, Photoshop Elements is faster and easier to use than Photoshop. If you can live without scripting and some of the more advanced tools in Photoshop, Elements is a terrific photo-editing tool.

SketchBook Pro can be downloaded from Alias as a 15-day trial. After the 15-day period is finished, some features will be disabled. You have choices of 25 brushes and unlimited colors in the full version. The tools act like you would expect, with no real surprises other than the simplistic (but useful) interface.

FIGURE 18.10

SketchBook Pro's interface is wonderfully simple, staying out of your way when you want to create.

Colligo Workgroup Edition

Target users:	People who collaborate with others
Web site:	http://www.colligo.com
Price:	$69.99 per computer

There have been numerous times when I've been at a meeting and people needed to share files, but didn't have a blank floppy or CD, or access to a network hub. With more computers having Wi-Fi built in, creating ad-hoc networks of users is becoming more important. Especially with Tablet PCs that don't include CD and floppy media, it is more important to have ways to collaborate with others.

tip

You can download a 15-day trial of SketchBook Pro. After the time expires, you will still be able to use it, but with limited functionality.

Colligo fills that void. Colligo Workgroup Edition enables ad-hoc workgroups to share files, printers, an Internet connection, Outlook calendars, and a digital whiteboard, and to chat. Figure 18.11 shows what Colligo considers its most important features.

Colligo is an easy-to-use application that lets you securely connect to others. To protect you from wireless pirates, Colligo ships with a lot of security built in. Figure 18.12 shows the basic connectivity interface, although there are many more aspects of the program. If you ever need to collaborate at the drop of a hat, Colligo enables you to do it.

tip

If you have ad-hoc meetings where you need to share data, Colligo can help facilitate that.

FIGURE 18.11

Colligo has numerous features that make sense for Tablet PC users.

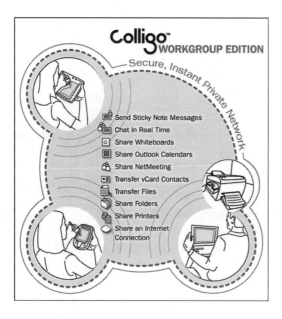

FIGURE 18.12
Colligo helps you connect with others, share files, and communicate.

Absolute Computrace

Target users:	Those concerned with data security
Web site:	http://www.computrace.com
Price:	$49.95 for one year of service

Computrace is part product, part service to help protect your Tablet PC from theft, and to help prevent data from getting into the wrong hands. Through various options, if your Tablet PC is stolen, Absolute Software can rid your hard drive of sensitive data and coordinate the retrieval of the stolen device.

tip

Computrace is a program and service that helps protect your data. If you have sensitive data on your Tablet PC, consider using Computrace to protect it. Remember, too, to keep your machine backed up.

Corel Grafigo

Target users:	People who need to sketch basic drawings
Web site:	http://www.corel.com/grafigo
Price:	$99.00

Corel Grafigo is a tool that lets you use your pen to sketch ideas. You can draw and erase sketches with pressure sensitivity. Shape conversion recognizes shapes and automatically converts them to perfect objects, smoothing out hand-drawn graphics. The first version was free, but now Corel charges for the application.

One particularly nice feature of Grafigo is its onionskin layers. With onionskins (shown in Figure 18.13), you can layer sketch upon sketch, allowing you to quickly try new ideas without redrawing the sketch each time.

Even kids can use Grafigo as easily as paper. In Figure 18.14, my then-three-year-old son drew his big brother's favorite thing: T-Rex. Grafigo is just plain easy to use.

tip

Use onionskins to try out multiple design options in a drawing. It helps the creative process and makes it easy to try new ideas.

FIGURE 18.13

Corel Grafigo has onionskins that let you layer your sketches. Here, two reception layouts can be tried easily.

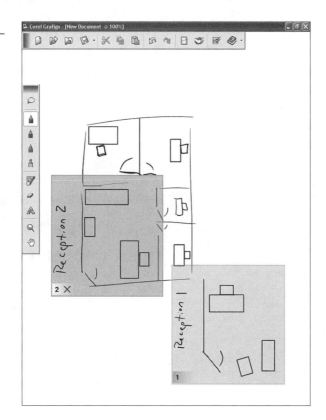

FIGURE 18.14

A drawing by a three-year-old in Grafigo.

Corel Painter

Target users: Graphic artists, digital artists, illustrators

Web site: http://www.corel.com

Price: $299.00

If you're into digital art or graphic arts, Painter is an incredible application. Coupled with a Tablet PC, it enables you to use fluid tools to paint, draw, sketch, and more. The effects can range from simple to complex. Figure 18.15 shows a painting done in Painter.

caution

You must have your Tablet PC set for 32-bit color in order to use Corel Painter, or you will have some very strange results in the palette.

In Corel Painter, You'll find a bevy of tools, including realistic watercolor and pastel media and numerous brush styles. The flexibility that Painter offers is almost unavailable even in traditional physical paint media—and that's saying a lot.

FIGURE 18.15
Corel Painter is simply the best graphic arts application for the Tablet PC.

You can design your own brushes using various shapes, colors, and pressure-sensitivity settings. With Corel Painter, you can paint without worrying about your clothes!

FranklinCovey TabletPlanner

Target users: People interested in managing their time and lives

Web site: http://www.franklincovey. com/tabletplanner.

Price: $199.95

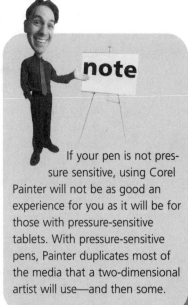

note

If your pen is not pressure sensitive, using Corel Painter will not be as good an experience for you as it will be for those with pressure-sensitive tablets. With pressure-sensitive pens, Painter duplicates most of the media that a two-dimensional artist will use—and then some.

Next to OneNote, FranklinCovey TabletPlanner is my second-favorite application for the Tablet PC. If you need to get a handle on life, and would like to use your Tablet PC to do it, TabletPlanner is a great tool.

Not only does TabletPlanner keep track of appointments and notes, it helps in some ways to make your life more, well, meaningful. TabletPlanner features tools to help you explore mission building, role assessment, and goal setting.

Figure 18.16 shows what TabletPlanner looks like in landscape mode.

FIGURE 18.16

TabletPlanner
looks like a
paper planner
in landscape
mode.

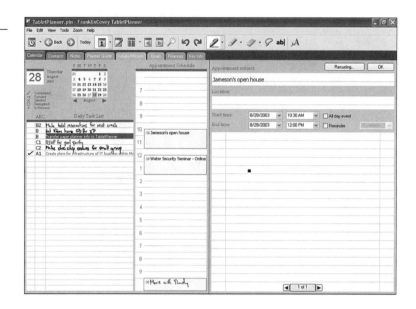

When you switch your Tablet PC into portrait/slate mode, TabletPlanner changes to
reveal a different viewpoint, as shown in Figure 18.17.

In addition to the basic planner features you'd find in paper organizers,
TabletPlanner lets you print documents to the FranklinCovey TabletPlanner print
device, which creates an image of the document that it stores in its Notes tab, as
shown in Figure 18.18.

As mentioned previously, the TabletPlanner features sections designed to get you
thinking about your mission, roles, and goals. You can store the results of this
process in TabletPlanner's Values/Mission tab.

But wait, there's more! What good would TabletPlanner be if it didn't synchronize
with Outlook? It does so with ease. The synchronization feature works great with
Outlook 2000, XP, and 2003. You can synchronize appointments, tasks, and notes
with Outlook, so it doesn't matter which application you enter the information into.
You can also convert your handwritten notes into text for pasting into other applications, or for clarity.

All in all, TabletPlanner is a fantastic tool that helps you keep the various aspects of
your life in order, letting you concentrate on doing rather than remembering.

FIGURE 18.17
TabletPlanner in portrait mode displays the Daily Task List with either the Appointment Schedule or the Daily Notes, but not both.

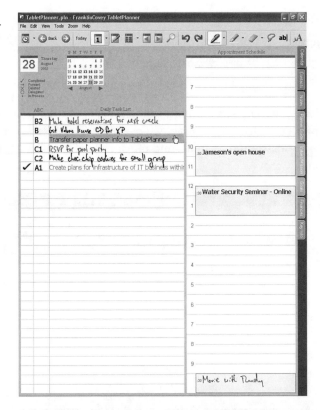

FIGURE 18.18
I "printed" to the Tablet-Planner printer to store the KnowledgeDog Web site in the Notes section of TabletPlanner.

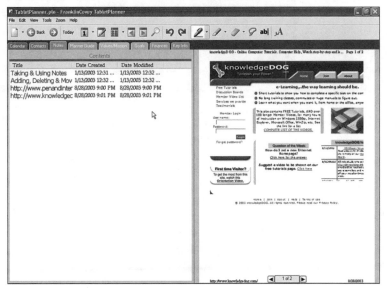

Groove Workspace

Target users:	Collaborative teams
Web site:	http://www.groove.net
Price:	$69 to $795, depending on version and number of licensees

Groove provides a collaboration platform that lets people work in shared "spaces" to keep up with project-related information. Groove features numerous tools for sharing files, hosting discussions and chats, and much more. Figure 18.19 shows the file-sharing portion of Groove.

FIGURE 18.19

Groove is made for collaboration. With various communication features and a knowledge repository, Groove can help your workgroup stay in touch and on the same page.

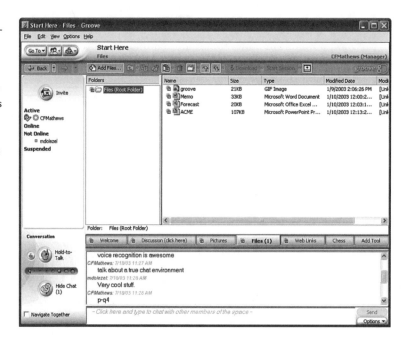

Groove works easily with Outlook and Office applications, and the Professional version even provides integration with Sharepoint Team Services. You can also extend the functionality of Groove by adding tools, such as a collaborative Chess application. Figure 18.20 shows Sharepoint Team Services integration.

FIGURE 18.20

Groove integrates with Sharepoint Team Services.

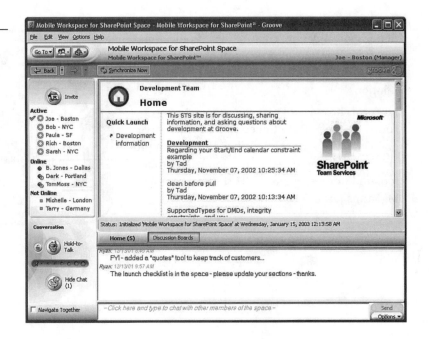

FIGURE 18.20

Groove integrates with Sharepoint Team Services.

Keylogix ActiveDocs

Target users:	Keyboard slaves (people who want to use handwriting only in forms and documents)
Web site:	http://www.activedocs.com/product/activedocsfortabletpc
Price:	$650.00

ActiveDocs streamlines the document-creation process by allowing you to automate document creation through wizards, as well as by allowing a totally pen-based input model. This means you can create forms with fields that can be filled in with handwritten notes.

Mi-Co Mi-Forms

Target users:	Forms-centric organizations
Web site:	http://www.mi-corporation.com
Price:	Unspecified, as it is usually part of a larger solution

Mi-Forms is one of the best-designed forms applications for the Tablet PC. It not only handles handwritten forms, it also has serious back-end data-integration capabilities, enabling a true enterprise-wide solution for forms design, capture, synchronization, and storage into enterprise databases. Figure 18.21 shows the architecture of the Mi-Forms solution.

Mi-Forms has several components, including Forms Designer, Data Collector, Mi-Forms Server, and Data Manager. All together, this system provides for rich pen-based form completion, routing, and storage. Figure 18.22 shows a sample Mi-Forms form.

tip

If you're looking for enterprise-level forms design, capture, and routing, Mi-Forms has the best solution on the market for most people.

FIGURE 18.21

Mi-Co thought through all the issues related to remote forms capture. Here is the architecture for the product.

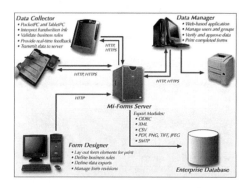

FIGURE 18.22

Mi-Forms lets you define zones in your digital forms to capture various kinds of data.

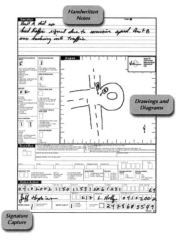

Microsoft Streets & Trips

Target users:	People on the go
Web site:	http://www.microsoft.com/streets
Price:	$39.95

Streets & Trips is perfect for those who travel a lot and don't always have access to an Internet-based mapping service. In addition to doing what Yahoo! Maps and Mapquest offer, Streets & Trips has an extensive database of hotels, restaurants, and other locations that help you plan a trip.

I used Streets & Trips on a 6,000 mile trip a couple months ago, and found it invaluable. While my wife took her shifts at the wheel, I could pull out my Tablet PC and plan/check/modify our trip. I could locate specific hotels or restaurants, and was even able to estimate costs for the trip. The

tip

If you plan to take a long trip and want to use Streets & Trips, invest in an inverter so you can power your Tablet PC during the trip.

mileage-, time-, and cost-tracking capabilities were right on. Figure 18.23 shows a portion of our trip into Wyoming, complete with stopping points. Streets & Trips also produces excellent maps if you still can't work without paper.

Streets & Trips also works with GPS units to track your progress on a map. If you need more business-oriented tools, look at Microsoft MapPoint, which adds business geographic and demographic analysis tools (such as locating all of your customers on a map). MapPoint can help focus your marketing campaigns and catch demographic trends in your data. MapPoint does everything else that Streets & Trips does.

Microsoft Visio

Target users:	People who need to create quick designs, diagrams, and charts
Web site:	http://www.microsoft.com/visio
Price:	$179.95 for Standard, $449.95 for Professional

Visio has been one of my favorite drawing tools for years. Now, with the Tablet PC, it's even better. Visio has always provided one of the easiest ways to create professional-looking diagrams. Just drag-and-drop shapes and connect them. Now Visio 2003 adds Ink functionality so you can make notes on your Visio diagrams. Figure 18.24 shows Ink on top of one of the diagrams I created for this book.

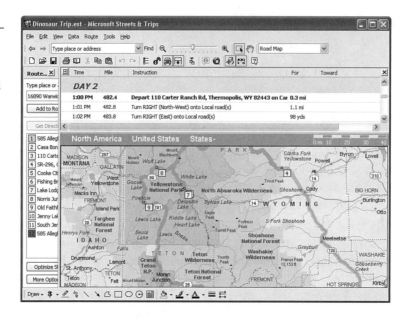

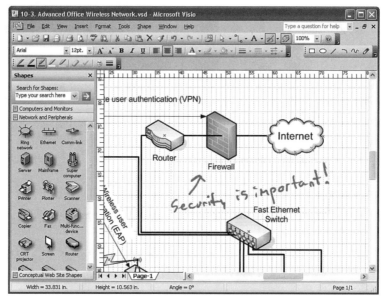

Mindjet MindManager

Target users: Idea generators and meeting coordinators

Web site: http://www.mindjet.com

Price: $189 for Business edition, $269 for Enterprise edition

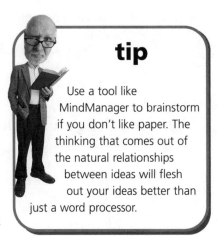

tip

Use a tool like MindManager to brainstorm if you don't like paper. The thinking that comes out of the natural relationships between ideas will flesh out your ideas better than just a word processor.

If you do a lot of brainstorming and spend a lot of time fleshing out ideas, MindManager is invaluable. I have used it on complex projects for which I needed to show relationships between thoughts.

MindManager uses the mind-mapping approach to brainstorming, which is a visual approach to the thinking process originally developed by Tony Buzan. MindManager makes the process simple for keyboard users and Tablet PC users alike. MindManager now supports Ink, enabling even more fluid thought. Once you have created a mind map in Ink, you can easily convert handwriting to text. Figure 18.25 shows a mind map created in MindManager using Ink.

FIGURE 18.25

MindManager is an easy-to-use mind mapping tool that helps you think through ideas in a natural way.

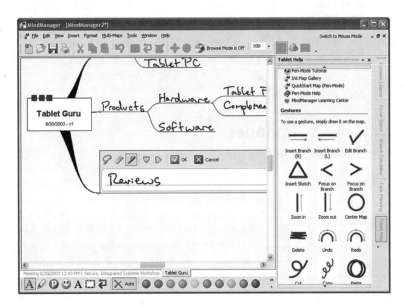

The Enterprise edition adds customizable templates and wizards. Both versions seamlessly integrate with Microsoft Office and Project applications, automatically creating PowerPoint presentations, Word outlines, and Project schedules based on the mind map. Future releases will include PDF export, Outlook integration, and team communication tools. This is a fantastic tool for knowledge workers.

ScanSoft Dragon Naturally Speaking

Target users: People who want to use voice dictation and command

Web site: http://www.scansoft.com

Price: $199.99

tip

Naturally Speaking improves dictation over Input Panel, but if you want your computer to read to you, ScanSoft also has RealSpeak, which has the most human-like voice of any text-to-speech engine.

Naturally Speaking is a natural extension for the Tablet PC. It takes speech recognition and control to the next level. Naturally Speaking works similarly to Input Panel's speech capabilities, but adds more commands and easier, more natural dictation capabilities. The speech engine is fully trainable and increases recognition accuracy over Input Panel.

ScanSoft has versions of Naturally Speaking for the legal, medical, and professional-services environments. It also has support for "talk and dock" functionality—allowing you to dictate into your Pocket PC and have it automatically transcribe when you dock with your Tablet PC.

Sensiva Symbol Commander

Target users: Everyone

Web site: http://www.sensiva.com

Price: $39.95

This is similar to the Leszynski inDirect software, in that it is used for gesture recognition and automation. Sensiva Symbol Commander enables you to use gestures to launch programs and perform operations instead of searching for links and double-clicking the icon. Symbol Commander Pro also has macro features for repeating repetitive tasks. Figure 18.26 shows Symbol Commander's gesture pad.

FIGURE 18.26

Symbol
Commander
uses gestures to
speed up routine
tasks.

Niche Tablet PC Applications

These applications are more for specific industries or niches. Because they are so specific in nature, I will not cover them other than to tell you what they are and where
you can find more information about them. This is not a comprehensive list, but
rather a list of the applications that I have looked into that appear to be valuable
for specific users. For more complete coverage of available applications, go to my
Web site at http://www.TabletGuru.com and look under the Software section.

Table 18.1   Niche Tablet PC Application List

Application	Industry/Purpose	Web Link
Allscripts TouchWorks	Physician office automation	http://www.allscripts.com
ColeConnect OrderPad 2003	Sales order processing tool	http://www.coleconnect.com
Criterion Real Estate Dashboard (R.E.D.)	Real estate	http://www.cc-re.com/red_tablet.htm
Cubistix MapSlate	Location analytics	http://www.cubistix.com/ solutions-MapSlate.php
CX Cyberplex/WEBfront Tablet PC Home Appraisal	Home appraisal	http://www.webfront.net/news/ devtemplatedetail.asp
Filbitron WriteTRAC	Sales-force automation	http://www.filbitron.com/software.htm
Finale Notepad	Sheet-music creation and editing	http://www.finalemusic.com

Table 18.1   (continued)

Application	Industry/Purpose	Web Link
MindGenius brainbloom	Brainstorming tool	http://www.ygnius.com
mTuitive Tablet ABC	Inspection and interviewing data-collection tool	http://www.mtuitive.com
Pen&Internet riteForm	Form tool for handwritten forms	http://www.penandinternet.com
Pen&Internet riteMail	Ink-based email and notes	http://www.penandinternet.com
Pen&Internet ritePen	Improved handwriting recognition	http://www.penandinternet.com
ScanSoft RealSpeak	Text-to-speech	http://www.scansoft.com
SketchUp 3D	3D sketching tool	http://www.sketch3d.com
TabletBlogger	Creates Web logs, or blogs, with Ink	http://tblogger.jrj.org/
xThink Calculator	High-end calculations using only a pen	http://www.xthink.com/product.html
xThink MathJournal	Math equation solving and graphing with only a pen	http://www.xthink.com/mathJournal.html

THE ABSOLUTE MINIMUM

Here are the key points to take away from this chapter:

- Numerous free applications can make your Tablet PC use more enjoyable. Download the applications and see if you like them.

- Tablet PC electronic document (and eBook) readers enable you to read digital content with your Tablet PC easily and comfortably. Keep all your reading materials with you in digital form.

- Your Tablet PC is the perfect platform for graphics work because you can use a pen for more natural painting and sketching. Try some of the available graphics applications if you have the need.

- Gesture tools, such as inDirect and Symbol Commander, help you access applications and tasks quickly through pen gestures.

- Movie Maker is a tool that can help you turn home video into good-looking and enjoyable video presentations.

- Colligo and Groove can help you connect to others. Both applications approach the issue from different perspectives, although there is overlap. If you work in a team that needs to communicate a lot, check them out.

- Computrace can help you locate a stolen machine, as well as protect that machine from data thieves. Use it as part of your data-security plan.

- TabletPlanner is the electronic version of the Franklin Planner for Tablet PCs. It can help you manage your life mission, roles, and goals, as well as keep up with tasks and appointments. Its synchronization with Outlook means you don't have to enter data twice.

- Mi-Forms by Mi-Co is a terrific tool for automating forms. Mi-Co has thoroughly thought through the process of forms design, completion, and data storage. It is one of the most complete solutions on the market for enterprise-level forms management.

- Streets & Trips is great for traveling and planning trips. It helps you get from point to point with all the stops in between. You can tie it into GPS receivers as well for following maps in your car.

- MindManager and brainbloom can help you generate ideas and think through issues more completely by utilizing mind-mapping tools. I highly encourage you to try one of these tools.

- Naturally Speaking can improve speech-recognition ease of use and capabilities. Use it if you find Input Panel's speech tools too limiting.

PART VIII

LEARNING RESOURCES FOR THE TABLET PC

A

ADDITIONAL RESOURCES

This appendix provides information about other places to go and other things to read that will help you get more out of your Tablet PC.

Web Sites

The following Web sites are locations that you can visit to get immediate information and help related to your Tablet PC. Note that I looked at numerous sites that are not in this list, as I only wanted to give you the sites that had the most value and that I feel are long-term players. Of course I'd prefer you go to MY site...

Tablet Guru

www.TabletGuru.com

This is my site, which will supplement this book. At the site, you will find discussion forums about Tablet PCs, product reviews, current news, and comparisons of various hardware and software. There will also be some hands-on training offered, as well as online video training courses (eventually).

If you like what you have in your hands, this site will be more of the same and then some. As the Tablet PC technology advances, I will be there to walk you through the updates and help you through the maze of hardware and software choices that develop.

Because you bought this book, you will have access to some items free of charge that I normally charge people for. Use the code ABGTPC in order to get access to special products.

Microsoft—Tablet PCs

www.microsoft.com/tabletpc

This is the Tablet PC Web site from Microsoft. Because Microsoft provides the operating system for all Tablet PCs, it has some good information about what the Tablet PC is all about, as well as about some of the partners with whom Microsoft has joined to make the Tablet PC successful. In addition, Microsoft includes case studies and general Tablet PC–related news.

Following are a few specific spots on the Microsoft Tablet PC site that are helpful.

Downloads for the Tablet PC

http://www.microsoft.com/windowsxp/tabletpc/downloads/default.asp

Most of the downloads found here are free, and add functionality to the Tablet PC. Some of these are discussed in Chapter 13, "PowerToys for Tablet PC," and others in Chapter 18, "Useful Software."

Office XP Pack for Tablet PC

http://office.microsoft.com/downloads/2002/oxptp.aspx

This is where you should go to add inking capabilities to Office XP, or to add additional Outlook integration to Windows Journal.

PowerToys for Windows XP Tablet PC Edition

http://www.microsoft.com/windowsxp/tabletpc/downloads/powertoys.asp

This site offers lots of applets that improve productivity and provide entertainment.

Tablet PC Newsgroup

http://communities.microsoft.com/Newsgroups/default.asp?ICP=windowsxp&sLCID=US&newsgroup=microsoft.public.windows.tabletpc

This newsgroup is one place to go to discuss the Tablet PC.

Tablet PC Product Information

http://www.microsoft.com/windowsxp/tabletpc/evaluation/default.asp

This is a helpful part of Microsoft's Tablet PC site if you want to learn more about how other organizations use the Tablet PC.

Tablet PC Developer

www.tabletpcdeveloper.com

You'll find this to be a good site if you're interested in creating applications for the Tablet PC. It discusses .NET and development practices. Some sample code and applets are available, as well as development news and links.

Tablet News

www.tabletnews.com

This site keeps track of the happenings in the Tablet PC world, and also keeps up with the latest Tablet PC models available. It has only a few software applications listed, but has a plethora of reviews of various applications and Tablet PCs.

Tablet PC Talk

www.tabletpctalk.com

This is one of the better sites. I like the news update, where you can subscribe to Tablet PC–related news items in email form. The site offers interviews with and feature stories about people who use the Tablet PC. It also has a good newsgroup section, and a section that compares all Tablet PCs. As I said, it's one of the best sites (although its design is lacking in some regards).

Tablet PC Buzz

www.tabletpcbuzz.com

Tablet PC Buzz is another news-based site with some custom content centered on a newsletter. You'll find a forum here as well.

Tablet PCs

www.tabletpcs.net

This site has many of the elements common to other sites (though lighter on content), and has an appealing design as well.

802.11 Hot Spots

www.80211HotSpots.com

This site has information about public and private wireless access points around the world. If you're in a good-size city, you may have some options for connecting to the Internet from your favorite coffee shop or restaurant, as well as at some hotels and other places; 802.11 Hot Spots can help you find those places.

Node DB

www.nodedb.com

If you're in a major metropolis, chances are there are Wi-Fi access points in your city. If so, Node DB is one of the sites you can go to in order to find them.

EZGoal Hotspots

www.ezgoal.com/hotspots/wireless

Another site that deals in wireless access point databases, this site is more difficult to navigate, but seems to have a richer data set.

Books

There are several books that I recommend you read in order to get the most out of your Tablet PC. Each of these books goes more in-depth to the topics that I covered here at the 30,000-foot view.

Because your Tablet PC is based on Windows XP, you will want to know the tips and tricks to making your Windows experience most effective, if you don't already. I've also included a couple of books on programming and a couple more on networking and Office 2003. There are certainly many other books that can help you, but with the Tablet PC being so new and rapidly changing, I'd recommend hanging out at TabletGuru.com, where I will keep you abreast of the most important news and related products for the Tablet PC.

Absolute Beginner's Guide to Windows XP

Shelley O'Hara

O'Hara's book covers numerous aspects of the Tablet PC, including printing, file management, using the Internet, working with videos and photos, and many other ways to get the most out of Windows XP. The material in her book is covered in the same manner as I've covered the Tablet PC here, so it's a great companion book.

Special Edition Using Windows XP Professional, Bestseller Edition

Robert Cowart and Brian Knittel

If you want much deeper coverage of Windows XP, jump into this book. Probably the most complete treatment of Windows XP in one bound volume, this book covers every aspect of what you need to know about Windows XP, and then keeps going. If you're really interested in the details of the operating system and stumping your friends on esoteric facts about Windows XP, get this book.

Building Tablet PC Applications

Rob Jarrett and Philip Su

The authors of this book are developers in Microsoft's Tablet PC group, so they have some in-depth knowledge about how to develop Tablet PC applications. The book deals a lot with the API (if you don't know what an API is, this book's not for you), and with the Tablet PC Platform SDK. This book will help you understand how to make your applications Ink-aware and to really leverage the power of the Tablet PC.

Tablet PC Software Development With .NET

Ed Holloway and Karen Watterson

Another good source of development know-how, this book also helps the reader understand Ink programming and leveraging the Tablet PC interface to make programs more usable.

Absolute Beginner's Guide to Networking, Fourth Edition

Joe Habraken

Here's a great book if you want to know more about connecting computers using common network devices. The Tablet PC is a great tool for communication with others across digital networks. Understanding how to set up a network at home or the office to properly leverage the Tablet PC's capabilities will help you achieve the promise of the Tablet PC.

Jeff Duntemann's Drive-By Wi-Fi Guide

Jeff Duntemann

Here's a good book that can help you thoroughly understand Wi-Fi networking. While my coverage gave you the basics, Duntemann's book will help you understand deeper aspects of wireless networking, how to get it set up, and how to connect.

The Wi-Fi Experience: Everyone's Guide to 802.11b Wireless Networking

Harold Davis and Richard Mansfield

This is a good book that will help you understand and implement Wi-Fi wireless networking. This book delves deeper into antennae and broader-range wireless than Duntemann's.

Absolute Beginner's Guide to Microsoft Office 2003

Jim Boyce

My coverage of Office 2003 dealt only with the Tablet PC–specific aspects of the applications in the suite, and did not touch on how to really leverage the tools outside the context of the Tablet PC. A book like this one that covers each application and the overall suite in more detail will help you if you're new to Office 2003.

You've probably been using some version of Microsoft Office for some time, but Office 2003 has some great new features that you will probably want to know more about.

Magazines

Currently, there is only one Tablet PC-specific magazine, listed here.

Tablet PC Magazine

Aeon Publishing Group, Inc.

www.tabletpcmagazine.com

This is the first magazine in print that addresses the specific issues of the Tablet PC. The people who created this magazine also created *Pen Computing*, solidifying their position as leaders in the field of pen-based computing. In *Tablet PC Magazine*, you'll find good information and reviews as well as advertising that will help you order related items.

B

QUICK REFERENCE

This appendix provides quick access to many of the most important configuration and usage tips from the book. If you need to know something fast, this is the place to turn.

Tablet PC Hardware Configuration

The following two hardware-configuration changes can help you get more out of the built-in buttons on your Tablet PC.

Power Button

You can access settings for changing the action of the power button in Windows XP by going to Power Options in the Control Panel, then choosing the **Advanced** tab (**Start**, **Control Panel**, **Power Options**).

Changing Button Functions

Open the **Pen and Tablet Settings** dialog box in the Control Panel (**Start**, **Control Panel**, **Tablet and Pen Settings**). The Tablet Buttons tab enables you to change the function of the buttons on your Tablet PC.

Windows XP Tablet PC Edition Configuration

The following items will help you customize some of the basic aspects of your Tablet PC for optimum use.

Change Handedness

Click on **Start**, **Control Panel** and select **Tablet and Pen Settings**. You can change handedness settings in the Settings tab.

Calibration

To calibrate your Tablet PC, click on **Start**, **Control Panel**, and select **Tablet and Pen Settings**. Then click on the **Calibrate** button for both the landscape and the portrait orientations.

Switching Between Portrait and Landscape

Under the Display tab on the Tablet and Pen Settings dialog box (**Start**, **Control Panel**, **Tablet and Pen Settings**), you can adjust the screen orientation and set the sequence that Windows uses when you change screen orientations.

Pen Options

The Pen Options tab is on the Tablet and Pen Settings dialog box (**Start**, **Control Panel**, **Tablet and Pen Settings**). With this dialog box, you can adjust the behaviors of your pen.

Start Menu Settings

If you right-click the **Start** button then choose **Properties**, you will see a dialog box that enables you to change the way the Start menu looks. You can choose between Start menu (Windows XP style) and Classic Start menu (Windows 2000/9.x style). For each option, there is a Customize button for changing basic settings, such as icon size and menu contents.

Taskbar Settings

On the same dialog box as the Start menu settings is a Taskbar tab. This lets you set taskbar properties such as showing the clock in the System tray and auto-hiding the taskbar to free up a bit more screen real estate.

Display Settings

The Settings tab on the Display dialog box (**Start**, **Control Panel**, **Display**) enables you to change the resolution and color depth of your display. Changing your screen resolution changes your screen real estate. The larger the numbers, the more information you will be able to see on the screen at once.

Windows Journal

For most people, Windows Journal is the application they use most often on their Tablet PC. The following tidbits are the few main points to understand about Windows Journal (see Figure B.1).

The Windows Journal Interface

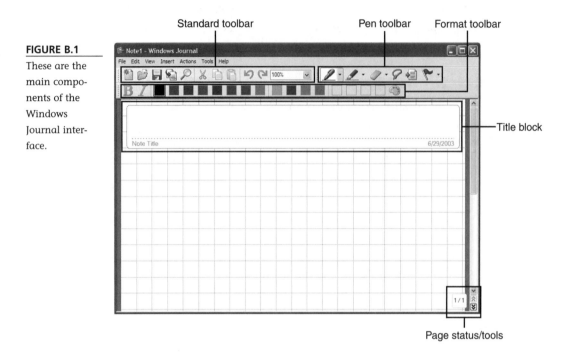

FIGURE B.1

These are the main components of the Windows Journal interface.

Export Notes

To export a Journal note, go to **File**, then **Export As**. You are given a choice as to the name you want to use to save the note, as well as to the file format—MHT or TIF. The file type you choose depends on what is easiest for your recipient to use. MHT is usually the best choice.

Using Templates

To use a template, tap **File**, **New Note from Template**, then select the template you want to use.

Setting a Template as Default

To set a default template, tap **Tools**, **Options** and select the template you want to use from the Stationery area of the Note Format tab. You can also create stationery to use as the default template.

Tablet PC Input Panel

For maximum handwriting recognition, keep words separated, use lowercase letters predominantly, and use cursive. Use the **Input Panel Keyboard** and/or the **Symbols Pad** to insert just a few characters or symbols. Table B.1 lists the gestures you can use within the Input Panel.

TABLE B.1 Gestures Available in Writing Pad

Gesture Sample	Meaning	Comments
→•	Backspace	Deletes the character to the left of the cursor, as does pressing the Backspace key.
•—	Space	Inserts a space at the insertion point.
⌐	Enter	Inserts a carriage return at the cursor.
⌐	Tab	Inserts a tab.
≥	Scratch-out	Tells the recognizer to ignore the handwriting before it leaves the input area. Can be used over a letter, word, or several words. Must block out most of the item to be deleted.

Speech Recognition

Following are the main commands used in speech recognition. Table B.2 lists the commands used in Dictation mode, Table B.3 covers handling common symbols and punctuation in Dictation mode, and Table B.4 lists commands used in Command mode. For a broader list, see Chapter 9, "Speech Recognition and Voice Control."

TABLE B.2 Common Voice Commands in Dictation Mode

Voice Command	Action	Example
Dictate into Foreground Application		
"Force num <number>"	Speak numbers instead of words.	Force num <2>
"New line"	Insert a single carriage return.	New line
"New paragraph"	Insert two carriage returns.	New paragraph
"Spell it <spelling>"	Spell a word exactly.	Spell it <humperdink>
"Spell that"	Spell a word in all caps.	Spell that <HUMPERDINK>

TABLE B.2 (continued)

Voice Command	Action	Example
Controlling Speech		
"Microphone"	Turns microphone off.	Microphone
"Voice command"	Switches to Command mode.	Voice command

TABLE B.3 Common Symbols and Punctuation

Symbol	Voice Command	Symbol	Voice Command
&	"Ampersand"	-	"Hyphen"
*	"Asterisk"	(	"Open paren"
@	"At sign"	%	"Percent sign"
\	"Backslash"	.	"Period"
)	"Close paren"/"end paren"	?	"Question mark"
,	"Comma"	"	"Quote"
:	"Colon"	;	"Semicolon"
"	"End quote"	_	"Underscore"
!	"Exclamation"		

TABLE B.4 Commonly Used Voice Commands in Command Mode

Voice Command	Action
Starting and Switching to Applications	
"Launch <application name>"	Starts the application you specify. You can also use "Open" and "Start" to do the same thing.
"Switch to <application name>"	Switches to the open application you specify.
Selection and Correction	
"Correct that"	Provides correction options for the selected text.
"Scratch that"	Undoes the last word or phrase dictated.
"Select line"	Selects the entire current line, from left margin to right margin.
"Select paragraph"	Selects the entire current paragraph.
"Select sentence"	Selects the current sentence.
"Select word"	Selects the word that the cursor is currently on.
"Unselect that"	Unselects the selection.

Voice Command	Action
Navigation	
"Go to beginning of line"	Moves the cursor to the beginning of the current line.
"Go to bottom"	Moves the cursor to the bottom of the current page.
"Go to end of line"	Moves the cursor to the end of the current line.
"Go to top"	Moves the cursor to the top of the page.
Uppercase and Lowercase	
"All caps"	Capitalizes all letters of the selection.
"Cap that"	Capitalizes the word or phrase selected.
"No caps that"	Uncapitalizes the word or phrase selected.
Editing Operations	
"Copy that"	Copies the selection to the clipboard.
"Cut that"	Cuts the selection from the document.
"Paste that"	Pastes the contents of the clipboard into the document.
"Undo that"	Undoes the last action.
Keyboard Simulation	
"Backspace"	Deletes the selection or character to the left of the cursor.
"Delete"	Deletes the selection or character to the right of the cursor.
"Enter"	Inserts a carriage return.
"Move down"	Moves the cursor down one line or cell in the document.
"Move left"	Moves the cursor one character or cell to the left.
"Move right"	Moves the cursor one character or cell to the right.
"Move up"	Moves the cursor one character or cell up.
"Next cell"	Moves the cursor to the next cell in the selection or the next cell to the right.
"Page down"	Moves the document down one page.
"Page up"	Moves the document up one page.
"Space"	Inserts a space.
"Tab"	Inserts or executes a tab.
Controlling Speech	
"Dictation"	Switches to dictation mode.
"Microphone"	Turns the microphone off.

Microsoft Office 2003 Ink Tools

Ink comes in three forms in Office 2003: Annotations, comments, and drawing and writing. Ink annotations can be hidden, while ink drawing and writing areas cannot. Ink comments are used only in Word 2003 for collaborative notes. Table B.5 lists the ways ink can be used in the various Office 2003 applications.

TABLE B.5   Ink Capabilities in Office 2003 Applications

Application	Ink Drawing and Writing	Ink Annotations	Ink Comments
Access	Yes (on the form in Design mode, and in the Handwriting recognizer field in View mode)	No	No
Excel	Yes	Yes	No
InfoPath	Yes	No	No
PowerPoint	Yes	Yes	No
Visio	Yes	No	No
Word	Yes	Yes	Yes

Index

D

How can we make this index more useful? Email us at indexes@quepublishing.com

How can we make this index more useful? Email us at indexes@quepublishing.com